Renner Learning Resource Center
Elgin Community College
Elgin, IL 60123

The Worlds
of Elie Wiesel

The Worlds of Elie Wiesel

An Overview of His Career and His Major Themes

Jack Kolbert

Selinsgrove: Susquehanna University Press
London: Associated University Press

© 2001 by Associated University Press, Inc.

All rights reserved. Authorization to photocopy items for internal or personal use, or the internal or personal use of specific clients, is granted by the copyright owner, provided that a base fee of $10.00, plus eight cents per page, per copy is paid directly to the Copyright Clearance Center, 222 Rosewood Drive, Danvers, Massachusetts 01923. [1-57591-050-0/01 $10.00 + 8 ¢ pp, pc.]

Associated University Presses
440 Forsgate Drive
Cranbury, NJ 08512

Associated University Presses
16 Barter Street
London WC1A 2AH, England

Associated University Presses
P.O. Box 338, Port Credit
Mississauga, Ontario
Canada L5G 4L8

The paper used in this publication meets the requirements of the American National Standard for Permanence of Paper for Printed Library Materials Z39.48-1984.

Library of Congress Cataloging-in-Publication Data

Kolbert, Jack, 1927–
    The worlds of Elie Wiesel / Jack Kolbert.
      p. cm.
    Includes bibliographical references and index.
    ISBN 1-57591-050-0 (alk. paper)
    1. Wiesel, Elie, 1928– 2. Holocaust, Jewish (1939–1945) 3. Authors, French—20th century—Biography. 4. Jewish authors—Biography. 5. Holocaust survivors—Biography. I. Title.

PQ2683.I32 Z695 2001
813'.54—dc21
[B]   00-063726

PRINTED IN THE UNITED STATES OF AMERICA

To my first pupil, my sister Esther.
The pupil was three; the
teacher was eight.

and

To my beloved Ruth—with thanks.

Contents

Preface	9
Acknowledgments	15
1. Elie Wiesel—A Life and a Career	19
2. Yearning for Childhood: Sighet	50
3. Remembering the Holocaust	59
4. "Indifference to Evil Is Evil"	72
5. The Rhetoric of Silence	80
6. In Remembrance of History	86
7. And Where Was God?	94
8. Hear Oh Israel: The Jewish People Are One	106
9. In Search of Jewish-Christian Dialogue	124
10. The Sanctity of Life	136
11. What Is Literature?	143
12. A Portrait of the Writer as Teacher and Scholar	163
13. The French Connection	172
14. And Yet—A Conclusion That Does Not Conclude	188
Notes	197
Select Bibliography	207
Index	211

Preface

WHY YET ANOTHER BOOK ON ELIE WIESEL? AFTER ALL, AN IMPRESsive number of book-length volumes on him have already been published during the years following his initial appearance on the international literary stage. During the last three years alone Wiesel completed his two-volume memoirs: *Tous les fleuves vont à la mer* and *Et la mer n'est pas remplie* (the first of these translated into English as *Memoirs: All Rivers Run to the Sea;* the second volume [*And the Sea Is Never Full*] in an English translation has just appeared. Also, during the last three years we have seen the publication of Philippe-Michaël de Saint Cheron's biography of Wiesel and an edited collection of proceedings at an international Wiesel colloquium held during the summer of 1995 at the cultural center in the Chateau de Cerisy-la-Salle, near Saint-Lô in Normandy. In honor of the writer's seventieth birthday, at least two other festschrifts were published in France and America. I must also mention other recent and well-researched monographs like Simon B. Sibelman's *Silence in the Novels of Elie Wiesel* and Colin Davis's *Elie Wiesel's Secretive Texts*. A few months ago, in his new book, *Great Souls Who Changed the Century,* David Aikman classified Elie Wiesel as one of the six "great souls" who transformed spiritual and moral life during the twentieth century, along with Billy Graham, Nelson Mandela, Solzhenitsyn, Mother Theresa, and Pope John Paul II. Aikman states that Wiesel "forced people to look more closely at the nature of human evil." Given Wiesel's prominence as a writer and as a force for exalted human values, I believe that there will always be room for yet another book on his thoughts, words, and visions. Wiesel is a writer who will continue to inspire others to write about his texts. No voice more eloquently than his defined the full scope of the Holocaust, arguably the greatest tragedy in history.

My main reason for wanting to write this book on Wiesel stems from the fact that I have derived much personal satisfaction, both from my readings of his literature and from my close association with him. Our paths have intersected in a number of venues. Out of these encounters there burgeoned within me an irrepressible desire to do my own study on Elie Wiesel and to examine him from the point of view of someone whose life has been deeply touched by contact with his works and presence. I hope to add new rays of light to those already projected by the other specialists of the subject.

My greatest challenge here—and I know that I have not entirely succeeded—was to develop a sense of distance between Wiesel and me. When one knows a man so well, it is not easy to discuss him in a fully unbiased way. Yes, being human, Wiesel is not a perfect, flawless person. He does have some detractors. There are a few who believed that he has drawn too much capital from the fact that he suffered poignantly in the concentration camps and built a career out of his memories in the camps. A few accuse him of being too aggressive in his quest for recognition. A few have even claimed that he allowed his friends and allies to orchestrate an overly concerted campaign to get him to be selected for his Nobel Prize. A few believe that he enjoys too much the limelight of presence at prestigious social and governmental events. He has had his stressful relationships with prominent figures like President François Mitterand of France, the justifiably recognized Nazi-hunter Simon Wiesenthal, the late writer and critic Alfred Kazin, and two or three others. With equanimity Wiesel acknowledges some of the animosity that surrounds his personality. In his own words he admits that some people have been "irritated" or "disturbed" by his renown and his "celebrity."[1] But the truth is that the majority of the critics who have read his works and know of his work as an internationally recognized humanitarian and humanist admire him passionately. For most of us he has become an heroic figure, a man worthy of the highest admiration. He has accomplished so many good works in his lifetime that I have deliberately decided not to search for blemishes. I have always adhered to the credo enunciated somewhere by André Maurois that "La vie est trop courte pour être petite" (Life is too short to be small-minded), and so I shall concentrate on the positive here and leave it to others to spend their time dealing with imperfections.

I have no illusions about my originality. I know that inevitably I will be restating some of the facts already expressed by other commentators. To some degree, all of us become repositories of information that accumulate within us as a result of our earlier readings and discussions. At the same time, I think that I can shed some new light on certain facets of Wiesel that have not yet been adequately treated, including the following areas: his views of literary art and creativity; his idea of the function of literature; the importance of the experience of teaching in his life; the crucial place of French culture and language in his professional and personal life; the principal themes that shape his texts and public speeches, themes that, when repeated regularly, lend to the totality of his work a sense of comprehensiveness and consistency. And I hope to demonstrate that these themes, based mostly on his belief in the sanctity of human life (perhaps the central tenet of his Jewish faith) form the most significant feature in the architecture of his lifework.

I know that in a single volume I shall not succeed in exhausting each of these themes; but I believe that I can at least cover all or almost all of the main topics in Wiesel's extraordinary production. I hope that others will continue my work by exploring more fully some of the thematic material outlined in my panoramic view here.

My strategy is to select and to focus my attention on those overarching ideas, thoughts, and themes diffused throughout the length and breath of Wiesel's texts. Whereas most of the already published works on this writer accentuate a particular aspect of his thought (i.e., God, silence, memory, humanitarianism, the Holocaust), I prefer to view him in a more global sense, one that covers the broad gamut of his many interconnected themes and views.

I cannot overstate one imperative that determined my strategy here: whereas most of Wiesel's commentators concentrated on his book-length works of fiction and on his anthologies of Hasidic/Judaic essays, I, for my part, have deliberately opted to penetrate into the universe of his thought by studying mainly the enormous quantity of his shorter pieces (the essays, public addresses, prefaces, articles, dialogues, interviews) scattered throughout the span of his career. Only occasionally do I refer to the better-known, longer books. If I am not mistaken, I do not believe that anyone has as yet systematically stressed, to the same degree as I have, the shorter, more casual, more incidental, perhaps even more spontaneous writings produced by Wiesel on a fairly frequent basis during about four decades of feverish activity.

As the reader will infer from the attributions in my endnotes, by far the most useful single source for my research was Irving Abrahamson's *Against Silence: The Voice and Vision of Elie Wiesel,* an admirable three-volume compendium of Wiesel's shorter texts. Given the scale and cost of this collection, relatively few Wiesel readers will have had much familiarity with the Abrahamson work. They will find it available only in some of our larger academic and public libraries.

At the end of my book I list most of the works by and about Wiesel in English and French, especially those that proved to be most helpful to me in the preparation of my work. Wiesel has attracted the greatest attention in America (where he lives and works), in France (which he visits very often and because he chooses to write mainly in French), and in Israel (a nation that occupies a special place in his heart). The books about Wiesel to which I owe a great deal include titles by Michael Berenbaum, Harry Cargas, Ted Estess, Ellen Fine, Albert H. Friedlander, John K. Roth, Carol Rittner, Brigitte-Fanny Cohen, Philippe-Michaël de Saint Cheron, and a few others.

I have decided to treat my subject by quoting copiously from Wiesel's own statements and texts, many of which appear in texts rarely seen by most readers familiar with his more popular book-length works. No one—not even his most expert commentators—can speak more eloquently that the author himself about the themes underlying his philosophy of life and literature. When I add my comments to Wiesel's statements, it is mainly to explain, to clarify, and to make them more meaningful. In doing so I hope that I can increase the reading public's appreciation of the significance of Wiesel's total *oeuvre*.

Once my decision was made in late 1989 to write a book about Wiesel's themes, I realized that I would need to revisit all of his texts and to approach them as segments of an organic whole. Soon it was apparent to me that although his texts were disparate and varied in form, they were unified by a set of dominant themes and thoughts that marked the substance of his writings from beginning to end. Together these themes and thoughts constituted a veritable philosophy of life, a coherent view of the human condition. Starting with his initial work, *La Nuit* [Night], and continuing through his recent memoirs, there seems to exist in his writings a certain unified design. In effect, in a personal discussion with me one day, Wiesel adamantly stressed that he had undergone little or no intellectual evolution since the day he launched his career.

Wiesel's personal experience struck a meaningful chord in my own life and in that of my wife, both of us having lost a number of close relatives during the Holocaust catastrophe.

For the most part, I have read each of Wiesel's works in the original French, as they appeared in Paris "hot off the press." I have always tried to read texts in the original language, especially if I possessed proficiency in that language; I believe that one comes closest to appreciating the real intent of the author if one reads the text in the very words and phrases of the original version.

For some three decades, Wiesel has faithfully sent me each of his books, always enhancing them with an affectionate inscription. A prolific author, he has published about one book a year. Already almost forty have appeared in print, not to mention his numberless minor pieces, articles and prefaces.

That Wiesel has retained even a kernel of respect for the sinful family of mankind, that he holds a degree of hope for the future of the human race, these are astonishing facts when we consider the extent of his suffering and the tragic losses he himself had endured during the Holocaust. Despite all that he had seen and endured in the camps of death, the humanistic values inculcated in his soul by his orthodox Jewish upbringing have shielded him from the despair, bitterness, and nihilism that might otherwise have resulted from the atrocities and humiliations witnessed at Auschwitz/Birkenau and Buchenwald. His faith in humanity forms a central firmament in his philosophy of life. After liberation from the nightmare Elie Wiesel emerged a badly scarred human being. More than a half-century later, he continues to be haunted by his memories. His published pages are scorched by the flames of memory. These pages stand before us as a powerful monument to the hell created by humankind on this planet during the middle of the twentieth century. By reminding readers of the depths to which men and women can plunge, he hopes to guide us towards a more lofty plane of human behavior. His essential message, I believe, is his warning that if we do not remember the evils of the past, we may one day be forced to relive them.

A personal anecdote is appropriate at this point. Around 1967 or 1968, the organizers of a public lecture series at the University of New Mexico invited me to introduce Monsieur Elie Wiesel to an overflowing audience on that campus. At the time he was known mainly for a single book, *La Nuit*, and two or three subsequent novels. Few could predict then that he would someday develop into an international personality and even a Nobel Peace Laureate. While I do not recall my exact words of introduction, it was Wiesel himself who, a quarter of a century later, reminded me that I was the first person to have predicted on that day that he would someday receive a Nobel Prize; but I was thinking of the literature and not the peace prize. As a token of his appreciation, Wiesel gave me a gift, one of the few available facsimiles of the gold Congressional Medal of Achievement presented to him by President Reagan at a White House Ceremony.

Elie Wiesel is more than a writer; he is a compelling international figure. He has even evolved, to his own embarrassment, into a kind of unofficial voice for the Jewish people of the world. In reality, he ought to be regarded as one of the truly eloquent spokesmen for not only the Jewish people but also for all of the suffering minorities around the world. No one speaks more passionately than he about peace, justice, tolerance, and ethical values.

Wiesel's story continues to unfold. On October 25–27, 1998, Boston University celebrated his seventieth birthday. In the presence of a distinguished gathering of personalities, including President Jon Westling, Saul Bellow, Cynthia Ozick, Ariel Dorfman, John Silber, and many others, Wiesel shared with all of us present at these festivities his remarks about his philosophy of life, literature, and humankind.

Acknowledgments

During the years of my research I sought the counsel of many persons. My first words of thanks must be addressed to Monsieur Elie Wiesel himself. Having granted me considerable time, he willingly responded to many of my questions, helped me to clarify some perplexing questions, and confirmed or helped me to modify some of my theories. Because Wiesel speaks in so many places, and because I have traveled or resided in some of the places where he spoke, I was able to visit with him on and off his lecture circuit for almost three decades: in New Mexico, San Francisco, Baltimore, Boston, Cerisy-la-Salle, France, on the Susquehanna University campus in Pennsylvania, at his Manhattan home, and elsewhere.

Thanks to Wiesel's intervention, I met lengthily with a number of his closest Parisian associates—with journalist Brigitte-Fanny Cohen, Ministry of Cultural Affairs official Philippe-Michaël de Saint Cheron, Gabrielle (Gaby) Cohen (who described with visible emotion the days when she taught French to the young Wiesel, and who showed me one of Wiesel's adolescent notebooks), the well-known Parisian Rabbi Josey Eisenberg, with whom I talked about Wiesel's preoccupation with the figure of Job, and so many other French men and women. Almost an entire week, during the summer of 1995, I lived not only in Wiesel's presence but also with scores of Wiesel specialists from throughout western Europe who had come to the Château de Cerisy-la-Salle to share their interpretations of Wiesel's texts with each other.

In Washington, D.C. I benefited from a stimulating discussion with Michael Berenbaum, one of the most perceptive authorities on Wiesel who was working at the time with Wiesel on the planning stages of the United States Holocaust Museum. Berenbaum had already written one of the exemplary books on Wiesel. Frequently I met with John Friedman, a close friend of mine, who had published one of the most insightful interviews with Wiesel in the *Paris Review*.

During the summer of 1991 I visited with an old friend from my days at the University of Pittsburgh, Dr. Richard Rubenstein, then Distinguished Professor of the Humanities at Florida State University, and presently the President of the University of Bridgeport. A well-known and provocative authority of Jewish theology and a brilliant writer, Rubenstein helped me to come to grips with some of the multilayered intricacies of Wiesel's complex positions vis-à-vis God.

I am also indebted to several advanced students in French literature at Susquehanna University who, under my supervision, worked on various themes I discuss here and who assisted me in the preparation of my bibliography: Stuart Glasby, Robin Hastings, Alexandra Stobb, and John Stonaker.

I am grateful to the Faculty Research Committee at Susquehanna University for providing me with a key grant that funded a portion of my travel to France. Special appreciation must be expressed here to the then-Vice President of Academic Affairs, Dr. Jeanne Neff, who generously assisted me with funds for several research trips.

A word of thanks is appropriate here for Mrs. Shirley Weaver, my devoted faculty secretary at Susquehanna, who voluntarily spent many hours before her computer as she prepared three earlier versions of the manuscript. Not only was she generous with her time, but she proved to be a most perceptive decipherer of my almost illegible penmanship.

I am most grateful to my son Shelley Robert, who spent many hours, once this project was concluded, doing the final computer phase of this work.

Finally, I thank my wife, Ruth, who shared with me so many of the Wiesel experiences and helped me to better identify certain facets of Wiesel's personality that might otherwise have eluded me. She also suggested certain felicitous ways of describing some of the ideas that I had difficulty verbalizing.

* * *

I should like to acknowledge the fact that the United States Holocaust Memorial Museum has generously granted me permission to make use of the many long and short quotations that originally appeared in Irving Abrahamson's *Against Silence: The Voice and Vision of Elie Wiesel*, a work that was pivotal in my research. Both Mr. Abrahamson and Mr. Wiesel have also granted me permission to quote from their works.

The Worlds
of Elie Wiesel

1
Elie Wiesel—A Life and a Career

MANY AUTHORITIES OF THE CONTEMPORARY SCENE CONSIDER ELIE Wiesel the voice and conscience of the Jewish people today. For many of us he has played this role during the last three or four decades. But, in fact, who else does speak for the Jews? The Israeli Prime Minister cannot represent the Jews of the Diaspora living outside the territorial limits of the Jewish state. Nor can any rabbinical leader speak for all Jews since they divide themselves into several branches, among which are the Reformed, the Conservative, the Orthodox, and the Reconstructionists. Many nominal Jews do not affiliate with any of these branches. Some are non-practitioners. Some are closet Jews. Others are even self-hating Jews who hide behind façades of "Gentilism" or atheism. But then Jews also divide along other kinds of lines of demarcation: some refer to themselves as Ashkenazi Jews (those who hail from eastern, western, and central Europe) and then there are Sephardic Jews (whose ancestors came from the Mediterranean region). Other splinter groups exist, but all of this only demonstrates how difficult it is to make general statements that sum up the positions of all Jews. In reality, no single voice can possibly speak for all segments of Judaism to the same degree that the Pope, for example, articulates the message of universal Roman Catholicism. Nonetheless, if there is any single voice who commands the respect of most Jews, it is that of Elie Wiesel.

If not Wiesel, who else? By virtue of his literary achievements, by his unique ability to express himself verbally, by virtue of his powerful Holocaust experience, and especially by virtue of his thoroughly Jewish soul, he seems to be the ideal person to serve as the conscience of most Jews throughout the world.

A modest individual, Elie Wiesel would surely deny his right to serve as the spokesperson of world Jewry. Despite this modesty, however, he *almost* acknowledged this fact when, before an interfaith audience in the cavernous Cathedral of Saint John the Divine in New

York City, he stated that "I am glad you mentioned that I'm here as a Jew, and totally as a Jew, meaning that I represent more than my own person. As a Jew, I think it is my duty to tell you that we feel more and more threatened by anti-Semitism and by historical revisionism."[1]

The writings of Elie Wiesel and his own personal existence are consubstantial. His texts truly mirror his experiences, feelings, thoughts, and visions. I therefore begin my discussion of his journey through time and space by describing the high points in this author's biography and his personal traits. When one knows Elie Wiesel the man, one also knows the kinds of texts he has produced. My exegesis of Wiesel's ideas and themes will thus emanate from the roots of his life story.

According to Ted Estess, a respected Wiesel authority, there were three major existential phenomena that shaped Wiesel's life: first, Sighet, his hometown, where he experienced the joy of childhood and his spiritual awakening; second, the Holocaust, a period of destruction during which the values he had acquired during his childhood were challenged; third, the post-Holocaust epoch when, having undergone a psychological reawakening, he was forced to readapt to a new reality.[2]

Abrahamson, another respected authority on Elie Wiesel, partitions the writer's career into three momentous events: the Holocaust, the rebirth of the State of Israel, and the passive revolt of the Soviet Jews against Communist persecution.[3]

The life of Elie Wiesel is that of a citizen of the world. Born and raised in the Carpathian mountains bordering Hungary and Romania, he spent a part of his adolescence as a prisoner of the concentration camps in Germany and Poland. His formative post-liberation days he spent in Paris and Normandy, France. As a journalist he was assigned to India, and later Israel. He ended up residing in New York City, but his life in America has frequently been punctuated with his trips to Europe, Israel and to every corner of America and to other nations of the world. Often he is called upon to deliver lectures to international audiences. His thin, angular, tormented face appears on the television screens of virtually every nation of our planet. A wandering Jew, he "seems almost to recapitulate the story of his people."[4]

Wiesel has referred to his wandering existence as an "itinerary," a most appropriate term to characterize his experiences as a world traveler: "The itinerary of a Jewish writer today begins, has to begin, somewhere in the Carpathian mountains, in Sighet, has to go through many stations like New York where I live now; Paris, where I had my formative years, where I studied; Moscow, Leningrad—the places where I discovered the Jews of silence who are silent no more."[5]

Let us now retrace this itinerary, deconstructing the architecture of this life and arranging the principal segments in some kind of order. Prior to the recent publication of *Tous les fleuves vont à la mer* [All Rivers flow into the Sea], the first volume of his memoirs, Wiesel had never recounted the story of his life in any kind of coherent order. We can retell the story of Wiesel's life, basing our narrative on his memoirs, also on the scattered fragments of his existence such as they insinuate themselves throughout his other writings, and upon numerous conversations with him in New York, Albuquerque, Baltimore, San Francisco, France and elsewhere.

Childhood

Eliezer (Elie) Wiesel was born on 30 September, 1928 in Sighet, Hungary (today in Romania). He was named after his paternal grandfather, who lost his life as a medic in the Austro-Hungarian army during World War I. His mother, Sara Feig Wiesel, a homemaker, spent her life raising her four children: his three sisters—Hilda, Batya, and Tsipora, and her only son Elie. Shlomo Wiesel, Elie's grocer-father, encouraged his son to study languages, especially Yiddish and Hebrew, as well as literature and sacred texts of Judaic culture. A devout Jewish woman, Sara Feig Wiesel encouraged her son to study Jewish mysticism and religious doctrine, especially the Torah and the Talmud. A learned woman, (her forte was German literature), she adored the works of Goethe and Schiller. The Wiesel household was truly a bookish world in which knowledge for the sake of knowledge was a cherished central value of life. Wistfully Wiesel recalls that "my mind had been reformed, stimulated, or tested [in] Sighet in Transylvania."[6] Besides Sighet, the writer cites Paris, Moscow, and Jerusalem as the key cities where his intellectual formation was most forcefully shaped.

At the time of his childhood, Sighet was a bustling center of Jewish learning. Out of the town's total population of 25,000, 10,000 people belonged to the Jewish community. Following the Holocaust, only about fifty Jewish families remained there. Miraculously, the Jewish cemetery of Sighet has managed to survive the destruction of Eastern Europe's Jewry. Thus, the destiny of Sighet's Jewish community reflects the tragic history of modern European Judaism. Hitler had *almost* succeeded in his "final solution."

Among his childhood memories Wiesel recalls his early violin lessons: rhetorically he once asked "What parents in Eastern Europe did not want their child to become a Jascha Heifetz?"[7] Music has indeed held a special place during his life. He enjoys singing or hearing others interpret the "nigunds" or ancient Jewish melodies drawn from the long tradition of Jewish culture. In addition to music, Wiesel confesses that "once upon a time I wanted to become a philosopher, so I studied philosophy—and began to write novels."[8] In effect, his first literary ventures as a child consisted of commentaries on the Talmud written at the age of twelve. Decades following his departure from Sighet, when he returned he was surprised to find among the hundreds of Jewish books that still remained in an otherwise destroyed community a copy of a book containing the same boyhood commentaries. This rediscovery confirmed his decision someday to become a professional writer.

The single human being who more than anything else (even more than his parents) influenced him most significantly was his maternal grandfather, Dodye Feig. An old Hasid (a member of a Jewish mystical sect founded around 1750), Feig inspired his grandson with his passionate tales of Hasidic deeds of the past, tales which one day would have a way of penetrating into the texts of Wiesel's most memorable books. Wiesel later wrote that "My grandfather Dodye Feig is one of those no longer alive, and yet his teaching is still alive, because I am."[9] The writer could only assume that this beloved old man had perished in the gas chambers of Bergen-Belsen, since much later after the war he stumbled upon a photograph of his grandfather in the archives of this notorious camp.

Besides his music lessons and listening to his grandfather's Hasidic folk tales, the writer recalls his almost daily sessions in the *Heder* (Hebrew School) in which his stern teacher taught him to read and pray in Hebrew. He remembers returning home in 1938 from his *Heder* when he overheard his parents discussing Kristallnacht (the night of broken glass). Only much later did he realize the full significance of this tragic event. From the start, Wiesel became a religious young man. He found in the weekly services of the local synagogue not only a source of religious inspiration, but also a center for community social life and above all a place where he could listen avidly to the many storytellers who recounted the folk stories that Jews love to share with children from generation to generation: "I used to go to the synagogue every Sabbath and listen to the *maggadim*. They were wandering storytellers who used to go from one village to another. They were the link between the villages, the witnesses from one culture to another."[10] One day, these very same tales, like those related to him by Dodye Feig, were to reverberate in so many of Wiesel's own books. And so, in a sense, Elie Wiesel became the *maggid* for the Jewish world of the post-Holocaust era. In effect, he became the modern day troubadour who traveled throughout the world chanting the chronicles of Jewish experience before both Jewish and non-Jewish audiences in many nations and states.

Happy were the days of Wiesel's childhood. Growing up in a tightly knit family of loving parents and siblings was indeed a joyful period. Sabbaths and High Holy Days were marked by prayer in the Synagogue. For his entertainment he listened with wonderment to old Hasidic tales and sang traditional folk melodies. The weekly Sabbath meals and the blessing of the candles, wine and bread were major events for him. All of these happy days in Sighet took place against the backdrop of the picturesque Carpathian Mountains, overlooking the neighborhoods of Sighet. These mountains have imprinted in him an indelible mark: "Having spent all of my youth in the shadow of the Carpathians, I am always drawn to mountains, for I love their silence and their dizzying mysteries."[11] In effect, so strong was the lure of the mountains for Wiesel that he never learned to enjoy the beauty of a seashore or the charm of the flatter topographies of the world.

The Holocaust

The bliss and security of Wiesel's idyllic childhood came to an abrupt halt with the arrival of Hitler's armies into the heartland of Hungary in 1944. In March of that year Adolph Eichmann, the notorious Jew killer, from his headquarters in the Hotel Majestic in Budapest planned the eradication of the entire Hungarian Jewish population of some 750,000, one of Europe's largest. With awesome swiftness and with the usual German efficiency Eichmann moved to implement his infamous plan of extermination. More than 400,000 Jews were killed in an incredibly short time.

Hungarian Jews learned from news stealthily trickling in from other countries in Europe about how mass killings of Jewish communities had already begun to take place elsewhere. Yet with a mixture of blind optimism and incredulity the Jews of Hungarian Jewish communities, including those of Wiesel's Sighet, remained hopeful that somehow they might prove to be the exception in Hitler's grand plan for the final solution of the Jewish problem. After all, had they not been protected for the past three years by the Hungarian government in Budapest that repeatedly insisted that as Hungarian citizens Jews in that nation ought to be spared the tragic fate of non-Hungarian Jews? But Hitler's government insisted that Jews were Jews, no matter what their nationality happened to be, and the patience of the German authorities finally ran out. Once Hitler decided that Budapest was using delaying tactics, the Nazis assigned substantial German forces to do the dirty work more swiftly. Between 1940 and 1944, the Hungarian Jews lived with their false sense of delusion, certain that they would miraculously be spared. Wiesel's parents shared this unrealistic sense of delusion and did nothing to escape, even when escape might have been possible. Their time finally ran out.

In the summer of 1944 the Germans arrived at Sighet. Paralyzed by a mixture of indifference and immobilism, the Christian majority, having lived for generations side by side with the sizable Jewish community, did nothing to shield their neighbors from imminent disaster. With utter passivity the Christian inhabitants of Sighet watched with indifference as ten thousand of their Jewish citizens were arrested, ordered to board waiting cattle cars at the train station, and were deported to factories of death in Germany, Austria, and Poland.

So ended the happy boyhood of Elie Wiesel. This marked the beginning of the tragic "Night" in his life. For eleven terrifying months the sixteen-year-old lad would endure the most humiliating torture human beings were capable of inflicting upon other human beings. His mother and his three sisters were instantly separated from him and his father as they entered the women's compound of Auschwitz. Never again would Wiesel see either his mother or his youngest sister Tsipora, both of whom must have been killed in the gas chambers or in the crematoria, only to be buried in mass unmarked pits along with tens of thousands of other victims. As for his father, the son watched helplessly as Shlomo Wiesel was brutally tortured and starved. Eventually he died of malnutrition. Wiesel's two older sisters, Beatrice (or Batya) and Hilda, managed miraculously to survive the nightmare, and years after the fall of Germany their brother succeeded in reestablishing contact with them. The gruesome details of his captivity Wiesel has masterfully recaptured in *La Nuit*.

With the invasion of Western Europe by the Allies, the subsequent-liberation of France and the Low Countries, and with the counter-offensive in eastern Europe by the Russians, German military might began gradually to disintegrate. In Buchenwald where Wiesel was transferred, the Jewish underground launched an uprising against their weary SS guards. With grenades and gunfire on all sides, the adolescent Wiesel and the other children could survive in the battle only by falling on the ground to escape being hit. After the brief battle, the German SS guards fled, and the Jewish prisoners seized control of the infamous camp. Six hours later on 11 April, 1945, Wiesel remembers with emotion how the United States Third Army arrived to liberate the tattered and starving remaining Jews who had not been murdered. Three days after his liberation Wiesel became seriously ill with food poisoning; his body had temporarily lost its ability to digest real nourishment. After his recovery, when he saw himself for the first time in a mirror, he was so shocked by his emaciated image that he shattered the glass with his fist. The moment he obtained a pencil and paper he took notes of his experiences in the heinous camp, while his memory of them was still fresh. He felt obsessed with the need someday to record for posterity the nightmare of Auschwitz and Birkenau. These notes would one day germinate into the fiery masterpiece that he called, aptly enough, *Night*.

Understandably, the Holocaust cast an incredible shadow over his entire existence. Despite the metamorphosis of his life, from a prisoner to a free man, he believed that he had remained unaltered from the days when he was a happy child in Sighet: "I am still the same person I was thirty years ago and forty years ago; I am still a child going to *Heder*, afraid of the *melamed* [the Hebrew school teacher]."[12] His nostalgic longing for the happy days of boyhood represents a major theme in his literature, as we shall see.

La Belle France

A free person, Wiesel now confronted a major dilemma. He assumed, quite logically, that his entire family had perished in the flames of the anti-Semitic upheaval. Where could he go? He did not wish to return to Sighet where he believed that his former Christian neighbors had assumed possession of the abandoned Jewish homes and the furnishings therein. The return of the Jews to their former homes would surely be greeted with hostility. Besides, Sighet symbolized for him the place where he had so mercilessly been robbed of his happy childhood. He was tempted to go to Palestine, the historic homeland of the Jews. But Palestine was then under British mandate, and, the British, fearing violent repercussions from the Arab population, imposed severe immigration restrictions on the few European Jews surviving the German camps. A stateless and family-deprived young man of seventeen years of age, Wiesel had no choice but to consent to board a train bound for Belgium, one of the nations willing to accept homeless Jews. However, at the request of General Charles de Gaulle, the leader of the newly liberated French nation, his train was rerouted to Paris. De Gaulle wished to create in France a haven for the homeless. France had traditionally opened her gates to the dispossessed and had always emerged a stronger nation as the results of the contributions made to her culture by new immigrants.

At first, Wiesel was assigned to reside in an asylum in Normandy supervised by the Oeuvres du Secours aux Enfants, a charitable children's aid society. There he received nourishment, shelter, and instruction in the French language. So proficient in French did he become that between 1948 and 1951 he felt comfortable enough with the language that he could enroll and study in the University of Paris's liberal arts program at the celebrated Sorbonne. He not only mastered French but he also took courses in philosophy, psychology, and literature. He made friends among the remnants of the Parisian Jewish community and supported himself through college thanks to a variety of part time jobs: e.g., as a choir director, a Jewish Bible and Hebrew teacher, a translator from Hebrew into French, and as a counselor in a Jewish summer camp for children. At the same time he dreamed of going to the newly established State of Israel: "In Paris I wandered around like a sleepwalker, looking for ways to go to Israel."[13] Elsewhere he confesses that "in Paris, with rediscovered classmates, I recalled our tumultuous discussions of the early postwar years! Should one go to Palestine or choose the universal message of Marxism?"[14] One of Wiesel's closest friends in Paris was Moshe Lazar, whom he had originally met in the Normandy children's home. In 1948 the two young men went together to a recruiting center designed to attract soldiers for the fledgling Israeli army. Lazar was accepted, while Wiesel was rejected for medical reasons. Lazar emigrated to Israel and later moved to America where he distinguished himself as a professor of comparative literature and as a dean at the University of Southern California. As for Wiesel, he remained in France. The two men always remained close friends.

Elie Wiesel seems always to have been susceptible to influences by his greatest teachers. Throughout his life, he had generously acknowledged his indebtedness to them. One of these teachers was Gustave Wahl, a philosophy teacher in Paris. This teacher had instilled in the young man a profound appreciation for the French classical writers as well as those of ancient Greece and Rome. Decades later Wiesel continues to quote from the great writers of France whom he read with the same zeal as if he were reading Hasidic and Tamudic texts.

While still a student at the Sorbonne, Wiesel accepted a job as a journalist for the well-known Franco-Jewish periodical, *L'Arche*. His dream of seeing Israel was finally answered when the magazine assigned him to cover events in the newly established nation. By 1952 he was also working for the Tel Aviv daily newspaper, *Yediot Ahronot*. At the time, this newspaper struggled from week to week merely to survive, and Wiesel was poorly paid during his years as a journalist. Today *Yediot Ahronot* has become one of the most successful newspapers in Israel. One of his earliest assignments with the paper was to cover events in India. It was there that he learned English, a language that was rapidly joining French—eventually surpassing it—as a major vehicle of international communication. In 1956, the Israeli newspaper sent its by then experienced foreign correspondent to New York City where his editor asked him to cover the proceedings of the fledgling United Nations.

America the Beautiful

Wiesel's first trip to America proved to be a critical event that totally transformed his life. Soon after his arrival in New York, he was struck by a taxicab in Times Square. Much of that year he spent in a hospital bed and a wheelchair. This convalescence gave him time to reflect lengthily upon the meaning of his life and on the damaging scars scorching his shoulders since his liberation. Massive guilt invaded his being: why did he deserve to be alive while so many millions of innocent victims perished? Some five years after his accident he wrote a short novel, *Le Jour* (translated into English as *The Accident*) in which he depicted an accident involving a young Jewish survivor of the camps who was hit by a taxi in the busy streets of New York. During his hospitalization the protagonist in Wiesel's novel undergoes a psychological crisis on reaching the conclusion that subconsciously he may have been seeking death through the accident in order to join the victims of the Holocaust. Like the young man in *Le Jour*, Wiesel has remained even today tormented by the fact that he was one of the few to have outlived the nocturnal hell of the German camps.

As he survived both psychological trauma and the physical pain of the post-accident days, he comprehended for the first time why, if one must choose between death and life, one must select life. He understood, too, that it would be counterproductive for him to persist in reliving the past, that he had no choice but to face the future with a more constructive attitude, that the time had come for him to do something positive with his life. Without forgetting the past, he would henceforth use the lessons learned in the Holocaust to dedicate his life to inspire others to create a world that would keep humanity from reliving the misfortune that he had witnessed. He sums up his vision of life in the following citation: "We [the survivors] could have told the world: 'We don't trust you anymore. If all your civilization and culture could lead to this dehumanization, this total failure of man, we want no part of it.' . . . [But we] chose to become neither antisocial nor asocial. [We] refused to deal in hate. [We] became scientists and artists, teachers and musicians; some even became writers."[15]

A reborn human being, Wiesel, on learning that his French travel documents were about to expire, decided not to seek renewal of his old papers but instead to apply for the appropriate green card in order to remain a resident in America. An American citizen since 1963, Elie Wiesel continued to write almost all of his literary works in French; but these have been translated into English almost immediately after publication in Paris. Also, he frequently returns to France, for it is there that he finds much intellectual stimulation among his close friends and professional associates.

Literary Débuts

In 1957 Wiesel joined the staff of the *Jewish Daily Forward* the most venerable and best-known Yiddish-language newspaper in America. In his memoirs, he often alludes to his almost desperate financial circumstances, both while he worked as a journalist for the Parisian *L'Arche* and for the Israeli newspaper *Yediot Ahronot*. He lived from hand to mouth, from day to day. But later, once he wrote his first book, *La Nuit*, and enjoyed his first literary success, his fortunes improved markedly.

In 1945, the year of his release from Buchenwald, he took a self-imposed oath never to speak or write about the abominable experiences he had endured in the camps. This terrible debasement of the human spirit he could not bring himself to describe. For more than ten years he remained silent, consumed by the gnawing need to remind a naïve world about the anguish of the Jewish victims but simultaneously paralyzed by his inability to find the language that could do justice to his ordeal. Since childhood Wiesel dreamed of becoming a storyteller, a writer. Could he now describe the indescribable? For ten years Wiesel remained true to his oath of silence, lacking the courage or psychological stamina to depict the horrors of the death camps. He disclosed that "It took me ten years before I felt I was ready to do it. I wrote my first book, *Night,* in Yiddish, a tribute to the language of those communities that were killed. I began writing it in 1955. I felt I needed ten years to collect words and the silence in them."[16] What finally emerged was an enormous tome of manuscript pages entitled, *Un Die Velt Hat Geshvigen* [And the World Remained Silent], the title reflecting the indifference of the world during the time that six million Jews were being slaughtered. The indifference of the world during the systematic eradication of European Jewry remains an obsessive theme throughout Wiesel's career.

Un Die Velt Hat Geshvigen was published in Buenos Aires. Because the work was written in Yiddish, a language that had declined considerably with the destruction of the majority of Yiddish speakers, it was a virtual certainty that the audience for such a work would remain very limited. Soon after its publication, the struggling journalist returned to Paris to interview a number of major French personalities, including the Jewish Prime Minister of France, Pierre Mendès-France, and the internationally known French-Catholic writer, François Mauriac, who had recently received the Nobel Prize for Literature. Although Wiesel never succeeded in meeting with the well known French Prime Minister, at least he succeeded in getting to meet the writer. Mauriac revealed an almost obsessive interest in regard to Wiesel's existence as a survivor of Auschwitz and Buchenwald. He urged the young Jewish journalist to rewrite his Yiddish opus in French—a language that enjoyed wide international prestige. He also urged him to abbreviate the scope of the story, making it a more tightly organized, concise work that would possess much more intense dramatic appeal. Wiesel allowed himself to be persuaded by the great French author, reducing the 888 pages of his Yiddish manuscript to 127 pages of gripping French text. He also attenuated some of the rage he felt against God as well as against a taciturn world and replaced this rage with a heightened degree of narrative tension. Also, the somewhat cumbersome Yiddish title, *And the World was Silent,* was transformed into the much more gripping title *La Nuit.* It certainly helped Wiesel to gain a large French readership once Mauriac volunteered to write the preface. But Mauriac went one step further: he introduced the Jewish survivor to Jérôme Lindon, a young, sensitive French Jew who presided over one of France's most prestigious publishing houses, Les Editions de Minuit, a firm that had assumed a role of leadership among avant-garde publishers in Paris. It produced some of the most significant titles of the French Nouveau Roman (New Novel) group, including new novels of Michel Butor and important titles by Samuel Beckett.

An impressive success from the outset in France, *La Nuit* also sold well throughout the Francophone world. Two years after its French debut, the work, masterfully translated by Stella Rodway, appeared in 1960 in America and Great Britain under the title of *Night.* Henceforth, the career of Elie Wiesel was clearly established, and he has since emerged as one of the most read writers of our age. Never did the nascent writer forget the critical role played by François Mauriac in helping him to launch his career as a writer.

Night, an autobiographical tale, chronicles Wiesel's personal experiences of childhood and those of his captivity in the camps. A riveting text, it holds the reader's attention until the final page. Parts of it, although written in prose, assume the rhythms and sonority of poetry. That it has been compared with Anne Frank's *Diary of a Young Girl* (1947) is both understandable and somewhat unfortunate; the two works are vastly dissimilar, except that both are written by youthful commentators who describe the terror of life for adolescents who witness the Nazi Era. *La Nuit,* for its part, is a compelling account of a child's existence in a universe of starvation, torture, barbed wire, executions, and gas chambers. It relates Wiesel's inner anguish as he agonizingly watches the decline of his father's health and ultimate death. Beginning with a picture of childhood bliss, the author goes on to dramatize how these early joys give way to the tragic moments that followed his deportation to Auschwitz.

Although commentators of Elie Wiesel cite him as the prime example of Holocaust literature, *Night* is, in reality, the only book in which Wiesel provides us with a direct reporting of what actually occurred in the death camps. In almost all of his other texts, Wiesel refers to the Holocaust indirectly or obliquely, either by innuendoes, fleeting references, or through the residual effects residing in the souls of survivors.

A landmark even in Wiesel's career, *La Nuit* gave him self-confidence in his ability to express himself through a subtle combination of words and silences. At last he discovered that it was possible for him to vanquish his inhibitions concerning the revelation of the private world of the Holocaust recollections with a public audience of tens of thousands of unknown readers. By purging his tortured soul of memories that had been consuming his conscience, he could at long last establish a more harmonious relationship with his inner self. Above all, he realized that indeed he possessed the requisite rhetorical gifts of literary craftsmanship and could henceforth go on to write on subjects of profound interest to him. Through literary creation this young author could now transform himself from a witness of death into someone who believed in the miracle of survival. Out of the ashes of the past there rose the flames of hope.

The Years of Maturity

Soon after the publication of *La Nuit* in 1958, the newly successful and now self-confident author wrote two more compact novels, both dealing with the experiences of survivors from the former death-camps. Blending autobiography with fictional inventiveness, he composed *L'Aube* [Dawn] in 1960 and *Le Jour* [The Accident] one year later. In *Dawn*, Wiesel portrays a Holocaust survivor who travels to the newly born State of Israel to participate in the dramatic struggle to win the right to establish a Jewish homeland in the face of Arab resistance. Essentially this second novel is built around the theme of the creation of a new nation despite seemingly insurmountable odds. As for *Le Jour*, the autobiographical plot mirrors the author's serious accident in New York City.

Much later, in 1987, Wiesel's three earliest novels, *Night, Dawn* and *The Accident* were merged into a single tripartite volume entitled *Night Trilogy* and became one of the writer's best selling literary works. These three titles constitute Elie Wiesel's earliest period as a literary artist.

Wiesel has since continued to publish approximately one volume per year. His prodigious productivity has provoked considerable scholarly curiosity. When someone asked him, "Do you have a regular work schedule?": here is how the writer responded:

> Yes, I have always worked from six to ten in the morning. I always have two projects that I work on at the same time, one fiction and one non-fiction . . . I do my research, reading and studying in areas relating to my writing.

> I work sixteen hours a day, and I work everyday except Jewish holidays and Sabbaths . . . If I have one problem with fiction, I go to non-fiction. One balances the other. Fiction is more taxing. I really can write anywhere—that's my journalistic discipline. I can work in a plane, in a café, anywhere.[17]

Wiesel confesses to writing his manuscripts with a picture of Sighet almost always placed before him. Always he wishes to remind himself, during the creative process, of the once joyful experiences of life within the vibrant embrace of his beloved family.

On analyzing his personal method of composing texts, he reveals that it is the first line of every book that forms his most challenging obstacle. Once the initial opening has been devised, and once he has satisfied himself with the sound, flow, and the words of the first sentence, the remainder seems to emerge quite readily. But the first sentence generally does not take form until he can hear within himself some kind of indefinable melody that rings in his ears. Out of this melody he develops the themes, ideas, and structure of the nascent sentence. Confessing further that he generally writes three drafts of each book, he consumes reams of paper to communicate the themes that both haunt and consume him. Finally there comes the inevitable work of reduction. Once these themes have asserted themselves, he launches the inevitable elimination of excessive verbosity, retaining the barest essentials. Most of the time only about ten percent of the original manuscript ends up in the published text of the manuscript. Like the nineteenth-century novelist Flaubert, whose process of creativity may have served as a model for the author of *Night*, Wiesel claimed that "A writer's whole heritage is in the choice of each word."[18] In the second draft, Wiesel labors to polish his structure, to reshape the paragraphs, to refine the transitional sections, and to improve upon his choice of vocabulary. While continuing to perfect and further reduce the text in the third and final draft, he senses "the symphony is already there."[19] Repeatedly he refers to literary creation as a kind of musical composition or as the work of a sculptor who tirelessly chisels away the non-essentials of a block of marble until only the absolutely minimal, critical mass remains.

Having produced three major novels, Wiesel finally mustered the courage to return to his native city of Sighet. It was a traumatic experience for him to encounter there so few Jews who remained from a once thriving community of ten thousand. Shaken by his return to the original site of his happy childhood, he vowed to write a fourth novel, one that would recapture the emotional impact of his return to Sighet. In *La ville de la chance* (1962) (translated as *The Town Beyond the Wall*) Wiesel forged a plot in which he depicted a young Jewish survivor who, on returning to his birthplace, walks like a bewildered stranger through the meandering streets of the town. Along the thoroughfares, the visitor sees in a window one of the city's residents observing him silently, indifferently. With riveting tension, the novelist provides us with a flashback to an earlier day when a similarly mute person watched through the same window as the Jews of the city were herded into cattle-cars bound for Auschwitz. For this novel, Wiesel received his first major literary award, the 1963 Prix Rivarol.

One of the most anguished moments of Wiesel's life was his inability as a religious Jew to explain the silence of God during his imprisonment in Auschwitz. How could God accept the acts of barbarism committed against hundreds of thousands of infants and young children? How could God have permitted such heinous deeds to take place? Where was Wiesel's God when thousands of elderly, sickly people were tortured to death in Treblinka and Bergen-Belsen? How could anyone explain the murder of millions of God's "Chosen People," the very people who had devised a concept of monotheism, a concept that has become the foundation for the great religious faiths of our universe? Out of the troubling questions Elie Wiesel constructed a new novel on the theme of man's relationship with God: *Les portes de la forêt* (translated as *The Gates of the Forest*), a work published in Paris in 1964 and the English in New York in 1966. One of Wiesel's most complex and philosophical works of fiction, *The Gates of the Forest* is built around the experience of a young Hungarian survivor of the concentration camps who, following his escape from captivity, ends up in a band of partisans who resist the German military forces from their refuge in a forest. Eventually, after the war, the survivor travels to America in search of a new life. But memories of the Holocaust continue to torment the protagonist. He cannot stop searching for answers to his questions of why God, the God of the Jews, refrained from halting the extermination of millions of guiltless human beings. Intermittently this young man hurls both recriminations against and declarations of love for God as he concludes by choosing the path of love for his fellow men rather the road leading to rejection of God.

After writing a series of semi-autobiographical novels concerning the Holocaust and its aftermath, Wiesel turned in 1966 to his first purely non-fiction, non-autobiographical book, *Les Juifs du silence* (translated that year as *The Jews of Silence*). Sent to the Soviet Union by the Tel Aviv newspaper, *Yediot Ahronot,* in 1965 and again in 1966 to write articles in Hebrew on the plight of the three million Soviet Jews, he composed his first series of essays on their unfortunate fate in a Godless state. This collection he soon rewrote in French as *Les Juifs de silence,* so that he could reach out to the consciences of Jews and non-Jews in Europe and America. Wiesel sought to provoke awareness among the non-Russian people about the tragic predicament confronting a whole population, one that was denied the freedom to worship according to its tradition. Everywhere in Russia he had encountered an environment of intolerance, discrimination, and persecution, both subtle and overt. From personal experience he knew well how another Shoah (Holocaust) could rapidly erupt in a climate of animosity and persecution.

Elie Wiesel ought to be credited as the first major writer to call attention to the plight of Soviet Jewry. In the preface to *The Jews of Silence* he wrote that "The pages that follow are the report of a witness. Nothing more and nothing else. Their purpose is to draw attention to a problem about which no one should remain unaware."[19] From that point on Wiesel assumed a new role in life: he became the indefatigable champion who called for the unconditional release of the Soviet Jews from their bondage. That he succeeded in his campaign is a fact of history. Since *glassnost* the trickle of Jewish emigration expanded into a mass exodus of Jews who won the right to leave their hostile environment to find a more welcome climate in Israel and elsewhere.

From the Shoah Wiesel had learned one valuable lesson: no longer must the world remain silent before the plight of any people, as had been the case during the era of Auschwitz. Silence and indifference were the scourges of humankind. Human beings bear a sacred obligation to relieve the pain of other human beings. From his powerful campaign in behalf of Soviet Jewry Wiesel learned a vital lesson: that of the power of the pen. Through his pen he could move a reading public to take action. But he also learned that he possessed the literary gifts to be not only a novelist but a persuasive essayist who could inspire action in his readers.

Following a second visit to Sighet, he published in 1964 a collection of short texts entitled *Les chants des morts* (translated into English two years later as *Legends of our Time*). Consisting of philosophical essays, short stories, and various personal anecdotes, this work summarizes his views on the question of survival following the excruciating experience of the Holocaust.

On the occasion of the twenty-fifth anniversary of his liberation from Buchenwald he wrote in 1970 *Entre deux soleils* (translated as *One Generation After*) in which once again he depicted his vision of someone who had miraculously survived, someone who could shake off the uneasy feeling that so many pressing human problems remained unresolved even a quarter of a century after the closing of the death camps.

Marriage and Fatherhood

At the age of forty, the then internationally recognized author married Marion Erster Rose, a woman of Austrian origin who had also been a Holocaust survivor. With his description of the wedding, Wiesel concludes the first volume of his recent memoirs. The wedding took place during the Passover holiday, a festival that symbolizes liberation from Pharaoh's Egyptian enslavement and also the renewal of Jewish civilization. For Wiesel too, married life signified renewal and apogée. From all appearances, the union of Marion and Elie Wiesel has been a felicitous relationship of two people who complemented each other—not only in their personal lives but also professionally. Marion Wiesel, multilingual in her own right, has become her husband's finest translator. Since 1969, the year of their wedding, she has translated most of his books from French to English. Her translations generally appear one or two years after the original Paris publication.

Three years after their marriage, in 1972, Marion and Elie Wiesel had their first and only child, a son whom they named Shlomo Elisha. With ostensible pride, the writer proclaimed that "I would like him to remember where he comes from, whose name he bears. He bears my father's name."[20] For Wiesel to have had a son seemed almost like a miracle. After all, most of the family had been exterminated. Thus Hitler's "final solution" would never be fulfilled. The very name that had nearly perished in the crematoria and gas chambers of Europe could now perpetuate itself through a newborn son! Here is Wiesel's passionate description of the wondrous birth of his son: "My son's first name is Shlomo. It was my father's name. His middle name, Elisha, , means "God is salvation." We [Jews] believe in names so much. I was the only son. I cannot break the chain. It is impossible that 3500 years should end with me, so I took those 3500 years and put them on the shoulders of this little child."[21] "Elisha" (as he is called in the family and who has since graduated from Yale University) accompanied his celebrated father to almost every significant ceremony in his honor-laden life. His presence was particularly meaningful when, at the age of fourteen, he stood at his father's side on the dais in Oslo, Norway when the Norwegian Monarch presented his father with the Nobel Peace Prize. After graduation from college, the son has gone into work in computer and information science.

As the twentieth-century's most renowned survivor—perhaps even the most famous survivor in history—Elie Wiesel has always been obsessed with the miracle of Jewish survival despite the millennia during which the Jews were victimized by assimilation, forced conversions, persecution, inquisitions, and the Holocaust. For Wiesel, his son Elisha represents a vital link in the ongoing chain of Jewish history. In his own modest way, Wiesel contributed to the history of a beleaguered people in their struggle to prolong their values and identity from generation to generation. Here is how he describes the responsibility that his son will have to bear for the rest of his life:

> And so I will tell my son that survival in itself is a virtue. It has become the virtue of mankind, and that virtue we [Jews] have taught mankind. It is important. I will tell my son that all the fires, all the pain, will be meaningless, if he in turn will not transmit our story together, to his friends, and one day to his children.[22]

As the son of a survivor, Shlomo Elisha Wiesel thus carries on his back an awesome baggage of history.

THE GRAND YEARS

After several ventures in the domain of non-fiction, Elie Wiesel returned to his more customary mode: the writing of novels. His unquenchable taste for novels had been recharged by the decisive and unexpected victory of the Israeli defense forces over the seemingly invincible military might of the Arab nations during the Six-Day War of 1967. Out of this heady victory he concocted a whole new novel built around the theme of Israel's triumph and its recapture of the Old City of Jerusalem. Like so many other pundits of history, he viewed Israel's electrifying success as yet another David-Goliath event. A year later, in 1968, he produced *Le mendiant de Jérusalem* (published in 1970 as *A Beggar in Jerusalem*). For many years this novel proved to be what was probably Wiesel's most popular title after *Night*. A bestseller in Europe and America, *A Beggar in Jerusalem*, arguably his most optimistic novel, relates the saga of a spectacular military victory and the joy of returning to pray before the west wall of Jerusalem, Israel's holiest shrine.

Despite the effervescent spirit pervading this novel, Wiesel continued to be troubled by the ongoing plight of the Soviet Jews. Thus, in 1968, he composed his first play, *Zalmen ou la Folie de Dieu*, (adapted in English as *Zalmen or the Madness of God*). The work premiered at the Arena Theater in Washington, D.C. Later televised on national public television throughout the United States, *Zalmen* proved to enjoy only limited success. Paradoxically, the writer who excelled in minimalist literary style buried his first play in layers of complexity and verbosity, so much so that it suffers from ambiguous symbols and overly detailed realism. The sole successful component in the play is the personality of Zalmen, an idiot in a small Russian town visited by a delegation of prominent American Jews during Yom Kippur. Beneath Zalmen's illusory ignorance there lurks a great deal of practical wisdom and much common sense.

Since Wiesel's earliest work, one notes in his total oeuvre the interchange between two alternating and recurrent trends: his predilection for autobiographical novels, universal themes and Jewish topics. Thus the novel *A Beggar in Jerusalem* (1970) was followed by a purely Hasidic work entitled *Célébration Hassidique: Portraits et légendes* (1972), translated as *Souls on Fire: Portraits and Legends of Hasidic Masters* (1972). One of his truly stellar literary achievements, *Souls on Fire* represents Wiesel's most eloquent statement on Hasidism. Drawing his inspiration from childhood remembrances of tales told to him and his sisters by his Hasidic grandfather, Dodye Feig, the author recreates a kaleidoscope of stories about the lives of some of the Hasidic masters, their *weltanschauung*, their ecstatic and mystical relationship with God, and the adventures of some of the leading Hasidic rabbis of Europe. Ubiquitously present throughout these tales is a visible Camusean influence: like Camus, Wiesel believed that in spite of depressing tribulations in human existence, people must resist the temptation to fall prey to despair. They must resist negativism and struggle to vanquish defeatism. Out of this struggle there grows a kind of cautious optimism that points us in the direction of hope.

Quite deservedly *Célébration Hassidique* received the Prix Bordon from the Académie Française.

In 1973, Wiesel composed *Ani Maamin* (in Hebrew, I believe), a work defying easy classification among the rubrics of literary genres. First published in France and subtitled *Chant perdu et retrouvé* [A Song Lost and Found Again], it appeared the following year in the United States as a handsomely bound bilingual edition in French and English. Written in blank verse and serving as a libretto for a cantata composed by the Franco-Jewish composer, Darius Milhaud, the verses in *Ani Maamin* simultaneously incorporate music, poetry, prayer, and theater. With its surging rhythms and dramatic biblical scenes, the reader or spectator cannot easily resist the compelling events portrayed by this passionate drama.

Wiesel's creative pendulum now swung back to the novel. In 1973, he completed *Le serment de kolvillág* (translated that same year as *The Oath*), a novel that gravitates around the protagonist, Azriel, a typical Wieselian madman. But this seeming madman comprehends more lucidly than sane or "normal" people that we live in a topsy-turvy world of irrationality, a world in which sane people commit unspeakable acts of torture and horror, while their "insane" *confrères* watch these acts with disbelief and shock. In the "cultured" nation of Nazi Germany, inhuman, despicable behavior was regarded as socially acceptable activity legitimized by the policies of the established state. In order to prevent a deeply disturbed young man from committing suicide, Azriel breaks a self-imposed oath of silence (hence the title) never to disclose to anyone that all of the Jews of his village, Kolvillág, had been killed by their gentile neighbors. Azriel, the sole Jew to have escaped the massacre, is thus the only witness to a heinous crime. He understands that once he dies, no one will be alive to preserve the memory of the fatal pogrom. As a result, he selects the young suicidally inclined man to serve as the potential carrier of his story from generation to generation. The young man is thus motivated to reject suicide, realizing that it is his moral obligation to serve as a link with a past that would otherwise disappear into oblivion. In Hebrew "kol" means "every," while "villag" is Hungarian for "village." Thus Kolvillág symbolizes all of those villages, those shtetls, where entire Jewish populations were eradicated during the pogroms or as a part of the Holocaust.

Wiesel's creative urge then swung from fiction towards non-fictional Jewish history. His new book, entitled *Célébration biblique: Portraits et légendes,* was published in Paris in 1975 and, one year later, in New York as *Messengers of God: Biblical Portraits and Legends*. Whereas in the earlier volume of Jewish non-fiction the principal characters were Hasidic figures, in the second volume Wiesel opts to feature the patriarchs and prophets from the Jewish Bible. The author transplants Abraham, Isaac, Adam, Job, and others from the ancient times, placing them in contemporary situations where they must react to the demands of the twentieth century. Interestingly, they witness the post-Holocaust era and try to apply the values they had asserted in the ancient Bible to the atrocities witnessed by them in the Hitler era. Like Camus' Sisyphus, these biblical giants counsel a wounded humanity to choose perseverance and faith over despair and faithlessness. Through the voices of the patriarchs, Wiesel sends us a message of life and hope and rejects the rhetoric of death and nihilism.

Wiesel's subsequent work, *Un Juif aujourd'hui,* appeared first in Paris in 1977; a year later it was translated into English and published in New York as *A Jew Today*. His third volume of essays about contemporary topics, *A Jew Today* expands the author's concern for the purely Jewish destiny to a vital interest in the fate of all other oppressed people: specifically the book deals with the people of Cambodia, Bangladesh, Blacks suffering under the then-apartheid of South Africa, the boat-people of Vietnam, the Palestinians forced to dwell in the refugee camps. The underlying theme here is quite obvious: Wiesel's belief in the solidarity and brotherhood of the human race. Repeatedly he reminds us that when one people suffers, we all suffer.

Once again the novelist/essayist tried his hand at the theater. This time he published the play, *Le Procès de Shamgorod (tel qu'il se déroula le 25 février 1649)* (1979). The play was later translated as *The Trial of God (as it took place on February 25, 1649)*. God is placed on trial for allowing a pogrom to take place in 1694 in which scores of Jews are murdered by their Christian neighbors. A Jewish innkeeper and three wandering Jewish minstrels conduct the trial, acting as prosecuting attorneys. Although they ostensibly accuse God of indifference to evil, in reality, it was not God who ought to be prosecuted but rather the accusers who did little to halt the atrocities. Wiesel maintains that it is not God who behaves in an evil manner but rather ordinary men and women. Only the guilty are guilty, those who perform the evil acts. But there is here a not so subtle suggestion that God, too, by being so ineffectual in permitting his creatures to victimize others, shares some culpability. And so Wiesel, once again, subjects his own faith to a supreme test. How can one remain a true believer when God allows such despicable crimes to occur? Unlike his first play, *The Trial of God* enjoyed considerable success, thanks in part to the superb performances of the casts in Paris, Oslo, West Germany, and on numerous American university campuses.

THE DECADE OF THE EIGHTIES

Year after year, Wiesel's productivity continued unrelentingly. In addition to his composition of booklength volumes, he traveled frequently from city to city, addressing university audiences, public forums, church and synagogue groups, television audiences. Through a lecturing agent, he secured assignments as a speaker in public lecture series both in the United States and Europe. In addition, he taught as a college professor every week, believing that it was essential for him to share his testimony with young people. Instrumental in organizing conferences on Soviet Jewry, he led an especially successful World Meeting in Brussels during February 1976. In his address to the delegates he enunciated a particularly eloquent statement on one of his favorite themes, Zionism and the state of Israel:

> He who threatens the State of Israel attacks the people of Israel. He who fails to denounce the lies equating Zionism with racism [referring to a United Nations resolution passed by the General Assembly on this subject] accepts the thinking of our enemies. We hold that Zionism, conceived in Jewish history, bears the nobility of the Messianic spirit—and that Jewish history, so oft the victim of racism, is ever the answer to racism.[23]

One fundamental conviction reverberates throughout his public talks: the inseparability of the Jews inside the State of Israel and those Jews who constitute the Diaspora around the world.

Wiesel launched the decade of the eighties with the publication in Paris of a new novel, *Le testament d'un poète juif assassiné* (1980), a work that earned for him two literary awards: the Prix du Livre International and the Prix des Bibliothécaires. One year later it was translated into English as *The Testament*. Deriving its inspiration from the author's ceaseless anguish over the plight of the Soviet Jews, the novel is structured as a confessional diary written by a Soviet poet, Paltiel Kossover, who was murdered during the Stalin era in 1952. The poet's only son finds his late father's diary and devotes much of his life to analyzing its text. With horror, the son learns of the barbaric torture his father had been forced to undergo. The analogy between the Stalinist gulag and the Nazi concentration camps is quite apparent. In Paris and New York, the major critics reacted to Wiesel's latest novel with thunderous praise. By now Wiesel had managed to draw the attention of the entire western world to the dramatic problem confronting the Soviet Jews, a fact that explains, at least in part, the novel's success. Another reason for the favorable critical reviews was the fact that in *The Testament* Wiesel's literary style and art had never been so felicitous.

Buoyed by the triumph of *Le Testament,* Wiesel applied his creative faculties to the composition of yet another novel, *Le Cinquième Fils,* published in 1983 and translated two years later by his wife Marion as *The Fifth Son.* Of all of his novels, *The Fifth Son* is the one work that takes place mainly in an urban setting of Manhattan, the site of Wiesel's home. We encounter there the son of Holocaust survivors who is being raised in a typically middle-class American milieu. (Did Wiesel use his own son Elisha as a model for the protagonist here?) Once again we encounter a typical Wieselian plot: a young man, Ariel, is obsessed by his insatiable need to demystify the murky past of his parents. Thanks to his persistent investigations into this past, he discovers, to his surprise, that his survivor-parents had once given birth to another son, also named Ariel, who had been murdered by the Nazis during the Holocaust. Ariel also discovers that his father had once been foiled in a plot to assassinate the German murderer of the first Ariel. Later in the novel, an indiscreet witness, a contemporary of his parents unable to keep a secret, revealed to the second Ariel that both of his parents had been brutalized and tortured so much by the Nazis that they have both become psychologically incapable of talking about their previous nightmare with their only son. Ariel then manages to travel to Germany for the purpose of avenging his parents and his late brother by attempting to slay the former SS officer culpable of the crimes. In prosperous postwar Germany, this ex-murderer had transformed himself from a Nazi war criminal into a highly respected chief executive officer at one of Germany's most prestigious industrial corporations. Once young Ariel comes face to face with the elegantly attired, suave ex-Nazi, seated in his luxurious corporate suite, he cannot bring himself to commit murder. Reflecting Wiesel's personal philosophy of non-violence, Ariel recoils before the prospect of becoming a killer himself. And so he returns to his native America with his vengeful mission unaccomplished.

Wiesel's subsequent novel, *Le Crépuscule au loin*, was published in Paris in 1987; one year later it appeared in English as *Twilight*. The central subject here is the line dividing sanity from insanity—a common Wieselian theme. As he wondered if a line of demarcation could truly divide the two, the writer concluded that it is the insane who most often commit the shameful crimes that debase human history. One of Wiesel's most complex works of fiction, *Twilight's* main action takes place in a mental institution in upstate New York. After a long, tireless search for a lost friend, Raphael, the principal character, finally locates him in a mental institution where he has been committed as an incurable inmate. Raphael arranges to visit the institution, interviewing some of the patients there, all of whom imagine that they are Biblical characters—such as Cain, Adam, Abraham, even God Almighty. In his quest to unravel the mysteries of his friend Pedro's existance, Raphael deciphers not only the reason for the latter's loss of sanity, but also he penetrates many of the crevices in the life of his family. As in the case of the earlier novels, Wiesel—possibly influenced by the experimental work of the French New Novelists—leaps back and forth, almost erratically, from past time to present actuality: in his bold chronological shifts, the novelist conveys to us the sensation of the interconnectedness of the past, present and imminent future.

The Nobel Peace Prize in Oslo

The decade of the eighties was for Elie Wiesel his most fruitful literary period. Despite his enormous productivity he continued to accept new assignments, new responsibilities. He yielded irresistibly to countless invitations to give lectures. Wherever he went, he made new friendships, cemented old associations, attracted larger and larger audiences of admirers. Many of these friends and associates around the world began to promote his candidacy for the Nobel Prize for Literature. Wiesel seemed like a natural candidate for such a prize. His admirers launched forceful, aggressive, concerted campaigns to persuade the Nobel selection committee of Wiesel's meritoriousness. Wiesel seems not to have discouraged any of these supporters. Why should he? Finally, what seemed to be the inevitable and logical outcome occurred. At long last, the Nobel authorities, in 1986, selected Elie Wiesel—but not for his attainments as a writer, rather the sum total of his humanitarian work around the world. In a word, they decided to present to him the Nobel of Nobels: the coveted Peace Prize. This decision made sense. After all, Wiesel had established his reputation not only as a consummate literary artist, but above all, as *the* international defender of human rights par excellence. Indeed he was a true spokesperson for international peace, tolerance, understanding, the rights of the underdog, *the* voice that chanted the message of the brotherhood of humankind.

On December 10–11, 1986, with his wife Marion and his son Elisha, Wiesel flew to Oslo, Norway to accept the award of his lifetime. At the gala festivities, in the presence of an internationally prestigious audience, Wiesel gave a truly stirring address of acceptance. Immediately afterwards, the text of his address was published in volume form in Paris as the *Discours d'Oslo* (1987). With typical modesty he questioned whether it was he who truly deserved the Nobel Prize; or was this award intended to recognize all of the Jewish people, especially the survivors? Perhaps it was meant as a memorial for the millions of victims:

> Do I have the right to represent the multitudes who perished? I have the right to accept this distinction in their name. I do not have the right to speak for the dead; no one can interpret their dreams and mutilated visions. And yet, I sense their presence this moment more than ever. The presence of my parents, that of my little sister. The presence of my teachers, that of my friends, of my companions . . . This honor belongs to all of the survivors. To their children. And through us, to the entire population of the Jewish people whose destiny I claim in its entirety.[24]

Wiesel then went on to outline the major themes that had formed the scaffolding of his published works: the Holocaust, the theme of memory as a countervailing force for man's natural tendency to wish to forget unpleasant chapters of history, the efficacy of silence, the sin of indifference, the aloneness of the Jewish people during the most tragic era of their long history, the still unresolved plight of the Soviet Jews, the ongoing persecutions of ethnic people by governments from the left and right, the necessity of championing human rights, even the rights of the Palestinians, the horror of violence, terrorism, warfare, the cult of universal peace; his confidence in the State of Israel, the millennia of martyrdom of the Jewish people, the indestructibility of childhood memories, and above all his unfailing faith in God.

Egal Aarvik, the Chairman of the Nobel Committee, for his part, responded that "Elie Wiesel has emerged as one of the most spiritual leaders and guides in an age when violence, repression and racism continue to characterize the world . . . Wiesel is a messenger to Mankind. His message is one of peace, atonement, and human dignity. His belief that the forces fighting evil in the world can be victorious is a hard-won belief."[25]

THE LAUREATE YEARS

Throughout the world the name of Elie Wiesel had become synonymous with the remembrance of the Shoah. Thus when President Jimmy Carter developed the proposition that the nation's capital should become the site for a national memorial honoring the memory of six million Jews and the millions of other victims of the Holocaust, it seemed reasonable for the American president to appoint the author of *Night* as chairman of the National Holocaust Commission. The main purpose of the commission was to plan for an appropriate monument to be erected in Washington to memorialize the tragic destruction of so many innocent victims during the atrocities of the Holocaust. And so, on a regular basis Elie Wiesel traveled to Washington to meet with the other distinguished members of the Commission. They debated heatedly about the kind of monument to create. Should it memorialize only the Jewish victims or also the other groups singled out by the Germans for extermination? After weeks of arguments it was decided that the Holocaust monument should include a museum and a library in which would be displayed mementos, documents, collections of relevant literature, photographs, and all other important material that could chronicle the Nazi-related Holocaust. An international effort was then implemented to collect historically authentic materials that could reproduce the atmosphere of the death camps and that could document the disaster.

The burden of administering an often contentious committee became onerous for an already over-committed Wiesel. He found it difficult to preside over a body of strong willed personalities. This kind of oversight was scarcely Wiesel's *forte*. He was simply not suited for the fractious politics of the group. Besides, it became increasingly harder for him to manage his time: his writing, teaching responsibilities, and lecturing assignments made the chairmanship of the Commission a too highly stressful onus. Thus, he reluctantly resigned from his chairmanship in order to return to a more normal life style.

His passion for writing controlled his existence. 1989 proved to be an especially productive year. He completed two significant titles: *L'Oublié* [The Forgotten One], his latest novel; and another volume of essays, *Silences et mémoires d'hommes* [Silence and Memories of Men]. In *The Forgotten One,* his central figure is a young man, the son of survivors (once again!). Malkiel, the young protagonist, searches for self-understanding by slowly puncturing the layers of secrecy created around him by his parents in order to protect their son from knowing their horrendous past. This time, the novelist adds to his all-too-familiar plot a new wrinkle: time-urgency. In his search for his parents' history Malkiel must move swiftly. His father, Elhahon Rosenbaum, is an ailing scholar who suffers from a degenerative disease that is slowly destroying his speech and memory. Soon Malkiel's father will be unable to tell his son of his past; nor will he recall events in that past. Wiesel suggests that Elhahon's disease has been caused by the traumatic suffering and torture he had undergone in the camps. As for his mother, Malkiel never knew her. She had died in Israel during his childbirth. To comprehend his roots, Malkiel must retrace both the events in his father's life during the *univers concentrationnaire* and also his activities in Israel where he had gone after the Holocaust.

L'Oublié has a secondary plot: Malkiel has fallen in love with a young American woman from New York who cannot comprehend or accept her sweetheart's obsession with the phantoms of his family history. Stylistically this novel manifests many of the traits found in Wiesel's earlier fiction (He seems unable to venture outside his already established mould by experimenting with wholly new directions.) And so once again we see dramatic contrasts between italicized and traditional print; staccato-like leaps from past to present to future; the plight of the children/survivors who are mystified by their parent's Holocaust past. Once again, *The Forgotten One* is marked by Wiesel's affinity for minimalist art: metaphors and figures of speech have been eliminated.

As for Wiesel's anthology of essays, *Silences et mémoires d'hommes,* it is arguably one of his most significant works of non-fiction to date. A potpourri of dialogue, tales, anecdotes, and essays, it begins with a truly remarkable chapter entitled "Au delà du silence" ("Beyond Silence"), an essay replete with some of the most candid revelations by Wiesel of his personal moments of life and of his fundamental credo of existence. With utter frankness he confesses his enormous indebtedness to certain of his teachers. He discusses some of the conferences he had organized. And then subsequently, he analyzes memory. Other selections include an essay titled "Six Days of Destruction," inspired by the six days of creation. It deals with the dilemma facing most Jews as they watched the advance of Hitler's German armies: should they flee or not? Most believed that the Nazis might somehow exclude them from their death machine. There then follows a chapter on the history of the *niggund* (traditional Hebrew melodies), a chapter on an exalted poem in tribute to Jerusalem and Judaism, another selection featuring an account of a trip Wiesel took to West Germany, where the former victim of German persecution addressed the Bundestag. There is also the text of Wiesel's deposition at the Klaus Barbie trial in Lyons, France, as well as Wiesel's analysis of the significance of the Dreyfus Affair. An essay on apartheid in South Africa is included, as is a chapter on the meaning of human freedom. We also find a Talmudic children's tale, an essay on war and peace, another on the crime of human indifference, and finally, an essay containing recommendations on how to read the Bible from a Jewish perspective.

In 1991 Wiesel published his ode to the Talmudic scholars who enriched his life intellectually and spiritually. He called the work *Célébration Talmudique*, and the English language version appeared almost at the same time as *Sages and Dreamers*.

The Teacher and Lecturer

During the most recent decade of his life, Wiesel has devoted a considerable portion of his life to teaching in the university classroom. When recently a class of Susquehanna University Honors students visited his home in New York City, one of them asked why he, as an internationally recognized writer, felt compelled to divide his time between creative writing and teaching. Instantly Wiesel responded that he "needed to keep on teaching because he needed to keep on learning."

Almost from the beginning, Wiesel designed for himself a dual career as a teacher and a writer. Between 1972 and 1976 he served as Professor of Jewish Studies at the City University of New York. Since 1976 he has held the chair of the Andrew Mellon Distinguished Professorship in the Humanities at Boston University, a situation requiring him to commute each week between New York City and his classroom in Boston.

A considerable portion of his time is devoted to his numerous speaking assignments throughout the world. Those of us who correspond with him regularly appreciate the quantity of these engagements, as he sends his typically cryptic six- or seven-line letters to his correspondents, datelined in many corners around the earth.

Often he informs us that he is about to leave for or has just returned from some remote corner of the earth. Before audiences everywhere—in synagogues, lecture halls, churches, auditoriums, parliamentary buildings, forums and theaters, television studios, and on campuses large and small—Wiesel delivers lectures, leads discussions, engages in interviews with journalists and personalities from the electronic media, meets with heads of state and especially enjoys encounters with other Holocaust survivors. Unable to say "no" often enough, even for the sake of his own health, he accepts a staggering number of speaking engagements. A compelling speaker, this seemingly frail man leaves an indelible impression on all who have witnessed his lectures.

Wiesel's life has been punctuated by a steady stream of prizes, awards, honorary degrees, citations, and recognitions. The article in *Who's Who in the World* devoted to Elie Wiesel, one of the longest articles in that volume, enumerated many of his awards, among which there are the following samples: the grand Prix de la Littérature de la Ville de Paris; Martin Luther King Jr. Award; the William and Janice Epstein Fiction Award and the Ethel S. Cohen Award, both of which came from the Jewish Book Council; the Congressional Gold Medal of Achievement; Commander of the French Legion of Honor; honorary doctorates from several dozen universities including Hebrew Union College, the Jewish Theological Seminary, Yeshiva University, Bar Ilan University in Israel, Boston University, Hofstra University, Yale, Notre Dame, Marquette University, and Susquehanna University.

Wiesel has granted many interviews to journalists and academicians who wrote treatises on him. Among the two most interesting are his interviews with Brigitte Fanny-Cohen and Philippe-Michaël de Saint Cheron (quoted extensively here). In one of his most memorable interviews (with John S. Freidman) for *The Paris Review* (Spring 1984), he provides us with what may well be his best description of his creative methodology:

> But there is never a struggle in the morning [when he usually writes]. I work for four hours without interruption. Then I stop for my studies. But

> these four hours are really mine. It is a struggle when I have to cut. I reduce nine hundred pages to one hundred sixty pages. I also enjoy cutting. I do it with a masochistic pleasure although when you cut, you don't. Writing is not like painting where you add. It is not what you put on the canvas that the reader sees. Writing is more like sculpture where you remove, you eliminate in order to make the work more visible. Even those pages you remove somehow remain. (page 136)

Literary composition brings him the fullest possible measure of personal satisfaction. He also seems to enjoy the time he spends in the college seminar, on the dais as a lecturer, and in the offices of presidents, kings, and prime ministers.

At times, this otherwise timid and humble man has demonstrated surprising candor and courage in the presence of some of the world's great leaders. He seems to have felt little timidity in criticizing the President of the United States when—before a worldwide television audience—he requested that President Ronald Reagan not trivialize the memory of the six million by traveling to Bitburg, Germany to lay a wreath in a cemetery in which so many SS officers are buried. At the opening ceremony for the National Holocaust Museum in Washington DC, he chided President Clinton for his inaction during the genocidal ethnic cleansings in the former Yugoslavia. Many believed that Wiesel's public declaration proved decisive in persuading the President of the United States to engage himself more actively in bringing a halt to the hostilities in Bosnia. An occasional confidant and a former friend of President François Mitterrand, Wiesel boldly expressed his disappointment with the French head of state when he learned that the latter had maintained a relationship with a former Nazi collaborator. During Mitterrand's second term in office, even though Wiesel had worked closely with Mitterrand to organize the first worldwide conference of Nobel laureates at the Palais d'Elysée, he abruptly halted his affiliation with the President when the latter refused to express remorse about his embarrassing World War II connections.

Elie Wiesel's most recent achievements are impressive: his two volume memoirs have appeared at last. In 1994 he completed *Tous les fleuves vont à la mer,* and in 1996 the sequel *Et la mer n'est pas remplie.* At last, Wiesel exposes his soul and his inner life to his public audience. Systematically, chronologically, and coherently, he explains his actions, he elucidates his thoughts, he reveals many unsuspected facets of his private life, and even divulges the name of some of the prominent figures with whom he has had less than cordial dealings. In 1998 he added a third volume to his series of "celebrations" of prominent figures in Jewish history: *Célébration prophétique: Portraits et legendes.* Somehow this latest work does not possess the same depth of pathos and passion as his earlier celebrations of the Hassids and the Patriarchs. But every great writer is entitled to a work or two that may not measure up to his or her earlier lofty standards.

One of the high points in his career took place in the well-known literary center of Cerisy-la-Salle, in Normandy, France, from July 3–10, 1994. In the presence of Elie Wiesel himself, and under the direction of Philippe-Michaël de Saint Cheron of the French Ministry of Culture, a large international audience of writers, scientists, philosophers, religious leaders from several faiths, political leaders, writers, and educators participated in a colloquium to honor the fiftieth anniversary of the liberation of the author of *Night* from his unforgettable imprisonment in the deathcamps. Two years later, in 1996, Saint Cheron published the proceedings of the Cerisy colloquium as *Elie Wiesel: Une parole pour l'avenir* [Elie Wiesel: A Word for the Future]. To demonstrate that the rupture between Elie Wiesel and Mitterrand did not at all terminate the Wiesel's relationship with the French government, this entire volume starts out with a powerful encomium of Wiesel by Jacques Chirac, the current President of the French Republic.

Perhaps the most memorable moment in the colloquium came when Wiesel himself conducted a Sabbath service and interpreted for his enchanted audience the Torah portion of that week.

2
Yearning For Childhood: Sighet

Almost all creative artists possess their personal world of recurrent or dominant themes and their unique trademark style. Their themes and style lend a distinctive, recognizable cachet to their works. Even non-experts readily identify the special "look" of the paintings of a Monet, a Van Gogh, or a Chagall. In the poems of Victor Hugo or Mallarmé the reader easily recognizes a special patina, singular rhythms, uncommon metaphors, and peculiarly personal vocabularies that distinguish their poetry from that of other poets. Therefore, it is not unreasonable for us to expect that in the texts of Elie Wiesel one senses a special kind of verbal music, a private world of characters, a singular vocabulary, a select cluster of themes. One of the themes that resonates most insistently in his books is his nostalgic longing for childhood—-the dream of returning to his days as a youngster raised in his tightly cocoon-like universe of his family, one that was intimately linked with the Jewish community in his native town of Sighet.

For Elie Wiesel life fluctuates between his memories of the past, on the one hand, and his reaction to present time as well as to his expectations of future time, on the other hand. Like so many Jews, he seems to be haunted by the memory of his own past and that of his people. For him memory consists of two highly dissimilar epochs: first, his pre-Auschwitz childhood and secondly, the somber period of adolescence in Auschwitz. Literature for Wiesel has become a form of memory, one that recaptures the joys and tribulations of the past. Through literature he seeks to find the interconnections among past, present and future.

Sharing the view of those psychologists who believe that the adulthood of most human beings is dominated by experiences in childhood, he senses that many of our adult behavioral patterns emerge out of the earliest days of childhood. What he wrote, felt, thought, and feared emanate from the reservoir of early life. Wiesel main-

2: YEARNING FOR CHILDHOOD: SIGHET

tained that he never entirely liberated himself from the memories of boyhood in Sighet: "As for my stories, you must see beneath every word the child I was and that perhaps I would still like to be today."[1] Abrahamson agrees that "In all of his work, one feels the presence of Sighet, . . ."[2] Estess sees in Wiesel's texts an unending search for the town that represents the childhood: "Elie Wiesel is haunted by the memory of Sighet [childhood], he is unable either to get away from Sighet or to find it again."[3] What does Sighet represent for Wiesel whenever he dreams of returning there to revisit the days of his boyhood? Sighet represents Jewishness—*Yiddishkeit*—; it stands for the universe of his *heder* [Hebrew school], where he learned Biblical Hebrew and studied the scriptures; it stands also for his Hasidic grandfather who fired his imagination with exciting tales about the ancient rabbis; it rings with the echoes of the wonderful Sabbath and High Holy Day observances in his home and at the synagogue. Whenever he longs for Sighet he remembers the mountainous backdrop of the Carpathians in the distance; he is reminded of the frequent visits of Jewish minstrel-like wayfarers who circulated from shtetl to shtetl with their fascinating tales and Yiddish songs. Wherever Wiesel travels his antennae search for sights, sounds, and smells that he hopes can transport him back to the lost era of Sighet. Even in so urban an environment as the Williamsburg district of Brooklyn he continues to dream, to search for a place and a time that have both disappeared: "I come there [Williamsburg] sometimes to soak myself in my childhood, perhaps to prolong it. Williamsburg might be able to be named Sighet."[4]

He yearns to find once again an existence stripped from him by the Holocaust, an existence of youthful bliss that had been devoured in the flames and lethal gas of Auschwitz, for his childhood had disappeared abruptly in Auschwitz and Buchenwald: "Attracted by childhood, the old man will search for it in different ways. As for me, I am searching for mine. I shall always search for it. I need it. It is necessary for me like a kind of landmark, a refuge. It represents for me a world that exists no more, a sunlit and mysterious realm where beggars were princes in disguise where madmen were sages liberated from their inhibition."[5]

In reality, Elie Wiesel has never ceased being a Jewish child reared in a profoundly Judaic community in Sighet. His reminiscence of that irredeemably lost era, between 1928 and 1944, and of a particular place in southeastern Europe, his shtetl of Sighet, pervades the verbal texture of his writings and speeches. As he relates his tales, it is as if the voice of his maternal grandfather, Dodye Feig, is speaking into the ears of young boys and girls of today, as if Dodye Feig had not been swallowed up in the poison of the concentration camps, as if yesterday continued into today. A sample opening sentence from one of Wiesel's tales: "Let me tell you a tale. It happened in our town. Everything happened in my town."[6]

Sighet, or the memory of it, transcends reality. Wiesel, the consummate literary artist, has transfigured his memory into something magical, something ethereal. He has alchemized an otherwise humdrum town in Carpathia into a heavenly Jerusalem, a town that is so lovable that it cannot really exist on the surface of our planet, but rather floats within a nostalgic utopia, one which he persuades his readers to seek: "That's where the town of my childhood seems to be right now. Not here, but up there, in a Jerusalem of fire, hanging onto eternal memories of night [the Holocaust]."[7]

In Wieselian literature two worlds are juxtaposed: the world of joyful Jewish youth in Sighet and the world of the tragic upheaval in Auschwitz, a place where he was transformed from a happy boy into a grief-stricken adult. The conflict between Sighet and Auschwitz, between a place of happiness and one of death, manifests itself throughout Wiesel's texts and lends to them that special Wieselean dynamic that exists in the literature of no other writer.

This tension between the vanished paradise of Sighet and the real world of the camps divides his childhood and his adulthood; it dominates both his psychological makeup as a human being and the literary expression of his texts.

With the destruction of the six million victims came also the disintegration of Wiesel's boyhood Sighet. Today that town in Transylvania has been metamorphosed into an unrecognizably different place. Whenever he returns there, he mourns for the Sighet that was, and he rejects the Sighet that is. The old town, with its once thriving Jewish community of 10,000, with all of the vibrant infrastructures developed by the Jews there, that old town lies buried within the fabric of boyhood memory:

> How does one mourn a city, a city which lost not its body, but its soul—a city which lost its Jews? Nineteen years ago, the last of the Jews were expelled from Sighet, the city in which we had built our homes and dreamed our dreams . . . When the war ended, I refused to return home. I was afraid I might find a city different from the one I left.[8]

2: YEARNING FOR CHILDHOOD: SIGHET

And when finally he mustered the courage to return to the place of his roots, what did he find there? "In Sighet the only synagogue still open holds thousands of religious books. I do not know their value, but they are important. Now they lie in dust, and nobody looks at them."[9] Wiesel hopes that young Jews from the United States, Israel, and Europe might one day return to Sighet in Romania to retrieve these forsaken books, that they might someday study their contents, and revitalize their contents. For what is the meaning of a book if no one is alive to read it?

Today, with the international borders redrawn, Sighet has been transferred from Hungarian rule to that of Romania. In July 1991, Wiesel returned there as a principal speaker for a special national day of mourning for the Jews massacred in the infamous camps. Pre-Holocaust Romania was once the home of some of the staunchest communities in all of Judaism. To Wiesel's surprise, he discovered that the roots of anti-Semitism remain alive and well in that nation: before thousands of people at the public ceremony of remembrance, anti-Semitic hecklers shouted obscenities at Wiesel, the survivor of Buchenwald, and made it difficult for him to complete his address. Some in the audience screamed at him that the Holocaust never existed, that it had been a fabrication of the Jewish imagination, as if all that the author of *Night* had personally witnessed had been little more than a dream.

Although the wonderful boyhood days of Sighet had evaporated into the smoke of the gas chambers, the memory of those days continues to haunt Wiesel and permeates his poetic prose. One can compare the lingering presence of Sighet in the soul of Wiesel with the memories of Marcel Proust's boyhood in Illiers, France as they perfume the pages of *In Remembrance of Things Past*. And just as Proust transformed Illiers into his fictional Combray, Wiesel has filled his pages with the fragrance of a paradise that had been once the town of Sighet.

What are the elements of the bygone Sighet that form the substructure of so many of Wiesel's adult writings? First, Sighet represents his Jewish faith. It was there that he was initially imbued with the religious laws, moral and ethical values, customs and celebrations, history and traditions, the Hebrew and Yiddish languages, and the way of life of observant Jews. Unlike the Jews of the United States, France, Canada or Great Britain, the Jews of the shtetls of eastern Europe were a largely unassimilated people; they lived in their own microcosmic districts and villages. They could readily be distinguished in their lifestyle from the ambient majority culture. For centuries they had lived as a separate culture imbedded within the macrocosmic national culture of their nation. When Wiesel longs for Sighet, he longs for days when he observed an unassimilated faith, one that had been untainted by the corrosive forces of neighboring regions. In *Signes d'exode* he links his dreams of childhood with those of a religious Jew: "Somewhere in the Carpathians, at the other end of my life, a Jewish child recites his daily prayers. In order to concentrate better, he closes his eyes and sways back and forth as if to exit from his daily activities. . . . I look at the Jewish child as he prays and who is afraid of looking; I listen to him; and I envy him. For him, for me, it was easy and simple, I feared God at the same time that I loved him."[10]

Whenever Wiesel dreams wistfully of the happy days of his Sighet boyhood, these reveries signify something special for him: they bring back the values of the Hasidic Jew. The Hasid confronts the question of faith from an entirely unique perspective—joyfully, fervently, merrily, and with dance, song, and passionate prayer. Unlike the dignified, restrained, and solemn worship characterizing most Christian or Reformed and Conservative Jewish services, the Hasidic ritual consists of an exuberant, unrestrained communion with God. And this joyfulness suggests for this author the dream of the lost paradise of Sighet.

For the Jew in Wiesel, the observance of holidays and of the Sabbath holds a unique significance. Especially meaningful is the seventh day of the week, the day when God reposed after six arduous days of creation. The color "white" reminds Wiesel of his boyhood days, for it is the color of the Sabbath dinner tablecloth as well as the *talith,* the traditional prayer shawl worn by men during their prayers in the synagogue. On the other hand, quite aptly, "black," the color of night, becomes a metaphoric representation for the somber days of the Holocaust. In Wiesel's special vocabulary, white and black alternate in dramatic tension with each other, just as Sighet alternates in his life with Auschwitz:

> When I remember the Sabbath in my town, the color I always see is white—the white napkin, the white kerchief my grandmother wore. After *schul* [synagogue services], with my grandfather and parents we would look for the strangers in our midst . . . Here in this town, a town so Jewish that the memory of its simplicity and generosity moves me to tears, the people understood the meaning of the word sovereignty. They also un-

derstood the burden of responsibility sovereignty imposes. Here I learned that whatever happens to one Jew also happens to me, and whenever one Jew stands in need, I also stand in need.[11]

There was also the nostalgic memory of the annual seders that took place during the Passover festivities. Of this magical holiday Wiesel later wrote that "The Seder transformed us in our very being. On that evening, my father enjoyed the sovereign authority of a king; my mother, sweeter and more beautiful than ever, resembled a queen. And we children, we were all princes."[12]

Above all, the dream of the lost boyhood Garden of Eden signified for this writer the indelible memory of his parents, both of whom were destroyed in the Holocaust. Not only did he recall the loving care they so selflessly showered upon their four children, but he never forgot their frequently expressed hopes that their only son, Eliezar, might someday become an important personage. The son did indeed manifest from his earliest childhood the traits of extraordinary intellectual prowess:

> If one's past were to begin with one's childhood, I would find in mine a dream—nurtured for their son over there, far away, in another time, in another place, in what used to be an indestructible Jewish kingdom—the shtetl . . . to be a good Jew, they would say, is important, but one has to think of one's future as well. In wishing to protect mine, they hoped to see me get both *smikhah* [ordination to the rabbinate]—and a doctorate—in anything.[13]

But just as the Holocaust eradicated the raptures of youth so did it also eradicate both of his parents, his grandfather, a sister, and many close relatives and friends.

The theme of lost childhood in Sighet is linked throughout Wieselian literature with the writer's frequent references to the teachers there who had shaped his intellect. He acknowledges that, to a large extent, he represents much of what his parents had transmitted to him as well as that which he had learned from those who served as the custodians of his education. One of Wiesel's capital works is devoted to the effective work of his teachers; in *Legends of our Time,* he has composed a book "about encounters with my first teachers, those who once upon a time taught me whatever I have learned. For it is in my hometown, in my childhood that I acquired whatever I know now and whatever I try to communicate now. It is still to them I turn whenever I am in doubt, whenever I need assurance, if not guidance . . ."[14]

Finally, the recurrent refrain of Wiesel's yearning for his boyhood Sighet contains nostalgic memories of his closest friends. With the boys and girls with whom he grew up in the excitement of real camaraderie, he exchanged confidences and played various games: "As adolescents, we tried to emulate David and Jonathan whom life set up in opposition to the world of adults with the intrigues and plots, which were sometimes clever and sometimes petty. Friendship must have isolated us and strengthened us."[15]

That the theme of Sighet and of boyhood reverberates throughout his fiction is evident from the frequency with which he depicts life in small eastern European towns where there once existed a vital Jewish communal life. From book to book the reader stumbles upon young protagonists with family lives and religious orientation not at all dissimilar to his own personal childhood.

Even in his purest fiction, an author seldom creates in a vacuum. It is normal for the author to reincarnate those places, people, and human traits that represent his or her most precious values. But since fiction is after all fiction—that is to say, something invented and fashioned out of the artist's imagination, the illusion must be created that the content of the novel is entirely fabricated by the writer out of the various visions he or she had during the course of the creative process. In reality, of course, much of this content emanates from the raw material of the artist's own experience. And because the artist cannot totally be disengaged from reality, the same raw material has a way of reasserting itself again and again in all of the other works issuing from the pen of that writer.

In her highly perceptive monograph on Elie Wiesel, Brigitte-Fanny Cohen quotes from her lengthy interviews with him, interviews in which she quite accurately calls Wiesel's incessant reference to Sighet and his recurrent dreams of childhood "obsessions." She points out that even though the towns of Wiesel's texts are not called Sighet—he resorts to names like Kolvillág, Shamgorod, and Szerencsevaros—these communities are none other than Sighet in fictional disguise. Cohen even calls Sighet "the principal character in his books." To which Wiesel responds unabashedly that "there are two cities that attract my glance, Jerusalem, always, and Sighet."[16]

Unsurprisingly Wiesel's fictionalized protagonists also resemble him strongly. In *Le Crepuscule au loin* [Dawn], his young hero Raphael grew up, like Wiesel, in the Carpathian mountain region, and also like him, was incurably attracted to madmen and beggars. On the

Sabbath Raphael distributed fruit and cake to them (as Wiesel handed out food to the madmen and beggars of his boyhood). Raphael, like Wiesel, lived in a state of frenzied anticipation of the coming of the Messiah. When Raphael later goes to Paris, his first impressions of the French capital are little more than pastiches of Wiesel's personal reactions when, during 1945, he went there after his release from Buchenwald.[17] Like Wiesel, the fictional Raphael feels a powerful fascination for things that remind him of childhood: Raphael says that "I see myself again as a child, at the house of study or the asylum, listening to my old friend speak to me of the worlds inside of worlds . . ." But these words rarely describe the way Wiesel himself reminisced about his own early experiences in Sighet.[18] In the *Messengers of God,* the once happy childhood of Cain and Abel is little more than the recounting of a similar childhood experiences by Wiesel and his three sisters.

"Whenever I want to write something good, I go back to my childhood. The soul of every writer is in his childhood, and mine was a Hasidic one."[19] This citation sums up the pivotal place occupied by Sighet and Wiesel's joyful childhood in so many of his literary texts. One can only wonder how Wiesel's life might have developed if only the Germans had never invaded Hungary and if the Jews would have been content to remain there after the defeat of Nazism and the departure of the German occupational force (assuming of course that they could have survived the Holocaust.) And what would he have dreamed about as an adult if he had not been savagely pulled out of that delicious moment in time and space in eastern Europe?

That moment in time and that geographical space Wiesel movingly described in *Paroles d'étranger:* "I would give much to be able to relive a Sabbath in my little town, someplace in the Carpathians. The whiteness of the table clothes, the blinking flames of the candles . . . It hurts even to think about it. That is what I miss the most: a certain peacefulness, a certain melancholy that Sabbath, in Sighet, offered its children, large and small, young or old, rich or poor. It is this Sabbath that is missing in my life. It reminds me that things have changed in the world, that the world itself has changed more. And me too."[20]

In reality, however, the world has changed much more than Elie Wiesel. Sighet has changed more than the young man who once lived there. In so many ways, Wiesel remains, even today, the young Jewish lad who, once upon a time, lived in a fairylike kingdom called Sighet.

But once the Nazis occupied that once magical town, once they had brutally forced all of the Jews there to climb into the waiting cattle cars, once these cars transported them to the gates of Auschwitz, Wiesel's Sighet had been transformed from a once joyful reality into a universe that lives on only in his dreams and yearning.

3
Remembering the Holocaust

No one can dispute Abrahamson's assertion that "Wiesel is by far the most significant writer to have made the Holocaust the major theme of his work, even as it has been of central importance to him."[1] In effect, largely because of Wiesel's efforts to compel us to remember the most atrocious event in human history, the Holocaust ranks both as the most compelling theme in his own writing but also as a major theme in almost all contemporary literature in Europe and America. Some universities nowadays even offer courses or programs on Holocaust literature and Holocaust studies.

Countless books have been published in many countries on the subject of the Holocaust. Educated people have developed a fascination with the fact that the policy of one nation could lead millions of human beings to be systematically eradicated or mutilated. Despite the intensity with which this tragedy has been depicted on the printed page, in movies, and the electronic media, the full extent of the agony and human suffering will probably never be fully recaptured, even in those books written by the most artful authors and historians. The Holocaust has provoked a crisis of conscience not only among Jews but also among Christians and even among Moslems. It has also provoked many complicated and far-reaching questions. Would the State of Israel have been created were it not for the tragic destruction of millions of Jews? Christians justifiably question their tormented souls about their complicity and indifference during the Holocaust. The Catholic Church has been particularly anguished over certain of its institutional policies vis-à-vis Nazism and Hitler. In effect, so troubling have been the tragic events surrounding the Holocaust that the Catholic Church, during an official service of forgiveness conducted at the Vatican by Pope John Paul, actually asked for public forgiveness for members of the church for the two millenia during which the Christian faith involved itself in crusades, the Inquisition, and the charge of deicide hurled against the Jewish people. The so-called neutrality of Switzerland and Sweden, the banking policies of the Swiss nation, even the early isolationism of the United States have been recently treated with suspicion by the historians.

Long after the fiftieth anniversary of the end of the Holocaust, many prefer to forget the catastrophe of catastrophes. Especially tormented are those who behaved with indifference before the evils of that event. Some prefer to obliterate in their consciences all traces of the memory of the Shoah. A few twisted souls, motivated by anti-Semitism or mischief, have even tried to revise history, claiming that the Holocaust never took place, that it was an imagined nightmare or, at most, an inevitable and normal consequence of international warfare. At a time when some seek to forget the unforgettable, to forgive the unforgivable, or to deny the undeniable, it is Elie Wiesel more than anyone else who has waged a veritable battle of remembrance. It is he who warns us that we must remain ever vigilant. Convinced that other Holocausts are not impossible, he warns against complacency and forgetfulness.

Firm in his insistence that the Holocaust must always be remembered, Wiesel emphasizes that "I consider the Holocaust to be the most important event in Jewish history and in human history, with the possible exception of the Revelation [the Ten Commandments] at Sinai, no other [event] even can be compared to it. It is an ontological event."[2] In another statement, he asserts that the Holocaust represents the most significant happening of this century, perhaps even of all centuries: "With the possible exception of the *Mattan Torah* [the giving of the Torah] at Sinai, of the Revelation of the Law at Sinai, this event is the most crucial one, for it weighs on a man's conscience and consciousness. As the central theme of our lifetime, it poses problems and challenges . . . The Holocaust calls into question all that was obtained through knowledge for the last thirty centuries or so: man's relationship to God, to society, to time, to culture, to his fellow man, and most important to himself. Everything must be reexamined."[3] No writer of our age was better positioned or qualified than Wiesel to reexamine these fundamental questions; after all, as a victim, survivor, and witness of the flame of Nazi wrath, he could construct an entire body of literature inspired by the theme of the Holocaust.

If Elie Wiesel's message is relevant for every inhabitant of our planet, it is even more relevant for Jewish populations because "All Jews are survivors. They have all been inside the whirlwind of the

Holocaust, even those born afterwards, even those who heard its echoes in distant lands. For the event, its magnitude and history, is not limited to one generation alone: Every Jew, everywhere, is and will be affected by its horror and stunned by the truth it contained."[4] It is a fact that hardly does a Jew exist in today's world who has not lost relatives, friends, and associates, or who has not been physically or psychologically marked by the events in the death camps. Understandably, Wiesel knew that Jews could be defined as the people who carried on their shoulders the haunting memories of this black period in human history: ". . . no Jew can be fully Jewish today, without being part of the Holocaust."[5]

It is not surprising that Wiesel's writings are seared by the fires of the Nazi era. The Holocaust appears and reappears throughout the pages and chapters of his texts. Even when he deals with the subject obliquely, it insinuates itself into the recesses of the author's sentences and ultimately disturbs the mind of the reader. Like a stubborn pain, one that refuses to vanish, the Holocaust asserts and reasserts itself in many of the passages composed by this death camp survivor, even when his literary plots depict characters one or two generations removed from the events of 1935–45.

In effect, Wiesel treats the Holocaust directly and in its entirety in only one of his works, *La Nuit*. There the "Event" occupies the epicenter of the whole book. After the initial opus, the author wrote mainly novels about survivors or the children of survivors, but he does not embark upon detailed accounts of what took place in the camps. In his more recent novels, the protagonists are contemporaries of his own son Elisha. But even there the fumes and the ashes of the Holocaust manage to exude indirectly to the surface of the text, ending up by profoundly contaminating the environment within which these more recent characters live.

The poet, Paul Valèry, wrote an immortal poem entitled "Le cimetière marin" [The Cemetery of the Sea]; had Wiesel written a similar poem to sum up his own experiences during the atrocious era of 1944–45, his poem might easily have been entitled "Le cimetière maudit" [The Cursed Cemetery] as he himself once called his own work.[6]

Wiesel's experience in life can be divided into two sharply contrasting epochs: the pre-Holocaust era of Sighet and the Holocaust era during and after the camps. Similarly, he divides Jewish history into two epochs: pre- and post-Holocaust. The Holocaust is viewed as "the end of an era, the end of the world,"—an end that made him wonder if the human race could begin its cycle of civilization all over again, once the night of destruction ended. For him the Holocaust was the logical and predictable "culmination of 2000 years of Christian-inspired anti-Semitism."[7] He stressed that during the two millennia popes, priests, and some Protestant leaders (like the much admired Martin Luther) either overtly or subconsciously taught, encouraged, inspired, and advocated animosity against the Jews. After centuries of inquisitions, banishments, persecutions, crusades, pogroms, mass executions, book-burnings, and gas chambers, it became finally necessary for Pope John XXIII to declare that enough was enough. Wiesel warmly applauded Pope John XXIII's momentous encyclical calling for a halt to anti-Semitism. In the eyes of Wiesel, the Holocaust stood not only as a decisive development in Jewish history, but it was also a key event in Christianity. At long last Christians admitted a degree of guilt in the tragic consequences arising out of an endgame that resulted in the destruction of six million Jews.

So devastating was his experience in the concentration camps that for many years Wiesel was too traumatized to speak to others or to write about what he had witnessed there. After liberation from Buchenwald, he faced a severe dilemma. Since childhood he has dreamed of the prospect of becoming a writer. It would have been effortless for him to have written about his pre-Auschwitz life, to wit, about his happiness as a Hasidic youth. But to write about the depressing episodes in the camps went beyond the limits of his physical or emotional strength. The joyful Sighet versus somber Auschwitz, a world of affectionate family life versus a world of starvation—these contrasting forces created an irreconcilable tension within his soul. Should he launch a career as a writer by recapitulating the joyous years of his life? Or, conversely, could he share with readers the anguish of captivity during the war?[8] Eventually he opted to launch his literary life by dramatizing the conflict between his two lives—those of Sighet and of Auschwitz. Ultimately he learned how to blend these two contrasting facets of life—hope and despair, celebration and grief.

The wounds inflicted on him by the Holocaust proved to be indelible (Brigitte-Fanny Cohen avers that the Holocaust became such an obsessive factor in his texts that his otherwise diverse writings were unified by this theme.[9]) Not at all content to be labeled a "Holocaust writer," Wiesel often rejected this appellation on the grounds that it did not take into account the many Hasidic, Judaic, Biblical and humanistic subjects on which he also wrote. Almost resenting this seemingly too-restrictive label, Wiesel argues vehemently that he has written many other books besides *Night*. He claims that in reality only five of his titles, at the very most, deal directly or indirectly with the Shoah, whereas in more than two dozen other works, he scarcely mentions the subject at all; and if he does so, it is only covertly. Here is what he tells Saint Cheron: "In the thirty books that I wrote [prior to 1989], only five or six treat this question directly; in the others, I exalt life and the Bible, Hasidism and the Talmud, the Midrash and mysticism, Jerusalem and the Jews of the USSR. Like Joshua ben Hattaniah, I believe that it is necessary not to live in mourning, in the memory of suffering."[10] In effect, in *Signes d'exode*, Wiesel even admits candidly that it is his objective to liberate himself from the obsession of the Holocaust.[11]

One factor must be taken into account: although Wiesel recreated with remarkable credibility the climate of the *univers concentrationaire* in *Night*, his successful resurrection of the nightmare did not come easily to him: it emerged only after his well-documented ten-year inner struggle. He could not readily find words adequate to describe the overwhelming emotions exploding within him to retrieve the irrational event: "The Holocaust could barely be conceived, let alone imagined. The few novels that have attempted to depict this catastrophe have therefore been failures as literature and even as history: Treblinka and art do not mix—and are forbidden to do so."[12] Elsewhere he suppresses the same creative impotence: "the experience of the Holocaust in Europe defies language and leads to a mystique of silence, or to madness itself. The experience cannot be communicated; one only knows it from within, where knowledge becomes an obsession."[13]

Furthermore, Wiesel feared the danger of trivialization and commercialization of the event that, in his view, was nearly a sacred experience. After all, when millions of lives were consumed in the flames and fumes, and when millions were tortured in their bodies and soul, mankind has no choice but to face up to this tragedy with the most profound emotion and prayer. Besides, none of the survivors extricated themselves from the atrocities unscathed physically or mentally. The greatest challenge faced by the witness of the tragedy was the task of developing both the verbal prowess and the appropriate reverential tone to transmit the revelation of an experience that for the most people might seem inconceivable. Wiesel has always felt that he had been awakened by a nightmare, only in his case the unpleasant dream was real. Nightmares are difficult enough to describe after one has awakened, but when they do actually occur, they become even more challenging to recreate with accuracy.

Despite all of his trepidation, Wiesel concluded that he had no choice but to return to the scene of the despicable happenings, at least literally, in order to provide his reading public with a personal account of the human barbarism in the concentration camps. With profound misgiving, many years after his imprisonment there, the former inmates of Auschwitz returned to that infamous place. Here are his recollections of that dramatic visit: "I lacked courage [to visit the camp] . . . I was afraid of the reawakening of old ghosts; the reminders of past twilights would be obscured by the commercialization of the present."[14] Knowing that the camps had been transformed into tourist sites, he feared encountering souvenir stands, snack kiosks, photographers, and tourist guides who did not truly appreciate the sanctity of the venue.

Wiesel's worst fears were realized when the electronic media, responding to a widespread public interest in the Holocaust, produced both mini-series and movies that purportedly depicted real episodes from the death camps. With unusual candor (for him) he lashed out against an NBC mini-series entitled "The Holocaust: "Am I too harsh? Too sensitive perhaps? But then this film is not sensitive enough . . . It transforms an ontological event into a soap opera. Whatever the intention, the result is shocking. Contrived situations, sentimental episodes, implausible coincidences: if they make you cry, they make you cry for the wrong reasons."[5] What Wiesel deplores mainly of this mini-series is the unconvincing mixture of romantic fiction and documentary. He does not believe that purely documented feature should be blended with fictional content. By mixing the two, the Holocaust becomes just another trite event, just another show. It loses its sacredness. In an interview with Saint Cheron, Wiesel stresses emphatically that one must avoid the banalization of the Holocaust."[16] An excessive array of slick and technically perfect images transforms the greatest and most sacred "Event" from that of a profoundly human tragedy into just another visual and entertaining spectacle. Once audiences become saturated with too many spectacles, they tend to become blasé, even indifferent to the real dimensions of the tragedy.

Even so respected a writer as Solszenitsen has been criticized by Wiesel for having banalized or underestimated the awesomeness of the Holocaust. If such writers have themselves not experienced the tragic drama of such an infamous place as Auschwitz, they cannot possibly appreciate the unique character of the Shoah. The author of

Night levels harsh criticism at the Russian novelist for failing to differentiate between Hitler's death camps and Stalin's gulags.[17] As Wiesel explains, the Shoah was an unprecedented event ending with the near-destruction of an entire people, their culture, and even an almost entire religious faith. In the same vein, he reveals his resentment at the cavalier manner in which the Soviets had memorialized the Holocaust, for example in their monument to the massacred victims of Babi Yar. Wiesel faults the Russians for having claimed that the Babi Yar martyrs had been murdered solely because they were Russian whereas, in reality, they were singled out solely because they were Jews. Not once did the colossal monument at Babi Yar even mention the word "Jew." Wiesel accuses the Soviet government of having diminished the uniqueness of the Holocaust.[18]

Which factors explain the uniqueness of this event? To this question Wiesel responds by noting that for the first time in human history, the extermination of an entire people became the central policy of a national government. In the eyes of the German government of the nineteen thirties and early forties, it was actually a capital crime merely to be Jewish. Of course the Jews were not the only ones slated for death; many Gypsies, homosexuals, and so-called "enemies of the state" suffered a similar fate; but they were murdered not because of racial, ethnic or religious reasons but rather because of their lifestyles or specific practices. Elsewhere, when mass killings took place—as in Cambodia or Biafara, they did not happen because of the state of being of the victims but rather because of political factors arising out of civil wars or desires for political power. The unique tragedy faced by the Jews during the Holocaust was aptly summarized by Wiesel in his statement that he had directed to President Carter: "Mr. President, it is true that not all victims [the millions killed during the Holocaust] were Jews, but all Jews were victims."[19] Unlike the burning of Jews in Spain and Portugal during the Inquisition, the Germans of the Holocaust era permitted neither flight from Europe nor conversion. At least the Iberian monarchs permitted non-Christians to survive if they were willing to depart from their homeland or if they would submit to conversion to Christianity. The Nazis, on the other hand, offered no similar options to their Jewish victims. Their single option was to participate unwillingly in Hitler's "final solution." The catastrophe was exacerbated by the fact that the murdered Jews were given neither a humane burial nor even memorial tombstones.

The Holocaust carries with it a supreme irony: the very people who gave western civilization the Books of Moses, where the act of creation is treated with absolute reverence, were doomed in Hitler's world order to total annihilation. Wiesel notes this irony as follows: "The people of creation were driven from creation. They were condemned to die for nothing, the very people sworn to sanctify life and the meaning of life."[20]

Given the extraordinary nature of the Holocaust, given also Wiesel's insistence that the description of such an event went far beyond the capability of language, what are the factors that explain his success in being able to recapture verbally much of what he had experienced? First, he saw, lived, and felt the hell itself. He was there. From firsthand experience he knew what hell was all about. A witness to Auschwitz and Birkenau, he possessed the most authentic credentials needed to delineate his testimony in moving and fiery words. Second, Wiesel seemed to have possessed a sense of history. He realized, early on, the historical magnitude of the "Event." Thus he could treat it with commensurate reverence and solemnity. He knew enough about human history to comprehend that the Holocaust was a happening without an antecedent. Therefore, he formulated a tableau endowed with the Herculean language that reflected the scope of the Shoah. He once wrote that "The Holocaust is a sacred realm. One cannot enter this realm without realizing that only those who were there can know. But the outsider can come close to the gates. One can never know and yet one must try."[21]

With his carefully chosen language, Wiesel did indeed guide these "outsiders" until they could stand at the brink of the precipice from which they could view the full scale of the tragedy of the abyss below. The ten long years of his gestation, prior to his writing of the story, served him well. They allowed him to organize his factual data, to select his words, to construct his paragraphs, and above all to gather the psychological and historical distance needed to accomplish his task. These ten years gave him the opportunity to maturate, to digest, to evaluate, to select, and above all to eliminate the nonessentials. This period of time also made it easier for him to adopt the best vantage point from which to recount his testimony. Furthermore, during this ten-year vigil, he learned to understand the critical relationship between words and silences. He came to understand that the Holocaust has to do with silence, even with silence in the words we say, a silence beyond the words, the deepest silence in us.[22] The depiction of the Shoah resembles a sacred worship service during which prayers of oral words alternate with silent prayers. Wiesel thus perpetuates a major tradition in French literature, that of the Theater of Silence (the tradition of a school of writers that includes Maurice Maeterlinck and Tristan Bernard)—in which the spaces between words are as vital as the words themselves, and in which the utterance of actors and the pauses between these utterances were equally eloquent. In *Night* Wiesel came close to Maeterlinck and Bernard in his delineation of the delicate, even fragile, equilibrium between the spoken and the unspoken.

The nomenclature assigned by society to designate the tragic happening in which six million Jews were annihilated continues to disturb Wiesel. Through overuse of the term "Holocaust," the experience has become devalued by post-World War II society and has lost some of the sacredness it deserves. When an entire people—the Jews of Europe—have almost been effaced, a term must be found that fully does justice to the scale of tragedy. At times Wiesel resorts to the word "Hourban," the ancient Hebrew expression denoting the destruction of the ancient temple of Jerusalem. At other times he prefers the more generic "Event," with a capital "E." He even refers to the Holocaust as *La Nuit* [Night], also as "darkness" or "flames" or "fire." Occasionally he uses "kingdom of night." But in truth, he has never resolved this dilemma to his satisfaction. It may be then that one of the reasons why Wiesel relies so heavily on his many silences stems from the fact that he seems unable to identify or invent the right word capable of encompassing the full gamut of these nightmarish experiences. He seems to suggest this in the following statement:

> What does the holocaust mean? The total oblation by fire, thus, if there is a word one must use in any event, it is fire. It is fire that dominates in this tragedy. Then, the term, implies being totally consumed, total sacrifice. Personally I do not like this word [Holocaust], but because it has been banalized, commercialized. People use it nowadays to describe any old thing.[23]

In another passage he explains further his struggle to select the most appropriate designator for the destruction of the European Jewry: "I prefer to use *Hourban* which evokes the destruction of the Temple. One might have to return to it in order to designate the Jewish Catastrophe."[24] In yet another statement he accepts the suggestion of Saint Cheron that Hourban ought to represent the extreme opposite of the term "the Exodus from Egypt." In his Nobel acceptance address Wiesel refers to the holocaust as "The Kingdom of Night."[25]

The literary works of Elie Wiesel have aptly been regarded by Holocaust scholars as the most eloquent expression of that enormous tragedy. Because he had so persistently and persuasively reminded us of our duty to remember what actually occurred, it is tempting for us to classify him as a "Holocaust writer." But this classification severely delimits his true stature among the writers of his generation. In truth, he transcends the label of "Holocaust writer" by frequently writing about much happier subjects: for example, he often deals with the joys of Hasidic worship, lighthearted Jewish folk tales, triumphant Biblical events, harmonious parent-children relationships. Wiesel clarifies his varied efforts to be much more than a "Holocaust writer" in the following passage:

> Does this mean that wound has cicatrized? It continues to burn. I am always incapable of talking about it. But I feel I am capable of *talking*—that is the change in me. . . . I evoke memories that precede my own, I sing the chant of the kingdom of the ancients, I describe engulfed worlds: I exist through what I say as much as through what I do not say. To protect the silent universe that belongs to me, I relate the one belongs to others. In order not to speak of what hurts me, I explore other subjects: Biblical, Talmudic, Hasidic or contemporary. . . . In other words, literature has become for me a way of diverting your glance. The tales that I relate are never those that I would like myself, that I ought to relate.[26]

In some ways, Wiesel's deliberate departure from the theme of the Holocaust in other literary directions can be interpreted as a form of self-imposed silence. By steering away from topics related to the Shoah, he assumes a posture of silence vis-à-vis this bitter subject. Instead he indulges in a kind of escapism as he shifts to other less depressing subject matter. But lest anyone be fooled the Shoah lurks always beneath the illusory veneer of the more joyful topics.

In a work written jointly with Friedlander, Wiesel traces the chronicle of the Shoah from its earliest stages through its crescendo and final aftermath. First Wiesel and Friedlander describe the prevailing rumors within the Jewish communities that the camps really exist, rumors spread by a few witnesses who manage to escape from their incarceration. The two authors then analyze the fears among the Jews that these rumors may indeed be true. And then the two writers note how the Jews were paralyzed by indecision—should they remain in their towns or try to flee somewhere? Soon indecision is followed by self-delusions and the Jews rationalize that the horrors of the rumors cannot possibly be true. With blind optimism they decide that the rumors are surely fictitious exaggerations or wildly imaginative fabrications. Their rationalizations are further bolstered by their religious faith: the Jewish God would never allow His chosen people to be unprotected; surely he will shelter them from this peril. Then come the arrests, round-ups, deportations. People begin to disappear from their communities. Next Wiesel and Friedlander paint the brutal ride of the prisoners in the cattle cars. Ultimately, the Jews of Europe find themselves surrounded by barbed wire, unable to escape, and facing the gas chambers and crematoria. Engulfed by the flames of hell, the prisoners witness mass exterminations, torture, thirsty children screaming for water in full view of supplies of water, innocent babies being killed like criminals, mothers sacrificing children, sons sacrificing fathers, siblings being separated, whole families being destroyed, the savagery of victims turning against each other in their struggle to survive, inmates who must decide if a bite of bread is more valuable in their mouth or in that of a parent or child, people losing their sanity in an insane world, others seeking consolation by clinging to a bit of music, humming a melody, or writing a poem. And in the midst of this inferno God remains silent.[27]

Few writers in western literary tradition have equaled, let alone surpassed, Elie Wiesel's *Night* in depicting the pathos of man's inhumanity towards man. With meticulous care and impressive artistic precision he portrays the metamorphosis of life into death, of day into night, of sanity into madness, and of love into selfishness. With concise sentences like these he summarizes the complex pathos of an otherwise unimaginable human drama: "The human machine had worn out. Their nerves had given way."[28] "One million children massacred: I shall never understand."[29]

Wiesel's literary success derives from his uncanny ability to find the right language, imagery, and syntax that could effectively transmit his personal pain to people who had themselves not personally experienced the ordeal of the Holocaust. Especially touching is his rhetoric concerning his separation from his mother and sister, Tsipora: addressing his dead mother he exclaims that "I continue to seek you, I try to halt the tide. I see you walking with my little sister, hand in hand, I see both of you, and my heart tightens up, tightens up. I suffer pain, I suffer pain and I do not know what to do to keep from screaming out. I suffer pain and I don't know what to say, what to do. What a life, what a life."[30]

But Elie Wiesel did survive—miraculously! During the aftermath of the liberation, instead of feeling grateful that he had outlived the

Holocaust, his moods oscillated between outbursts of guilt at having survived, on the one hand, and expressions of thankfulness that he was still alive, on the other hand. He was especially grateful that he had lived long enough to father a son who would perpetuate the tradition of Judaism and the patrimony of a family that was otherwise doomed to disappear. Referring to his lost friends of childhood, he asks "what have I done to deserve to survive them. For the most part, they are no longer in this world."[31]

For Wiesel the most poignant suffering stems from the fact that in the aftermath of the Holocaust there exist some who prefer to forget this troubling era. He is also pained that others dismiss the Shoah as one of the many inevitable consequences of international warfare. Above all he has been distressed by those few who have gone so far as to deny the reality of the tragic events of 1939–45. How does a witness who has lost both of his parents, a sister, and many close relatives deal with those who deny these losses? How does one who has lived through this history cope with those who deny the same history? On being reminded that several "treatises" have been published in which self-proclaimed historians allege that the Holocaust never occurred, the embittered Wiesel simply refuses to respond to these preposterous allegations. Nor has he been willing to engage himself in argumentative disputations with the deniers and historical revisionists. Calling them "morally deranged" persons, Wiesel singles out especially Professor Arthur Butz of Northwestern University and former Professor Faurisson of the Université de Lyon (France), both of whom had published especially vitriolic books asserting that the Holocaust was little more than a figment of the Jewish imagination. Here is a typical reaction by the author of *Night* to the Holocaust deniers:

> But today the greatest injustice is being perpetrated: the obliteration of those memories, the erasing of those events . . . A movement is afoot not only to rewrite history but also to destroy it and in so doing to humble and humiliate those teachers who still remember but who carry their wounds secretly. If we are to believe these morally deranged, perverted, so-called historians, the Holocaust never took place, the victims did not perish. Auschwitz is a fraud, Treblinka is a fraud.[32]

Wiesel accuses the revisionists of trying to murder the six million Jewish victims yet another time, by depriving them even of the legitimacy of their deaths. But it is not only a handful of academicians against whom this surviving witness manifested his scorn. He was equally shocked that some German politicians, seeking to justify the camps and to whitewash a shameful chapter in German history, claimed with a false sense of innocence that the camps were little more than legitimate prisoner-of-war internment centers established by the Germans at a time when their country was fighting to save its cultural traditions from being destroyed by the Allied powers.[33]

That the voices of the "morally deranged" revisionists were not entirely unsuccessful in subverting the credibility of the Holocaust is apparent in various incidents that shocked Elie Wiesel. The most recent event took place on July 1, 1991—nearly half a century after Treblinka—when, during a memorial service commemorating the death of the 900 Jews of Iasi, Romania, a spectator, described by the *New York Times* as "a middle aged, well dressed woman" provoked pandemonium in the packed Municipal Theater by repeatedly shouting 'Lies!' and by interrupting a speech in which Elie Wiesel, the Nobel prize-winning author, eulogized the victims and delivered a warning about renascent anti-Semitism. As he tried to speak, a woman rose from the front row to shout: "It's a lie. The Jews didn't die."[34] The article did not report the response of the main speaker who had been drowned out by the din.

Even though he had undergone excruciating physical and moral pain, even though he had suffered immeasurable family losses, even though he has had a difficult time coping with the Holocaust deniers and revisionists, even though he has seen the lingering effects of anti-Semitism during the half century after Auschwitz, Elie Wiesel continues to live with hope. He refuses to lose all of his faith in mankind. He refuses to allow himself to slide into a quagmire of despair. Like Camus's Sisyphus he faces the future of human history with determination and cautious optimism. In the wake of the Holocaust, he once wrote: "Upon the ruins of Europe, on the scorched earth of Germany, yesterday's candidates for death began to build a Jewish future."[35] He has done more than his share in building this future. His texts have become a message that calls upon humanity to continue in its pursuit of that still elusive brave new world.

4
"Indifference to Evil is Evil"

DURING THE BLEAKNESS OF THE HOLOCAUST, ELIE WIESEL AND THE inmates in the concentration camps universally wondered if the outside world really knew what was taking place in those despicable camps scattered all over eastern Germany, Poland, Czechoslovakia, and Austria. It seemed inconceivable to the prisoners that the massive exterminations could possibly occur without anyone in the other countries being aware of the atrocities in the camps. Wiesel revealed his bewilderment at this situation as follows: "A key word of any vocabulary, 'to know,' disturbs our vocabulary. On trying to communicate our experience, we were anxious to discover who knew what and when. The excruciatingly painful question has been haunting us for years. Did the world know what the killers were making the victims undergo?"[1] Assuming that the sheer scale of the murder of millions of human beings could not possibly have gone unnoticed, Wiesel posed a question heavily laden with irony: "In a world that punished an ordinary thief, would campaigns of mass murder be ignored? It seemed impossible, unbelievable."[2] Out of questions like these there emerged in Wieselean literature a constantly recurring theme: indifference to evil is evil. After liberation, Wiesel wandered around the world, trying indefatigably to discover whether people in other lands knew about the camps. If so, why did they remain silent? Why did they not protest? Why did the others remain passive? Sadly Wiesel's years of research led him to the conclusion that the world did indeed know much, that news had certainly leaked out; but it was easier for outsiders to look away without intervention in what many rationalized to be an internal German affair. In his Oslo Nobel address, Wiesel summed up the situation with bitter terseness: "The world knew and remained silent."[3] Worst of all, Wiesel had come to realize that once the world permitted the colossal tragedy to occur without reacting in any way, the door had been opened so that in the future other killers could inflict similar crimes against other segments of the human population, and they could do so with impunity. Why do civilized nations tolerate monumental slaughters of whole populations—even today? Because the Holocaust had established a precedent. During the wholesale slaughter of Christians in Beirut, Lebanon, the world watched inactively. This is what Wiesel told Brigitte-Fanny Cohen during an interview with her: "I think that the world accepts nowadays the massacre of the Christians because it accepted the massacre of the Jews, yesterday."[4]

The worst human crime, according to Elie Wiesel, is indifference. Frequently he labels indifference as "neutrality" that is to say, people simply do not take sides one way or the other. Aloofness implies that one does not care. "Neutrality always disquiets me," he informs Saint Cheron.[5] In *Signes d'exode,* his distaste for neutrality or indifference is transformed into a plea for compassion:

> Humanity has conquered space, but it has not changed the hearts of men. Is it possible that we learned nothing? All of those wars that continue to ravage tens of countries! All of those victims who fall under the bullets of terrorists! All of those thousands of children who are dying of hunger—yes, of hunger—and of sicknesses—yes, of sicknesses—in Africa and in Asia. Why is there so much hate on our planet? Why is there so much indifference to hate, to suffering, to the anguish of others?[6]

A disciple of the early existential writers, like Camus and Sartre, he insists that we must take sides, that we must make choices, that we must make commitments. Otherwise we do not exercise our responsibility as human beings.

Indifference and neutrality can only result in the destruction of human life on our planet. This is the central message enunciated in most of Wiesel's novels: "Indifference, passivity, and resignation all lead to decadence. When you are in love, you are not neutral, you are not indifferent."[7] But this literary man is not only a disciple of modern authors like Sartre and Camus; consciously or unconsciously, he seems to have adopted the attitude of an earlier French writer, the well known André Gide, who, during his long career, advocated that individuals should live their lives with fervor, enthusiasm, and passion. Gide emphasized that each moment in life was important, and that we should live each moment fully, even with frenzy. Wiesel, for his part, sees fervor as an antidote to indifference and neutrality. "Whatever the road you have followed and you are about to take," writes Wiesel, "whatever you do, do it with fervor. Fervor is one of the most precious of gifts—and of rewards as well."[8] When one is fervent, one cannot be indifferent. Human beings can shield themselves from indifference to crime and evil by adopting strong positions, by feeling strongly, by believing in certain ideals passionately. During the celebrated trial of Adolph Eichmann in Israel, Wiesel did not solely blame the monstrous inhumanity lurking in the Nazi's soul; he also accused the German people of the crime of "acquiescence," the crime of tolerating barbarous behavior by their leaders and by those who enforced governmental policy. Through indifference, the German populace conspired unwittingly with the Nazi criminals. Additionally, men like Eichmann were supported directly or indirectly by the millions of anti-Semites in Poland, Slovakia and the Ukraine, Romania, Hungary and elsewhere. When Wiesel speaks of "indirect support" of Nazism, he is really referring to those who, by their indifference, did not actively oppose the rise of anti-Jewish movements in their countries. Such indifference to evil could only strengthen the Nazi killers in their determination to exterminate the Jews.[9]

Printed on the congressional gold medal presented to Elie Wiesel by President Ronald Reagan are the words, "Indifference to evil is evil." This slogan contains perhaps the trademark message Wiesel believes that he can communicate to others. These words sum up succinctly the basic thrust of that which he has sought to tell his readers in his books. Below are samples of other similar statements scattered throughout his texts:

> We must also learn the dangers of indifference and neutrality. In times of evil, indifference to evil is evil. Neutrality always helps the killer, not the victim.[10]

> In morality as in literature—or in any field of human creativity—indifference is the enemy; indifference to evil is worse than evil, . . . This is true of individuals as it is of communities.[11]

> We have learned that if evil strikes one people and others do not react, evil has its own dynamics. I wish we could stop evil.[12]

In addition to fervor and passion as countervailing forces against indifference, Wiesel proposes yet another remedy against this scourge: action. Every human being must *act* against evil in a way that is consistent with one's capabilities and talents. In the case of the writer (like Wiesel, for example), action assumes the form of storytelling, that is to say texts and sentences. Whenever he gives addresses around the world, he underscores the need for action against the sin of sins: indifference.

Better than any other commentator of Wiesel, Ted Estess has summed up Wieselean verbal action as the most effective remedy against indifference: "Action comes to occupy a large place in Wiesel's sensibility because in the Holocaust he experienced so catastrophically the consequences of the failure to act. In Wiesel's view, it was indifference on the part of the executioner and spectators that brought about destruction of six million. And storytelling is Wiesel's action against indifference and in support of Friendship."[13] With resentment, Wiesel reacted against those who turned their backs on the victims and their plight. In Wiesel's eyes, indifference is hardly different from complicity with the assassins. He was especially incensed at the refusal by the Americans and other nations to permit the steamer, *Saint-Louis,* laden with many Jewish refugees escaping the flames of Hitler's Germany, to dock either in America or other ports. Tragically, the ship returned to Europe where the refugees were arrested and sent to their deaths in the camps: "They knew in Washington. When the *Saint-Louis* asked for asylum, the United States turned them away . . . No one in the United States, Great Britain, Switzerland, Sweden, or the Vatican found it necessary to go on the radio to warn us [the Hungarian Jews who had not yet been arrested by the Germans]. Their failure to warn, I submit, was complicity of a criminal nature."[14]

Wiesel's disillusionment with President Franklin Roosevelt and Prime Minister Winston Churchill is an open secret. Despite their reputations as men who cared about Jewish destiny, both demonstrated little more than benign indifference towards German criminality against the Jews. Wiesel notes that neither the American president nor the British prime minister raised his voice against the massacres in the camps. Nor did they do much to alleviate the suffering of the inmates there. The Jewish writer makes much of the fact that neither leader authorized his armed forces to do anything substantial through the considerable military means at their disposal. Wiesel often asks why the Allies had even refrained from bombing the railroad tracks carrying the cattle cars crammed with Jewish prisoners bound for their death in the camps: "Why weren't the railways to Birkenau bombed by either the Allies or the Russians? And the Russians were so close."[15] Not only was Wiesel ashamed of the indifference to evil by the governmental leadership of the Allied powers; he was also outraged at the silence of the Jewish leadership in America. The most distinguished Jewish leader of the time, Rabbi Stephen Wise of Cleveland, having been informed of the tragic conditions within the camps, did little to alert the American Jews or to bring pressure upon the government to take concrete action: "But I am mostly ashamed as a Jew. . . . Jewish leaders did not make speeches until very late . . . nothing—I insist—nothing was done . . . And what did American Jews do to aid their brothers in Europe? . . . Wise knew that 2,000,000 Jews had already been exterminated. How could he pledge secrecy? [Wise had promised the American State Department not to divulge the details of what he had learned from governmental communiqués in order not to alarm America's Jews or to create uneasiness in the United States.]"[16]

What Wiesel did not realize was the extent to which American Jews were disunited during the forties. Nor did Jews in America truly appreciate, prior to the establishment of the America–Israel Public Affairs Committee (AIPAC) after the founding of the State of Israel, that even though their numbers were relatively small in comparison with the total American population, they could harness sufficient strength in certain key states and urban areas to exert considerable influence on the formulation of public policy in a nation founded upon the principle of representative government. Above all, during the early forties, the Jews of America did not really have an Elie Wiesel as one of their outstanding citizens to enunciate their collective aspirations. At that time in history, Rabbi Stephen Wise was the leader of a myriad of disorganized, individualistic organizations, most of which could not develop any national consensus. Moreover, Rabbi Wise seems to have been the kind of leader who was reluctant to "rock the boat." Silence, discretion, political correctness and passivity characterized his leadership style. Even though word had been leaking out of Europe concerning the atrocities of the Nazis, their behavior was so unbelievable that people regarded these rumors as preposterous. Despite occasional articles (usually buried deeply and discreetly in the back pages of the *New York Times*) about the events of the concentration camps—many Jews and non-Jews believed that such heinous activity could not occur in an age of enormous scientific achievement and lofty cultural accomplishments. In hindsight, Wiesel has come to understand the inertia of American Jewry during the period of the Holocaust: "Because the Jewish people could not get together, for political reasons. Also because Roosevelt asked them not to raise a fuss. That is the truth—the Jewish people in its most critical hours did not have the leadership that it deserved and that it needed."[17]

Wiesel opines that the only nation to have manifested real concern about the Jewish plight was Denmark, a nation that managed to smuggle virtually all of its Jewish citizens in small boats to Sweden. Wiesel is convinced that if the Poles, Hungarians, Lithuanians, Latvians, Slovaks, and others had manifested a similar high regard for human life, millions of Jews would have also been saved.

With such obvious worldwide indifference to their situation during the Nazi era, Jews felt abandoned and eerily alone on a planet in which they had almost no friends or allies. The aloneness of the Jewish people in an indifferent world—this constitutes one of the most poignant themes in Wieselean literature. The author believes that the isolation felt by the Jews at their greatest hour of need results inevitably from the rampant anti-Semitism that filled the world. Secretly, perhaps unconsciously, most Europeans preferred to insulate themselves from the Jewish tragedy because they either did not care or else hoped that "the Jewish problem" might simply evaporate once the Jews could disappear entirely. On isolating themselves from the pending disaster facing the Jews, Europeans essentially let the victims suffer by themselves. Wiesel has always maintained that if the European nations surrounding Germany had protested vociferously against Hitler's earliest anti-Semitic campaigns during the early nineteen-thirties, the Nazi plans for extermination would have been nipped in the bud before they could gather momentum. Had the Catholic Church in Rome publicly condemned Hitler's crusade against the Jews, had France and the United Kingdom vehemently censured German anti-Semitism, had the United States taken a clear and strong position at the outset, had the international community staged dramatic demonstrations in opposition to the Nazi policy— had all of this taken place, Hitler might have been deterred from his plan to destroy an entire people. Instead, the widespread policy of disinterestness, of non-intervention in Germany's internal affairs, provided the German führer with the assurance that once he proceeded with his brutal campaign, he could do so with impunity. An obviously bitter Wiesel wrote that "Hitler was convinced that he faced no enemy, no resistance."[18]

Once Hitler knew that the Jews stood alone, that they had no friends or advocates who cared about them, they became an easy target for extinction. Thousands of years of anti-Semitism had had their effect. And so "The killers killed and the world was silent. The killers were able to kill because the world was indifferent. . . . Let's face it, the world did not care, humanity was unconcerned. . . . Hitler understood it."[19]

Today historians pose troubling questions: Why did the Jews of Europe not resist annihilation? Why did they not revolt? The alleged non-resistance of the Jews is one of the truly painful charges to which Wiesel felt compelled to reply. In the first place, he notes that the Nazis were so cunning in devising a policy of gradualness, a policy of slowly incremental moves that by the time anyone realized the implications of the mounting tragedy, it was too late. In the second place, Wiesel stresses that the Jews of Europe represented only a tiny minority in most countries (except for Poland), and they were scattered throughout so many nations that their power base was highly fragmented. They could thus not offer much resistance in any single place against Hitler's mighty Wehrmacht. Even major powers like France collapsed after a few weeks of resistance. In contrast with the rapid collapse of the armed forces of France, Holland, Belgium, Poland, Norway, and elsewhere, at least the Jews in the Warsaw ghetto were able to hold at bay the German military units for several months, and Wiesel makes much of this fact. Also he accentuates the importance of various Jewish underground resistance movements in the forests of eastern Europe and in cities like Vilnius, Lithuania. What makes Wiesel especially acrimonious is the fact that these pockets of Jewish resistance received almost no help whatsoever from the local Christians populations, whose anti-Semitism was apparently stronger than their fear of the Germans. Wiesel is particularly resentful that today more people ask why the Jews seemed so acquiescent than those who wonder why the world was so indifferent. Once again Wiesel sees this situation as a classic case in which the victims are blamed more than the killers.

In a fit of outrage, the usually mild-tempered Wiesel wrote that "If the intellectuals, the lovers of mankind, the proclaimers of ideals had not slept peacefully while the sky over Auschwitz was aflame, we would not have had to ask the question: Why didn't the Jews revolt?"[20] Wiesel had frequently complained that post-Holocaust commentators seem to blame the passivity of the victims more than the cruelty of the murderers or the indifference of the world: "The world refused to look. When the Jews were being murdered, the world was indifferent. Now it asks why the Jews did not fight."[21] When all is said and done, the Jewish author emphasizes that when the Jews did

4: "INDIFFERENCE TO EVIL IS EVIL"

belatedly launch their rebellion in the Warsaw streets, no one came to their aid: "The first civilian uprising was the Jewish uprising of the Warsaw Ghetto. And no hand was stretched to the ghetto with help. Poland, Hungary, Romania, all countries forgot the Jews and the Jewish fighters. Even our friends forgot us . . ."[22]

The shameful and shameless indifference of the world during the Holocaust persuaded Elie Wiesel to make a decision that henceforth he would dedicate the rest of his life to combat the cowardly reluctance of people who, in the womb of their own security, refrain from involving themselves in situations where their neighbors have been endangered. This is a central theme of his Oslo Address in which he explains the rationale for his decision to combat hunger, injustice, persecution, intolerance, racism, prejudice, ethnic hatred, and above all else indifference. Henceforth his remaining years would be devoted to the cause of human solidarity and to that of brotherhood.[23]

In *Paroles d'étranger* the author writes that "If we fight for the victims of today, it is because those of yesterday have been forgotten, abandoned, left to the whim of the enemy. It is by thinking of the past that we aspire to save our common future."[24] With this Wiesel tells us that history must never be allowed to repeat itself.

5

The Rhetoric of Silence

As we have demonstrated earlier, Elie Wiesel is much more than a fulltime writer: he teaches, lectures, counsels major world leaders. For many years he was also a journalist. Above all, however, he is a writer! In all of his work, he depends upon words, sentences, paragraphs. Language is his tool of the trade. He writes in French, Hebrew, Yiddish, English. He can also function somewhat in German and Hungarian. In whatever language he selects to write, words become the soul of his métier. If words serve as the tools that make his works possible, they often become—paradoxically—major impediments or barriers to his art of communication. While Wiesel the writer/speaker/teacher/journalist cannot function without words, these same words become painful, tyrannical hindrances that constrict and constrain.

In Wiesel's creative activities, one discerns a pendulum oscillating between his desire to express his thought and experiences, on one hand, and his personal frustration at not being able adequately to transmit those same thoughts and experiences on the other hand. His career has been replete with awesome frays between words and non-words (or silences): "Words separate me from myself . . . In searching for silence, in digging into it, I started to discover the perils and the powers of the spoken word . . . Words seem stale, foolish, inadequate, artificial, anemic; I wanted them to be fiery . . . The language of night was not human but animalistic, even mineral-like: raucous cries, howling, muffled sighs, savage complaints, blows of the cudgel."[1]

What does a writer do when he is overpowered by the irrepressible urge to communicate a verbal message, but his words do not have the power to express what he wishes to say? The events of the Holocaust, the pain felt by Wiesel, the grief suffered by him at the loss of his family and closest friends—these are the traumatic experiences that often transcend linguistic description. He once told Brigitte-Fanny

5: THE RHETORIC OF SILENCE

Cohen that "I know that words do not have the power of transmitting the message that I carry inside of me, nor even a fragment of the message. In vain do I try to say the unsayable in order to express my impossibility of saying [these things]. If I succeed in convincing a reader or an auditor that we cannot communicate this experience, I would not have spoken in vain."[2] Wiesel thus believes that his mission as a writer/speaker has been achieved even if what he says is not the whole truth, but at least it conveys a reasonably accurate shadow of the truth. In the unique case of the Holocaust, the whole truth can never really be retrieved by the witness to an auditor or reader who was not present at the scene of the event. However, even a portion of the truth is preferable to total silence.

In effect, the texts of Elie Wiesel, both written and spoken, consist of an ingenious interplay between words and silence. That a professional writer should reveal his lack of faith in the power and magic of language is an uncommon phenomenon. After all, what other tools are available to the writer? It is even more unusual for a devout Jew like Wiesel to suspect the efficacy of language. Jews have traditionally enjoyed, deservedly, the reputation of being the people of the Book. The central tenets of Jewish faith emerge out of their reading and analyses of the Torah, a sacred work constructed of words, sentences, syntax, accent marks—in short, all of the accoutrements of language. How could such a deeply religious man like Wiesel doubt the potential of language? His skepticism about language alternates with his celebration of language. His ambivalence on the subject is reflected by the way he combines a judicious suppression of words with an equally judicious enthusiasm for words. Through his painstaking manipulation of utterances and taciturnity he has somehow managed to construct the texts that he eagerly transmits to his readers.[3]

Wiesel does not idolize language for the sake of language. He does not consider language to be an end in itself. Rather, for him, language is merely a tool, a literary aid. It possesses the power of uniting people and also of dividing them into sects and cults. Wiesel, for his part, chooses to utilize language as a dynamic force that brings people together. While language can be used both to clarify issues and to cloud them, he prefers to use his texts to elucidate and clarify issues, not to obscure them.

The issue of language—how it functions in the process of communication between an author and his public—this issue has always been a key element in how Wiesel views literature. This is so possibly because he opted to write in an adopted language, French, rather than in one of his mother tongues. This explains in part his fascination with Samuel Beckett, the Irish writer who also preferred to write in an acquired language, French, instead of in English or Irish. Wiesel also admired Beckett because "The impossibility of human communication is, by the way, the main theme of all of his work."4 (This is of course also true of Wiesel's works.)

The consideration of the role of language in literary creativity occupies an important place in Wiesel's thinking. In fact, the conflict between words and silence has always been a traumatic obsession for him. We can identify at least three major elements that explain this conflict. First, Wiesel seems governed by what the French call *pudeur*, a reticence to speak too freely about people's private lives. This *pudeur* is certainly apparent in his discussions of his own personal life. An almost untranslatable term, *pudeur* suggests the idea of reserve, modesty, the need to conceal one's emotions. Thanks to his *pudeur*, Wiesel has always found it painful to write overtly about his personal life with his wife and his paternal relations with his son. Even in his recently published two-volume memoirs, where, at last, he reveals more about his marital and paternal situation than ever before, the reader senses that the author does not tell everything, that he holds something back; his self-avowed *pudeur* prevents him from making full disclosure. Saint Cheron recognizes this trait in Wiesel both as a human being and as a literary figure: "All of his work strikes us by its *pudeur* [Saint Cheron uses the term dénûment here] and by its style stripped down to the bare essentials."5

The second element in Wiesel's silence is his basic philosophy of life, a philosophy in which he stresses that the finest literary texts are those in which the densest, the most complex subject matter ought to be stated in the smallest possible number of words. Wiesel must then be regarded as a minimalist, one who seeks to convey his message by limiting himself to the unavoidable essentials, and nothing more. At all costs, his ideas must be stated with few frills and sparse verbal ornamentation. Consciously he chooses to express his thoughts in simple, clear, uncomplicated, and straightforward language. The extraneous details have been eliminated. Each word must have a purpose. And each word must be chosen so that it is as pregnant with meaning as possible. In this respect, Wiesel's literary art is consistent with the finest traditions of French classicism, a movement for which he had much admiration.

That Wiesel waited ten years before he plunged into his literary career corroborates both his fascination with the use of language and his fear of resorting to it. During this ten-year gestation he waged his battle between words and silence. His desire to "communicate the uncommunicable—("communiquer l'incommunicable," to cite Saint Cheron).[6] Eventually the desire to tell his story became irrepressible. In *Signes d'exode* Wiesel admits his difficulty in "describing the indescribable."[7] At a rare moment of candor he confesses his fear of language: "I felt I needed ten years to collect words and the silence in them. . . . I am obsessed with silence because I am afraid of the spoken word, even of the written word."[8] Interestingly, an American professor, Simon Sibelman, has written an entire monograph on Wiesel's obsession with silence, entitled *Silence in the Novels of Elie Wiesel*.

How to depict verbally the horror of the concentration camps? This was the central challenge facing the writer as he prepared to enter the realm of literature. He knew that he would have to overcome not only the inadequacy of vocabulary, but also the awesome task of interspersing language with the appropriate use of silence. Even grammatical construction raised many barriers. The events of the Shoah were so illogical, so irrational that they did not readily conform to the established contours of syntactic logic. As Wiesel composed his sentences, he posed many questions; for example: "Can you even communicate Auschwitz by structuring it in literary form?"[9] In the end, however, he learned that by deftly alternating meaningful moments of silence with well-chosen language, he could vanquish the obstacles arising out of the grammatical constraints.

In his novels Wiesel likes to interrupt the flow of spoken dialogue between his characters by inserting into their speech pregnant pauses of silence, leaving it up to the reader's imagination to fill in the voids between the words. In *Night*, for example, as a mother passes in front of suffering children in the concentration camp, she becomes mute and even turns her eyes away from them, pretending to ignore their pain by distancing herself physically and physiologically from their wailing and their pain. Without uttering a single word, her gestures and taciturnity suggest to the reader the intense agony she obviously feels at the plight of these children. In *Twilight*, the protagonist visits an asylum for the mentally retarded in which the loquacious patients speak profusely among themselves. Their chatter actually deflects our attention from their inner feelings. But whenever they wish to convey a meaningful message, they become speechless. Wiesel seems to imply that words can often mask the truth, whereas silence speaks with eloquence. In the major

Wieselean novels, whenever the characters suffer intensely, their pain is transmitted to us much more effectively through silence than through speech. Wiesel has written that "Silence does not always signify absence of speech; it signifies also presence beyond speech."[10]

In some of Wiesel's other novels some of the most fascinating fictional personalities are those who have lost their speech, who have become either totally or partially mute. Their tongues have been frozen by their recollections of the brutal experiences they witnessed in the Holocaust. Even God, traumatized by the atrocities committed by the human beings He had created, has been rendered speechless. The silence of God, the inability of God to play an active role by expressing His outrage, that silence and that inability to act are both major themes in Wieselean texts. If for many of the survivors of Treblinka and Auschwitz, God has died, for Wiesel, at least, his God remains very much alive; but He has become inexplicably speechless and paralyzed by the shock of witnessing human evil.

Silence need not at all be considered as an enemy of literature. When managed skillfully by a writer, it can, ironically, be seen as a potent tool that enhances the writer's ability to communicate a compelling message. In literary works, one encounters all kinds of silences—those that drown out speech entirely and those that enrich it. Wiesel's silence is the kind that enriches language. Once he wrote as follows: "Of course, my silence is meant to be a very eloquent silence, a shouting silence."[11]

Following his famous ten-year wait, Wiesel made a conscious decision to bring silence to a halt. He knew that unless he ended his muteness and resorted to language, the Shoah would gradually evaporate into the mist of passing history. He realized that his testimony needed to be recorded; otherwise it would disappear with his own death someday. In the name of the six million he became the instrument that would keep their memory alive. It thus fell upon Wiesel's shoulders to assume the responsibility for reminding the world for all time to come that the Holocaust had destroyed millions of lives, a rich cultural heritage, and almost an entire civilization. For the author of *Night* it became a sacred duty to fill the universe with the haunting memory of those who had been destroyed.[12] If the lives of these innocent victims had been demolished, at least Wiesel's books would guarantee that the story of their destruction would remain forever.

There is something mystical or spiritual about Elie Wiesel's fusion of language and silence. This mystical, spiritual quality even lends to

5: THE RHETORIC OF SILENCE

his prose a certain poetic quality. In fact, one might say that Wiesel's prose combines poetry, prayer, chanting, and many quiet moments that are interspersed between the uttered words. For the highly regarded twentieth-century French critic, Abbé Bremond, prayer emerges out of poetry; in fact, the two were almost consubstantial. For Elie Wiesel too, there is an inextricably close relationship between the two. As he chanted the Kaddish and the Yizkor, those well-known Jewish prayers for the dead, he recited the poetry of memory honoring the deceased. This kind of poetic prayer has always been a central part of the Hebrew religious service. Remarkable also in this service is the vital interplay between spoken or chanted prayer, on the one hand, and solemn silence (referred to as the Amidah in the Jewish prayer book), on the other. As in the Jewish prayer service, one finds in the literary endeavors of Elie Wiesel an impressive harmony between poetic language and eloquent silence. This harmony between the spoken and the unspoken forms the core of Wiesel's oeuvre. Here is how he came close to defining his own entire body of literature: "When a thousand words are pressed into a single line, a poem is born. In Literature the weight of silence determines the weight of art."[13]

6
In Remembrance of History

WHAT HE HAD EXPERIENCED, WHAT HE HAD WITNESSED IN THE FACtories of death, Elie Wiesel vowed never to forget. And he did not forget. For him memory developed into one of the *idées fixes* that imperiously dominated much of his existence. In the second volume of his memoirs, *Et la mer n'est pas remplie,* he acknowledges the relentless action of his memory:

> Everything that touches upon memory fascinates me through the mysterious force that it releases. It wishes to embrace everything, to retain everything, and enlightens only some fragments. . . . Memory is one of the key words in my works and my quests, and, to be truthful, I never know what it is and what it is made of. For me memory is what poetry was for Aristotle: more than history, it is what contains Truth. I know that it is indispensable to me. For my writing. For teaching and sharing. Without it, what would I be? Without it, life has neither meaning nor destiny.[1]

Having made a solemn commitment never to forget the Shoah and having acknowledged that the reality of daily life as well as the anticipation of the future makes it necessary for us to deal with current and imminent situations, Wiesel made a conscious effort to interweave "past and present, present and future."[2] He knows that the present represents the prolongation of the past and that the future is little more than an outgrowth of the present.

Convinced that the Jewish people, of all people, are the most uniquely qualified to serve as the memorialists of the past, he asserted that for Jews history signified, quite literally, the collective, continuous, and indomitable remembrance of their past. A highlight of every Jewish religious service is the Kaddish prayer during which mourners remind themselves on the anniversary of the deaths of loves ones of how much they owe to their late family members. And during the holiest holidays in the Jewish calendar, especially on Yom

Kippur, a crucial portion of the synagogue service, Yizkor, is dedicated to the remembrance of the dead. In post-Holocaust services at the synagogue, a special prayer has recently been added to mark the memory of the six million. In short, to be a Jew signifies to become a link between the past and the future. And so Wiesel wrote: "In general, you take any chapter in Jewish history and you will see that somehow it reflects both the present and the future. The Bible has been called the book of history, but it is the book of history. But it is the book of the future, not of the past."[3]

Ashkenazi Jews (those who trace their roots to northern, central, and eastern Europe) generally assume the names of their ancestors. Wiesel notes that there exist among Jews innumerable Abrahams, Jacobs, and Isaacs since the same names tend to be repeated as symbols of continuity; the Abrahams, Jacobs, and Isaacs of the future will continue to multiply in coming generations in remembrance of those who live today: "They do not die. And whatever happened to them has been transmitted in a kind of collective memory which we inherit."[4]

Wiesel attributes one of the causes of anti-Semitism to the fact that other peoples have envied and resented the fidelity of Jews to their forefathers, to their language, to their customs and values, and to the message contained in the Torah. In brief, Jews have remained faithful to the ongoing cumulative memory of a whole people, a memory that will automatically and inevitably evolve into a future heritage. Those who remain outside of the boundaries of this heritage feel a certain enmity against those who live within the confines of this heritage. Excluded from the inner circle, outsiders feel resentment against those who regard themselves to be privileged to occupy the inner spaces of the circle. Out of this resentment there grows a feeling of anti-Semitism.

In their unbroken concatenation of historical continuity, Jews, probably more than any other people, feel compelled to maintain their ties to past history. As the most tragic single event in their history, the Holocaust has recently been added as yet another link in the chain of history. The Shoah occupies a privileged place in Wieselean memory. For the author of *Night,* this memory ranks as the apex of all memories. He considers this tragedy to be one of the two most momentous happenings in all of Jewish history. By the sheer scope of the numbers of victims murdered or scarred for life as well as by the fact that it was unprecedented, the Holocaust cannot easily be labeled. For want of a better term he uses the generic "L'Evènement" (The Event), with a capital "E" or else the Hebrew term "Hourban" (the destruction of the ancient temple of Jerusalem).

A witness is someone who has *seen, felt,* and *experienced* with his or her own sensory apparatus. A witness is someone who has *suffered* great pain or *rejoiced* at festive occasions. By merely remembering and describing happenings at which the witness was present, he or she becomes a link with the past. As Wiesel noted,

> A witness is a link—a link between the event and those who have not participated in it, a link between past and present, between man and man, and man and God. Being a witness, I would like to be that link between Arabs and Jews, between Jews and Christians, between Jews and Jews. I am glad that Arabs recognize that I do not oppose them or spread hate among them. There is enough hate in the world.[5]

Through the witness, time frames can be connected with each other. Through the witness, people from one generation can also be connected with those who lived in earlier generations.

In his role as a witness/survivor Elie Wiesel believed that he had no choice but to bear the torch of memory from generation to generation. In this role, he relates not only what he endured but also what others suffered. Transcending the limits of his personal experience he makes it his duty to read the testimonies of the other survivors who wish to share with others what they saw and lived during the momentous tragedy. In *Signes d'exode,* for example, he incorporates the texts of *La chronique du Ghetto de Lodz* [The Chronicle of the Lodz Ghetto]. In truth, he fears that unless he sets the example of recounting the Shoah, others may be reluctant to do so.

Wiesel reminds all who will listen to his voice that an entire civilization had been eradicated by the Nazis. The culture-destroyers obliterated most of the shtetls of eastern Europe, the communal life of the inhabitants throughout eastern Europe. They burned down whole libraries of Jewish books. They melted down thousands of objets d'art of Judaica. They destroyed ancient cemeteries. They murdered the madmen and wayfarers who wandered from town to town. They eliminated the Jewish shops and the Hebrew schools, the celebration of the Sabbath and both the sacred and secular festivals of the Hebrew calendar. With his novels and essays, Wiesel celebrates a whole vanished civilization. And so we may aptly think of his writings as a monument to the millions killed in the camps and as a memorial of a disappeared world.

Whereas the history of human civilization is marked by notable examples of vanished cultures, most of these evaporated in the process of historical evolution, e.g. invasions and warfare, natural disasters, decay during the passage of centuries. In contrast, Euro-Jewish culture disappeared not from natural corrosion but rather from a deliberate, systematic and national program of destruction. The eradication of Jewish culture in Europe forms the bedrock of Wieselean literature. In his reincarnation of the Holocaust, Wiesel serves simultaneously as a chronicler, historian, storyteller, memorialist, and personal witness. With his vivid memory and highly developed literary skills, Wiesel has been one of the truly authentic messengers of the Holocaust tragedy. Much more than fiction, his novels may well be viewed as stylized archives of the Holocaust and belong to the annals of modern Jewish history.

Because so many of the characters in Wiesel's novels lost their lives or survived the period of the atrocities in a state of physical or emotional damage, these novels may be viewed as a literary cemetery in which lie buried millions of people. In a touching poem, Wiesel the memorialist notes that "They [the Jewish victims] did not even have a cemetery/We [the survivors or witnesses] are their cemeteries."[6]

Of all of the definitions that Wiesel assigns to his own role as a writer, it is that of a witness who remembers what he saw to which he attaches the greatest importance: "I speak simply as a witness of the last twenty-five years."[7] But Wiesel is much more than a living witness. He is one of the major chroniclers of his people. He believes that the Holocaust ought not to be studied as an aberration, an isolated event, or an accidental phenomenon of modern history. Actually, he sees the Holocaust as the culmination of four thousand years of anti-Semitism, in general, and of two thousand years of Christian hostility, in particular. Abrahamson emphasizes these points when he calls Wiesel "the chronicler of the 20th-century Jewish experience, which he links to forty centuries of Jewish history. Wiesel is obsessed with Jewish history. For him Jewish history is forever alive in the present."[8] Ironically Wiesel has been reproached by some who reject his assertion that he did not, after *Night*, depict the Holocaust in his ensuing works; others reproach him for writing about nothing except the Holocaust. Still others accuse him of capitalizing on his Holocaust experience by writing best sellers about it. They believe that he has converted a tragedy into an activity that generates material gain and ego-satisfaction.

The truth is that Wiesel has been psychologically incapable of overcoming the weighty burden of memory. If he cannot, by his own admission, do justice to the immensity of the horrors he has witnessed, neither can he erase them from his memory. Uncontrollable inner pressures keep exploding within his soul until he cannot contain the memories that he feels he must share with others. And so he expresses these explosive feelings inside of himself by writing books. Saint Cheron calls Wiesel "a master of Memory"[9] because so much of what he has written is little more than the expression of ineradicable recollections that refuse to disappear. Wiesel recaptures his memories of the "Event" not because he seeks fame and fortune, but really because he can do nothing else. He believes it to be his sacred mission to remember so that the victims will never be forgotten. And when Brigitte-Fanny Cohen asked the writer what he would like to transmit to his son, he replied "la mémoire . . . Toute ma mémoire." ["Memory . . . All of my memory."][10] In effect, his novels contain numerous examples of fathers who seek—often in vain—the power of transmitting to their offspring their memories of the Holocaust. But these novels also contain instances when children attempt frustratingly to penetrate the cocoons of memory that burden the shoulders of their parent/survivors who had been interned in the camps.

As we shall see in one of the ensuing chapters, Wiesel is one of those writers for whom literature does not exist as an end unto itself. In his eyes, literature is little more than an instrument by which a profoundly human message is transmitted to an audience of readers. In his transmission of a message or a lesson, Wiesel believes that he is doing his duty as a Jewish author who perpetuates Jewish traditions. Let us remind ourselves that a crucial part of the Jewish religion consists of the commandment to the faithful observer of Judaism that he or she must transmit the story of the Jewish past to the children growing up within that faith. Wiesel notes that "One single obsession marks the entire history of the Jewish people: transmission."[11] Convinced that this people would cease to exist were it not for their passion to communicate their collective memory to their children, Wiesel stresses that the most potent force linking Jews to each other around the world is their insistent need to remember Jewish history and to remind their offspring of all that took place during the millennia of that history. The Passover festival, built around religious worship at the Seder table, requires the reading of the Haggadah, the story of the exodus of the Jews from their enslavement in Egypt. Similarly Jews recount to their children (as Wiesel does in some of his books) the tribulations Jews were forced to suffer at the hands of their Gentile persecutors. And they also remind themselves of their occasional victories against their oppressors. Wiesel regards Jewish survival as one of the miracles of human history. In his novel *Twilight*, a mysterious voice tells the protagonist, Raphael, that "You will remain behind [after the Holocaust]. Always. You will observe and you will not forget . . . Promise me that you will survive. Thus you will wait for the return of those who are absent. And you will welcome them into your memory. In you they will have a refuge, if not a tomb."[12]

Within the kingdom of Jewish (and Wieselean) memory those who are absent are also present. Behind the backdrop of the present there lurk events, objects, and people from the past. When Wiesel sees a commonplace chimney, his memory reminds him of the crematoria of Birkenau.[13] When he hears the noise of a train rolling over tracks, he recalls the cattle-cars in which the Jews of Sighet were transported to Auschwitz. These recollections transmute themselves into the language of texts. And these texts really become Wiesel's odes to the past. He knows that his language may endure much longer than the granite and marble monuments of the cemeteries. Even after books had been burned—as was the case when Jewish books and torahs had been incinerated for centuries—the ideas in these burned pages and the oral language contained on paper and parchment outlasted the ashes of the bindings and the books.

Despite Hitler's highly developed technology of destruction, despite the German plans for the Final Solution, the Nazis failed in their attempt to eradicate Judaism as a major worldwide religion. Jewish language proved to be more powerful than the powerful *Wehrmacht!* In *Sages and Dreamers,* Wiesel vividly portrays the martyrdom of Rabbi Hanina Ben Tradyon, who, draped in the parchment of the Torah, was burned at the stake by his persecutors. As the rabbi's body melts in the flames, he shouts to his disciplines that he can see the Hebrew letters, words, and sentences of the venerable scroll soar above the flames and float towards the heavens above. Ideas and words outlast the ardent flames.

In their attempt to record the positive achievements of past civilizations, historians have the obligation to remind future generations of the unspeakable acts of evil committed by the peoples of the past: "There is evil in the world; you must not forget this."[14] Once the human race remembers not only the exalted accomplishments of its creative minds, but also the tragedies of the past, it will be able to devise strategies that help people to avoid repeating the mistakes already made: "Literature will through words save humanity from itself."[15]

Immediately after his liberation, Wiesel took a solemn oath never to forget what he had witnessed. In *Signes d'exode*, where he has expressed some of his most important ideas, he describes that oath with total candor:

> We told ourselves: if one day, miraculously, we'll come out of this, we shall devote our life to being a witness, to telling the agony of a people in the midst of general indifference, to telling about the solitude of the elderly, the glance of mothers, the smile of children walking towards death; if we survive, we used to tell ourselves, out of each day we shall make an offering, and out of each night a prayer so that, out of the ruins of creation, there might be born a new hope announcing a generous dawn for future generations.[16]

In another passage, he utters a similar thought: "We [the surviving witnesses] must serve as living, integral links between the dead and future generations so as to save the dead from death and the others from forgetfulness."[17]

Night, Wiesel's most commonly read book, reaches its crescendo when the adolescent narrator (Wiesel) expresses himself in the style of a litany. The same words, "Never shall I forget," are chanted over and over again until the jagged edges of these words are transformed into a blade-like force that penetrates with razor-sharp acuity into the reader's conscience. Here is Wiesel's celebrated incantation:

> Never shall I forget that night, the first night in camp, which turned my night into one long night, seven times cursed and seven times sealed. Never shall I forget that smoke. Never shall I forget the little faces of the children, whose bodies I saw turned into wreaths of smoke beneath a silent blue sky.
> Never shall I forget those flames which consumed my faith forever.
> Never shall I forget that nocturnal silence which deprived me, for all eternity, of the desire to live.
> Never shall I forget those moments which murdered my God and my soul and turned my dreams to dust.
> Never shall I forget these things, even if I am condemned to live as long as God Himself. Never.[18]

Wiesel did indeed emerge out of the cinders and the smoke and the world of barbed wire. He believed it to be his mission to become the chronicler, historian, witness, and human cemetery of all that he had seen. Through his accounts his pen would keep alive the memory of the past and would join the history of the human race. His printed pages have since become the tombstones that honor six million.

7

And Where Was God?

ONE OF THE MOST COMPLEX SUBJECTS AN AUTHOR CAN TREAT IS HIS or her conception of God. In Elie Wiesel's case, this subject seems especially bewildering, even painful, so much so that he confronts the issue of God with obvious ambivalence. Given his religious upbringing during childhood, his later adolescent experience in the Godless universe of the death-camps, and his more recent struggle to define his views of the nature of God, one readily appreciates the dilemma he faced in his life.

As a child he was taught to be a God-fearing, observant Jew who did not question the traditional beliefs of his Jewish heritage. Like most orthodox Jews he grew up believing in the day when the Messiah would lead his people to a perfect life in some kind of Shangri-La. Like most orthodox Jews the young Wiesel was confident that God would protect his people from all peril. However, during adolescence, as an inmate at Auschwitz/Birkenau, much of his religious fervor and his confidence in God's effectiveness were severely jolted. He had, after all, witnessed so many scenes in which the prayers of the most faithful Jews seemed utterly futile, provoking no response whatsoever from a seemingly silent, perhaps even indifferent God. The faith Wiesel had once felt prior to his incarceration had been undermined. It was almost as if God had vanished or had somehow been consumed by a swirling void, an absence of sorts.

Some critics have interpreted certain of Wiesel's statements, especially in *Night,* as evidence to support their theory that in Auschwitz God had somehow died for Wiesel. For many years thereafter Wiesel has been repeatedly denying this contention. What is undeniable is that Wiesel's religious faith had been shaken in the Holocaust, that it had undergone some kind of metamorphosis. More than a half century after his liberation, his faith continues to evolve discreetly as he moves more closely towards the faith that he had once possessed as a child.

7: AND WHERE WAS GOD?

Given the complexity of the subject and also the fact that the theme of God appears to have shifted, it is not surprising that Wiesel's religiosity has inspired during the years a variety of sometimes-contradictory interpretations on the part of the critics. In my own effort to comprehend the place of God in Wiesel's life and career, I was compelled, as a non-specialist in theology and religion, to seek counsel from some of the more recognized authorities in the field. However, I intend to combine some of my own intuitive reactions to Wiesel's ideas about faith as they are enunciated in his texts.

Among the many commentaries on Wieselean religion, I find it especially helpful to refer to *The Vision of the Void* by Michael Berenbaum as well as to the chapter "Richard L. Rubenstein and Elie Wiesel: An Exchange," in *Holocaust—Religious and Philosophic Implications,* edited by John K. Roth and Michael Berenbaum, both of whom rank among the most respected authorities on Wiesel today. Also I have found extremely illuminating my personal discussion on Wiesel with Richard Rubenstein at the latter's former residence in Tallahassee, Florida. (The bibliography at the end of this book includes most of the works I consulted on Wiesel's philosophy of God.)

God, or man's relationship with God, is one of several ubiquitous themes resounding throughout Wiesel's writing. To the question, "Does Wiesel believe in God?," one must respond with an unequivocal "yes." It is patently wrong to categorize this author as an atheist or an agnostic. Adhering to the traditional Jewish position that God has always existed and will always exist, Wiescl would be the first to concede that since Auschwitz his belief in God has been both uneasy and anguished. Berenbaum sees in this uneasiness a kind of "void." Here is Berenbaum's assessment of Wiesel's position vis-à-vis God:

> Wiesel's theological vision is of the void. Where previous Jewish theologians found some security in God and his revelation, in man and his creaturely status, and in Israel and its divine mission, Wiesel now finds an abyss of chaos, madness, and radical insecurity. Wiesel's fundamental experience is one of absence in a world that once was pregnant with Presence. Where Wiesel formerly experienced God, he has come to encounter the void.[1]

But here one could differentiate between "void" as a synonym for total disbelief, on the one hand, and "void" as a feeling of uneasiness, on the other hand. How could Wiesel truly view God without anguish during the days of Auschwitz and Buchenwald? God's apparent silence or indifference could not at all reassure the genuine believer that Wiesel had once been during his childhood.

After the calamitous Holocaust period, how could a devout Jew maintain the same degree of religious intensity as before the upheaval? Among the crematoria, gas chambers and firing squads, how could a prisoner's faith not have been eroded? Wiesel's religious doubts further increased after liberation when he first went to Paris, a city that at the time became the Mecca of Sartrean existentialism and its related atheistic undertones. After all, Sartre and his disciples preached that God had not created man, but rather that man had created God. With passionate feeling, the young Wiesel, in the throes of a slow recovery from the physical and psychological damage inflicted upon him by the Holocaust, found himself enflamed by the exciting texts of existentialism that were so widely circulated throughout the French capital. In these texts God had been virtually eliminated as a factor in human existence. The Jewish lad from Sighet found himself inebriated by the lessons promulgated by the great French existentialist philosophers of the day. Wiesel's profoundly traditional Jewish faith seemed to absorb some of the atheistic elements contained in existentialism, and, paradoxically, Judaism and existentialism seem to have coalesced in Wiesel's soul. Saint Cheron points out that the Jewish survivor's faith had already been "torn apart and traumatized after the Catastophe,"[2] so that it may have been ripe for the message that existentialism was then promoting.

With the passage of time, Wiesel has begun, with increasing frequency, to reiterate his belief that human beings must once again return to their faith in God. If he has not yet formulated a satisfactory rationale to explain God's silence during the Holocaust, he has not been able to deny the existence of God. His most convincing statement to date on the subject of his current state of faith has been spelled out in his recent memoirs (*Et la mer n'est pas remplie*). Here is an important portion of that statement:

> Is this to say that I have reconciliated myself with God? I continue to protest against His apparent indifference with regard to the injustices that ravage his creation. With the messiah, perhaps? He ought to have revealed himself earlier, much earlier. Maybe Kafka is right: the Savior will not come on the last day, but on the day after that. And my faith in all of this? Certainly, I could abandon it. I would have the right to do so. I could invoke many reasons, six million reasons to justify my decision. But I do not do so. I feel myself incapable of distancing myself from the road

traced by my predecessors. Without this faith in God, that of my ancestors and of my father, my faith in Israel and in humanity would be diminished, weakened. I choose to maintain this faith which, in the past, gave wings to my soul. I would not be the man that I am, the Jew that I am, if I betrayed the child in me, the one who thought he had to live in God, if not for God. In truth, faith in God, I have never abandoned it. I affirm it, and I reaffirm it, for I feel the necessity [to do so.] I had to clarify this point before, I return to it. Even in the heart of the Kingdom of Night, I continued to pray. Certainly my faith was wounded, overwhelmed, and it still is today. There was an explosion, but not a rupture.[3]

During Wiesel's post-Holocaust years he has struggled to find an accommodation between his damaged vision of God, on the one hand, and his ongoing fidelity to the traditional values of his childhood years, on the other hand. Richard Rubenstein aptly calls Wiesel's internal struggle "a tension between two opposing polarities."[4]

The reader, who studies closely a key text in *Night*, cannot help but detect the serious deterioration of the writer's faith in God as he watches helpless and innocent victims, especially the children, being pushed to their violent death by the Nazi executioners. In the same work, on at least one occasion the writer refused to join observant Jews near him in their chant of the Kaddish prayer for those about to die and for those already murdered. By Wiesel's refusal to chant this prayer (in which the devout proclaim the magnificence of God), he revealed his resentment against God's apparent disinterest in the human condition. Nonetheless, the baggage of religious fervor that the Jewish adolescent had been carrying on his shoulders since childhood did not allow him to go so far as to deny the existence of God. Instead of denial, he hurls Job-like accusations at his God, holding Him at least partly accountable for millions of atrocities. With sincerity Wiesel reasoned that although the crimes had been committed by God's creatures, God the creator of these creatures ought not to be absolved of some of the responsibility for what had taken place: "I did not deny God's existence, but I doubted His absolute justice."[5]

In the camps his disappointment in God had made him angry. For the first time in his life he dared to ask questions and to protest against God's indifference. And so he asked: Why did God allow this to happen? What did God's silence mean? Why did innocent babies suffer the same destruction as adults? After Auschwitz, the religion of Elie Wiesel altered itself from an earlier willingness to proclaim God's inherent goodness to a fearless readiness to hurl accusations at the Almighty and to demand explanations for God's unconscionable and inexcusable silence.

To pose questions is one thing. To believe that God had perished altogether is another thing. Instead of denial, Wiesel began to protest, to blame, to challenge a God who had too deeply disappointed him.

In his questioning of God, the narrator of *Night* assumed the role of an accuser or a prosecutor, one who placed himself on a collision course with the Almighty. But let us note that this collision course evolved entirely within the frontiers of Judaism. As a devout Jew, Wiesel believes that the worshipper should never reduce his role to that of a docile valet who believes blindly that his master can do no wrong. On the contrary, the devout Jew must hold God accountable for His behavior. As a former inmate of Auschwitz, he believed that he had every right to impeach his Lord. To do so was even his solemn duty. Why should God be allowed to be absolved of His poor behavior towards His people? To blame the Lord was even a Jewish duty. This is exactly the theme in Wiesel's play, *The Trial of Shamgorod*, when God is actually brought before the court of mankind and placed on trial. It is here that Wiesel makes his position on God very clear:

> I believe it possible to accuse God and remain not only Jewish but well within the Jewish tradition. I would go one step further and say that perhaps *this* is the Jewish tradition—that in such times men should get up and turn to God and ask the ancient question, "Lamah Hashem? Why of all things did you do that?[6]

Questions like this one arise unrelentingly throughout Wieselean literature. Here are other examples of the author's accusatory questions directed at the Almighty (most of these examples appear in Abrahamson's anthology of Wiesel's shorter pieces):

> This is probably the most important question [the question of God] related to the Holocaust, maybe because I was so religious. I came into the war with my tefillin in my bags and with payes [the phyllacteries worn by the religious Jew]. So to me it was rather a shock. The Jewish child that I was had to choose during one long moment between adoration and curse—worse, maybe they are one and the same.[7]

> When you try to remember the Holocaust, you must inevitably confront the question: where was God? What did he know? What did he do? In other words, can one still believe in God? And conversely, can God still have faith in man?[8]

If you were the God of the Jews, and not simply the God of the Jews but the God of pity, a father to his children, where were you?[9]

Wiesel's incessant preoccupation with the mystery of God's absence during the era of the concentration camps added a potent theological dimension to the otherwise literary and esthetic elements in his texts. Thus he not only narrates a riveting story; he not only portrays interesting characters; he not only paints haunting literary landscapes; but he also adds his personal theological and religious anxieties to the texture of his literature.

In his revelations about his religious anxieties, Wiesel deals with the complex relationships between men and God. As he analyzes these relationships he does not question whether God exists, whether God ever existed, or whether God will continue to exist in the future. It is a given in Wieselean thought that God has existed, does exist, and will exist. The question of God's existence is a nonissue. His primary interest is in determining the extent to which God takes an interest in the destiny of humankind. To what degree is God committed to the welfare of the human race? One fact is certain: Wiesel seems unable to separate God from his created beings. For him God exists *within* each woman and man He has created. God and His creatures are inseparable. Having accepted the basic condition that God had created man and woman, such as this creation has been described in the Genesis portion of the Hebrew Bible, Wiesel goes on to study the reasons for God's intervention or nonintervention in the condition of the human race. Wondering about the interconnectedness between man and God, Wiesel raises multiple questions about God's awareness of the human plight: "When we speak of God, it is much more about the God in us. *It is a certainty* [emphasis mine] that we are not alone in the world, that something is better than what we think we are. Theologically, of course, the problem is whether God is aware of the human being."[10]

In the eyes of Elie Wiesel, God is not so lofty, so awesome that He hovers *above* mankind; rather He exists at the same tier as his human creatures, and He lives together *with* them and *within* them. God stands "à côté de l'homme et non au-dessus de lui," ["alongside of man and not above him"], as Saint Cheron phrased it in his summation of Wiesel's religious views.[11] Thanks to this side-by-side relationship, it is possible, if not essential, for human beings to converse with, and even, when necessary, to protest against God. Communication between men and God lies at the core of Wiesel's religiosity. Wiesel the Hasid knew the importance of communication between man and God. In his confrontation with God, he does not write as a theologian whose interest it is to speak *about* deity, but rather as someone who brings himself into an ardent state of mystical connection *with* God. Thoroughly familiar with the prophets and patriarchs of the ancient Jewish scriptures, he understands how these great figures placed themselves in intimate communication with God. This theme of communication between men and God explains the author's fascination with the prophets, and it is fitting that one of his most recent books is called *Célébration prophétique*. Faithful Jews believe that they, not unlike the prophets, have every right to enter into conversations with the Almighty, that they have every right to protest against the injustices that God permits them to suffer: "For to quarrel with the *Ribono Shel Olam* [the Almighty] is entirely Jewish, just as it is truly Jewish to accept the divine g'zar din, the decree of pain and agony, and of punishment. Neither Jeremiah the prophet, nor Jonah, nor Job feared to come to grievance against the Almighty."[12] Wiesel believes that every Jew has the right to enter into intimate dialogues with God: "The Jew, in my view, may rise against God, provided he remains within God . . . One can be a very good Jew—and yet be against God . . . I have not made my peace with Him. My struggle with God goes on."[13]

Even during his bleakest days in the deathcamps, the author of *Night* believed that there was a God, one who ought not to be blamed for the crimes themselves, since it was human beings who actually performed the atrocities. If God was guilty of anything at all, it was for the crime of silence and indifference. And surely silence and indifference are serious enough to merit criticism, even outrage. In *Night*, Wiesel admits his sense of outrage against the Almighty when he wrote that "I was the accuser, God the accused."[14] In *Dawn*, the novelist depicted a madman committed to an institution for the mentally retarded who imagines that he is God. In this episode Wiesel hurls the harshest kind of accusations at God, wondering if God can ever be thought of as blameless; in effect, the novelist comes close to charging Him with at least conspiratorial responsibility (for the Holocaust). Wiesel even wonders whether God has gone temporarily mad during the era of Auschwitz. In his Nobel address in Oslo, Wiesel accuses God of having "veiled his face" precisely at the moment when people needed Him most.[15]

Understandably, some of Wiesel's critics have used his vehement accusations against God as evidence in support of their contention that for him God had died in Auschwitz and Buchenwald. Surely the author came perilously close to the precipice of the rejection of God. Yet somewhere deep in his soul an inexplicable force restrained him from plunging into the abyss of religious nihilism. Yes, it is true that where he hoped to find the warm and compassionate God of his youth he encountered, at the most critical moment of his life, what Berenbaum calls a "void." The latter writes:

> In a sense, the entire corpus of Wiesel's writings is an attempt to confront absence [of God], to describe the beauty that preceded it [his boyhood days of faith], the pain of separation, the yearning for return, and the failure of all efforts to return. The void that Wiesel experienced was precipitated by the gap between his religion and the realm of history.[16]

Despite his inability to find a God who seemed to have vanished, his deeply rooted Judaism remained so vibrant inside of himself that he never renounced his faith completely. To this day, Wiesel remains a faithful Jew—albeit a disappointed Jew—one who stubbornly clings to the hope that one day he will find the glowing warmth of the God he once had worshipped with such undivided fervor. During his childhood Wiesel had entered into what he called an unconscious pact with God and took a vow that he would always believe in Him. This pact he refers to as an "alliance." He sees this alliance between human creatures and their God as an agreement that allows the believer to criticize, to protest, and to take issue with God, but only so long as these disputes of conscience occur within the bounds of religious faith, as he once stated in an interview with Saint Cheron: "One must go against chance, but never against the Alliance. That is to say, that within the Alliance, I can protest against God, but not outside of the Alliance."[17] In the same statement, Wiesel confesses that once it had been difficult for him to address prayers to the Almighty, but nowadays he has no qualms about reciting his prayers. Within the circumscriptions of Judaism, one has every right to express anger, disappointment, and indignation against God. After all, isn't this consistent with the precedent set by the prophet Job? In yet another text, Wiesel elaborates on this point: "I think a Jew can be a Jew with God and a Jew can be Jewish against God, but he cannot be Jewish without God."[18]

    The key to understanding Elie Wiesel's philosophy of religion is to remember that he has always remained a faithful Jew, in the fullest sense of the term. To be such a Jew means that the believer never stops yearning for God, even when this yearning seems futile. The authentic Jew must also accept the premise that order and security in life are attainable only through faith because faith has the power to protect us in a world that is otherwise chaotic and confusing. This is why Elie Wiesel has during most of his life been a strict practitioner of the rules of his religion: "Certainly I believe in God. I lead a religious life that is as intense as possible; I respect the Sabbath. I go to synagogue, I say prayers."[19]

Being a devout Jew in his daily routine of life signified much more to Wiesel than the belief in monotheism. Being a devout Jew meant also to appreciate, study, and love the Talmud, a work that he considered to be possibly the finest work of literature ever devised by the human mind: "The Talmud is a great masterpiece. Perhaps the greatest. No other civilization has produced such a prodigy of literature and philosophy. Nothing can equal or come close to the biblical and talmudic texts."[19] Among the masterful texts of Jewish literature, Wiesel has an especially strong predilection for the Book of Job. To this day, he likens the experience of Job during his darkest hour with his own sense of hopelessness in the concentration camps.

Wiesel's belief in God has influenced his philosophy of literary and artistic creation. Maintaining that God is the only creator of all life, he affirms that true creation can solely emanate from the actions of the divine being. Humans are not capable of creating anything out of nothing, unless they are assisted in their work by their Lord: "We can re-create; we are too weak to create. But we can re-create: we can complete; we can achieve what He [God] began."[20] Conversely, because humans lack the power to create out of a void, they ought to desist from destroying what God has created. "In Jewish tradition, since God is the source of all life, to kill is to usurp God's proper place."[21] Consequently, Wiesel avers that humans may be justified in killing others only under a single circumstance: self-defense, and only if self-defense preserves one's own life. Even then, one should act in self-defense with the greatest degree of anguish and reluctance, and only as a last resort. This rationale explains Wiesel's arguments in justification of the lethal action undertaken from time to time by Israel's Defense Forces; Israeli soldiers may kill only when engaged in a last-ditch effort to prevent the destruction of the Israeli people.

Wiesel, the observant Jew, believes in the efficacy of prayer. Regularly he attends religious services of one of Manhattan's most established synagogues on the East Side. An active member of this congregation, he also frequently attends services in other synagogues when his lecturing tours require that he be out of town during the Sabbath and on other holidays. Maintaining that prayer is the primordial duty of the Jew; he wrote that "Most of us need prayer to challenge God. Also we need prayer to help us to mourn."[22]

In the eyes of Elie Wiesel, Judaism is comprised of many interconnected components, among which figure the following: belief in God; acceptance of the sacredness of the Talmud; daily prayers; and compliance with the Jewish code of ethics. Ethics he defines as those laws that govern relationships among humans and the rapport between individuals and society. Excluded from Wiesel's definition of ethics are the laws and customs that govern relationships between humans and God. The highest form of ethical behavior, Wiesel opines, occurs when people protest against injustices inflicted by human beings against other human beings.[23]

Now that more than fifty years have elapsed since his liberation from Buchenwald, Wiesel's disappointments with God have mellowed substantially. Nowadays he argues that God ought not to be blamed entirely for those misfortunes and pestilences in which the human race has been decimated. Categorically rejecting arguments in which priests and other religious officials contend that God alone ought to be held solely responsible for the Holocaust or for epidemics like AIDS, he criticizes those who claim that mankind is punished by these pestilences and cataclysms because of our prior sinful behavior. Wiesel criticizes such specious statements by noting that the Nazi killers had destroyed at least one million infants and young children, people who had clearly been too young to have sinned. Also some of the victims of AIDS are newborn babies who were incapable of culpability of any sort: "It is scandalous. To say that AIDS is the consequence of sin is absolutely inadmissible, unacceptable. To play on the misery of men and to exploit their suffering for political ends or, what is worse, for religious purposes is a shame. I am outraged, hurt, that certain people dare to utter such words."[24]

When all is said and done, Wiesel is proud of his Jewish heritage, proud because Jews have gladly been willing to share with all of humanity their monotheistic concepts. He opines that if Jews had limited their belief in one God to their own population, God would have become little more than the Lord of a "tribe." Thanks to their generosity in sharing monotheism with the Gentile world, Jews have transformed their God into the "Master of the Universe." Furthermore, by universalizing their God they have enriched the culture and civilization of all people: "Our contributions to other cultures are numerous. There is no . . . literature where we have not given our song."[25]

The single issue that outrages Wiesel more than any other is the charge that he was the source of the "God is Dead" Movement that erupted after Auschwitz. Yes, there were moments in the camps when he refused to join his fellow prisoners in the camps in their recitation of prayers. But he insists passionately that he had never stated that God was dead. "The theologians of the 'God is dead' theory took me as their prophet and I resented it. On the contrary, I never said God is dead."[26] Conceding that he had posed questions like "Why does God not answer?", Wiesel declares that the real problem is "not that God is dead; the problem is that in some men the *idea* of God died or that the idea of man died in some men [the Nazis]."[27]

Yes, it is true that during his search for God within the abyss of the Night, Wiesel found only a "void," as Berenbaum phrased it. But in an exchange with Richard Rubenstein, the author elaborates on this question:

> Therefore, I never speak of God now. I rather speak of men who believed in God or men who denied God. How strange that the philosophy denying God came not from the survivors. Those who came out with the so-called God is dead theology, not one of them had been in Auschwitz. Those who had never said it. I have my problems with God. Believe me. I have my anger and I have my quarrels and I have my nightmares. But my dispute, my bewilderment, my astonishment is with men.[28]

If Wiesel did indeed not find the God he was searching for, he certainly did suffer not only from the physical abuse heaped upon his young body by his German captors, but also from the bitter anguish caused by the realization that he could not rely upon God to bring relief to him at his most desperate moment of need. Rubenstein accurately recaptures the anguish of the young prisoner by calling him a "skeptic who has problems giving up the idea of God."[29] By posing questions Wiesel did indeed assume the attitude of a skeptic, but he refused to cross the invisible divide that separated skepticism from the total denial of God. Once again Rubenstein correctly describes Wiesel's major anxiety as one of "tension between belief and unbelief."[30]

Anyone who reads Wiesel's texts cannot help sensing the dramatic tug of war that exists there between the forces of traditional belief and those of disappointment in God's absence. But even during his worst crises, Wiesel avoided the pitfall of "unbelief." Tenaciously clinging to the teachings he had inherited from his ancestors, he was unwilling to break with these millennial beliefs.

And so this is the reason why many, especially the Jews of America, view him as the one person who represents the conscience of Judaism in a world when Jewish conscience is besieged by a myriad of un-Jewish influences. Wiesel's voice carries resonance to many, if not to most of his co-religionists, particularly to those who find themselves embattled in a war against assimilation within the tidal wave of a dominant Christian society. Succinctly Saint Cheron sums up the otherwise complex, nuanced, occasionally ambivalent, and often seemingly shifting pronouncements found in some of Weisel's texts about God. Citing the central theological questions raised by the troubled writer—Where was God during the Shoah?—Saint Cheron replies: "To answer this question is impossible, but not to raise this question is equally impossible."[31] There are indeed no easy answers to Wiesel's questions; perhaps there are no answers whatsoever.

8
Hear Oh Israel: The Jewish People Are One

THE SIX HEBREW WORDS IN THE PRAYER KNOWN AS THE SHEMA represent the first words of prayer Jews are supposed to teach their children at the start of their lives and are also the final words pronounced at life's conclusion. The Shema is also the most resounding prayer in the entire Jewish liturgical prayer: "Shema Israel, Adonoy Eloheinu, Adonoy echod." ["Hear Oh Israel, the Lord is our God, The Lord is one."] Elie Wiesel not only sees the Lord as one; he also sees the entire Jewish people, scattered around the planet, as one. One of his most persistent themes is the oneness, the solidarity of the Jewish people. And so he celebrates their traditions, history, values, culture, contributions to world civilization, and their religious doctrines. Above all he insists upon the unity of this people, despite the fact that they are dispersed in many lands, speak many languages, and belong to a rich diversity of national cultures. No one better than this ex-inmate of Auschwitz understood better the enormous price Jews have had to pay during thousands of years of suffering and tragedy for their right to uphold their heritage. Wiesel provides Jews in Israel and the Diaspora with a calm voice of reassurance. With remarkable generosity, he always lends his support to Jewish causes whether they are connected with the security of the Israeli State or with the countless Jewish philanthropies around the world.

In his emphasis of Jewish diversity within the unity of Jewish culture, Wiesel resorts to terms like "a symphony, a pluralistic movement."[1] What does it mean to be a Jew within the multi-chromatic tapestry of Jewish culture and tradition? In one's definition of "Jewishness," should one adopt an ethnic approach? Is there even a satisfactory definition for what it means to be a Jew? Do Jews constitute a race, a religious denomination, a tribe, a cultural entity, a historical tradition, a national-state (as in the case of the State of Israel), a collection of minority communities residing inside of larger nations scattered around the globe? The answer to these questions is probably "all of the above" or parts of each element or of some of these elements. Throughout their history friends and foes have sought to define this complex people, sometimes emphasizing certain characteristics, sometimes others. Often these traits have been abused for politico-socio-economic-theological purposes.

As one of the most universally respected Jewish personalities of our day, Elie Wiesel's views of the Jewish people are a fascinating subject for us to explore here. To the various definitions of Jews he adds his own: "What is it to be Jewish? To be Jewish is to be a part of a collective memory, to be a part of the Jewish people."[2] Elsewhere he calls Judaism "a tradition . . . To understand, you must accept the idea of collective memory—that whatever happened to your father, to your grandfather, to your ancestors is part of you. So whatever happened to them—something of it remains inside you."[3] Thus Wiesel sees the Jews of today as a connecting link in the chain that fuses Jews of the earliest past with those of today, and even with Jews yet unborn.

The writer classifies in a single mold two other sectors of the Jewish population: those who were personally violated during the Holocaust and those who were spared the nightmare of the death camps: "Yet, I submit that a Jew today cannot—he cannot—be a Jew if he does not take upon himself the experience of the Holocaust, or at least the tale of that experience."[4] In this assumption the writer is probably right since it is difficult to find Jews living in far-flung places like Argentina, Canada, the United States, Australia, South Africa—places thousands of miles from Treblinka and Bergen-Belsen—who did not lose some of their relatives or acquaintances in the crematoria or in the gas chambers. To be a Jew means to have suffered, directly or indirectly, in the catastrophe. This fact explains why Wiesel can justifiably speak of Jewish solidarity.

Jewish solidarity is based not only on historical continuity but also on a kind of geographical dimension that extends from continent to continent. "Every Jew is a geography," the author of *Night* once stated in a private conversation with one of his friends. He meant that no matter where Jews dwell, no matter what their citizenship may be, all Jews share a common destiny. Despite their dispersion in dozens of lands, they identify themselves in a unique way with the State of Israel. Even those few who reject Zionism react to the existence of the Israeli state in a peculiarly Jewish manner that differentiates them from the non-Jewish world.

Like most Jewish leaders of the past three decades, Wiesel has insisted that Jews were morally obligated to concern themselves mightily with the plight of the millions of Russian Jews in the former Soviet Union. To a large degree, Wiesel must be credited with the worldwide movement that eventually culminated in the former Soviet government's relaxation of restrictions on Jewish emigration to Israel and elsewhere. His work, *The Jews of Silence,* served as an eloquent manifesto in its arousal of international resistance to the repressive measures of the Soviet regime against its Jewish population. In both volumes of his recently published memoirs (especially in the second), Wiesel describes the critical role he played in pressing the Russian government to relent in its anti-Jewish policies.

Wiesel's geographical perspective extends far beyond Jewish life in Russia and Israel. Fervently he believes that Jews everywhere must embrace the fate of all Jews in *every* nation of the world, especially in those nations where their security is in jeopardy: Ethiopia, the Sudan, Lebanon, Syria, Iraq, and so forth. Jews constitute a single people with a single destiny, no matter where they reside. Here is what he pronounced in one of his countless interviews:

> To be a Jew means to assume and to claim the destiny of the Jewish people, with its joys and its fears, with its anxieties and its hopes . . . As for me, I am as indebted to David as I am to Solomon. I am as indebted to the Baal Shem Tov as I am to his adversary, to Jeremiah as to Isaiah. I accept Jewish destiny in its totality. This is what it means to be a Jew.[6]

Solidarity also implies absolute equality among all Jews throughout the world. A sense of parity must govern the lives of all Jews; among them everyone is equal, no matter what the social, economic, professional, or national categorization. The poorest disenfranchised Jews of Ethiopia are equal to the most affluent and prestigious Jews of Paris, New York, or Tel Aviv. All Jews share responsibility for each other; all must fulfill similar duties towards each other; all are entitled to the same degree of respect. This is what Wiesel believes.

Wiesel emphasizes the difficulty of being a Jew in a world in which, historically, Jews have been singled out for incessant persecution, discrimination, hatred, and even destruction. In their confrontation with history, Jews have borne an inordinately heavy burden of suffering simply on account of their status as Jews. This message Wiesel has enunciated again and again throughout his writings and speeches. As Jews review their long history they can boast not only of tragedies but also of numerous triumphs. When one Jew grieves, all Jews grieve; conversely, when one Jew rejoices, all rejoice. This is what

Wiesel means in his use of the term "solidarity." Here is how he expresses this thought:

> Each Jew represents all Jews and is Jewish history... because each of us is responsible for the past and future of Israel, because each of us carries within himself the vision of Sinai and the flames of Khourban... One cannot be a Jew today if one does not take upon oneself the totality of Jewish existence.[7]

With meticulous detail and loving care Wiesel enumerates the many aspects of Jewish experience. The first component of Jewishness comes from the exalted place in Jewish lives of education. The writer has persuaded himself that without the benefits of education Jewish tradition would erode and eventually disappear. He once wrote that "A community without schools cannot survive. Wherever there were schools, the community remained. Israel would not be Israel, Jews would not be Jews, and we would not be what we are if we were to give up our commitment to learning. Our schools are essential to the survival of the Jewish community."[8] Schools mold the essential Jewish traditions and values into a single, indivisible, and durable culture, since it is there that the Hebrew language and the sacred texts of the faith are taught.

Jewish education has always been constructed upon the cornerstone of texts. Because texts are comprised of words, language assumes an awesome importance in the life of the Jew. In other religions, buildings, artistic artifacts, statuary, and music play a preponderant role in helping the religious tradition to continue. But in Judaism, religious life is perpetuated through words, texts, prayers. In lieu of edifices, shrines, mosques, what matters most are spiritual values and the texts in which these values are expounded. Wiesel wrote that "Man can understand only through words. Jews have never believed in buildings. Judaism is words... The only way for us to communicate what has happened in the past is through words, whether they speak of past glory or of past disaster. Only words."[9] In his own personal life, Wiesel claims never to have seen his grandfather or father without books in their hands. Nor does he recall rooms in his family home devoid of shelves laden with books: "They [his family] were not the only ones to live with this passion for books. Most of the Jews of my town, and of the other towns, had the same passion."[10] Today the visitor in Wiesel's home is immediately impressed by the fact that each room there serves as a repository for books. The writer confesses that whenever he travels, his baggage consists mainly of books and the materials he requires for the composition of his own books. His definition of hell is a place without books. For him existence without books is intolerable. He needs them to fuel his intellectual faculties.[11]

The transmission of history cannot easily take place without books. History is really the memory of the human race, and without memory life loses much of its validity. Were it not for encounters with texts, life for the Jew would have been dramatically different. In these texts, one confronts those courageous personalities of the Jewish Bible, especially the patriarchs and matriarchs of Biblical times. Take, for example, the case of Abraham: "Abraham: the first of a lineage, a founder of nations. The first to cry out against darkness and its idols, the first to proclaim that God is God, therefore that the task of man is to be human. After him, history will . . . follow a different course; nothing will be the same as before."[12] Wiesel sincerely believes that unless people anchor themselves deeply within the roots of their own culture, unless they maintain their collective memory, they will be doomed to disappear.

Without language the dynamics of memory and history simply do not function. Jewish liturgy—the basis for Jewish continuity—can, like all other liturgies, only be transmitted through verbal expression. Liturgy and prayer serve a dual purpose: first, as a force for religiosity and, second, as a force for historical continuity. Wiesel affirms that Jews can be defined, even classified, according to the degree of their acceptance of and respect for the textual content of their Bible, their Torah, their Talmud. He believes also that the very language in which these sacred texts have been recaptured, Hebrew, is much more than a tool of worship; it is also the record of the rich history of an entire people. Wiesel hopes that the typical Jew will always consider his or her own personal and family heritage as the logical outgrowth of the history of all Jews. Out of this idea he constructs the fundamental elements of his notion of Jewish solidarity. This is what he means when he declares that "To be a Jew is to take upon oneself the fate and the history of the whole Jewish people."[13] In *Signes d'exode*, he added that "To be a good Jew, what does this mean? It means to assume Jewish destiny in its fullness."[14]

Since texts of Judaism have been accumulating from century to century, one may safely assume that to this chain of texts readers will someday add the texts of Elie Wiesel. When future historians attempt to comprehend the saga of Jewish existence in the second half of the twentieth century, they will, in all likelihood, turn for their source material to the writings of the author of *Night*. In his own way, Wiesel will have added his own layers of history to the countless pages of prose and poetry, sacred and profane, that reflect the millennia of Jewish life on earth. Ted Estess aptly points out that Wiesel's oeuvre, both fictional and non-fictional, represents yet one more chapter in the relentless flow of Jewish history: "[The Wieselean novel] like all Wiesel's narratives, reaches beyond itself into the long history of Jewish experience."[15]

A central feature in the life of the Jew consists of waiting for the arrival of the Messiah. In contrast with the Christian world, for which the Messiah had already come some two thousand years earlier, Jews, for their part, wait, anticipate and hope for a still unfulfilled promise to occur. As Wiesel put it, "for us what matters is to await the Messiah."[16]

In some of his novels Wiesel depicts a stranger, someone who drops into a town to insinuate himself discreetly into the lives of the protagonists. Through the tales recounted by this stranger, he gains the power to enrich the lives of the other characters in the novels who listen with fascination to the tales recounted by this wayfarer. Traveling from hamlet to hamlet, from shtetl to shtetl, this wandering Jew or troubadour ignites the lives of all those who hear his magical tales. All of his listeners come away from these stories with fiery hopes and expectations. During his childhood days in Sighet, Wiesel encountered various vagabond-like figures who narrated to their receptive audiences tales of Jewish adventure. So stimulating were these tales that the young Wiesel and the other children of Sighet awaited each of these visits with much expectance. Of these unusual storytellers Wiesel wrote that "For a Jew, the stranger [his term for storyteller] suggests thus a world that it is a question of inhabiting, embellishing, saving."[17] More than an entertainer, the stranger is also someone who transmits a significant message to those who hear his tales: "The stranger . . . is a king, a messenger."[18]

The Wieselean wanderer/stranger/storyteller may be viewed as an outgrowth of the Messianic tradition in the Jewish Bible. One day such a figure will descend upon the earth to "embellish" and "save" all those who inhabit it. And as Jews wait and pray for his coming, they hope that the Messianic stranger will bring with him a much-needed amelioration of the human condition.

It is not enough for human beings to wait passively for the coming of their Messiah. Wiesel stresses that the wait must become a committed, active, and even aggressive preoccupation. One waits aggressively by becoming an *authentic* Jew. What does Wiesel mean by Jewish authenticity? True Jews are those who refuse to conceal their uniqueness within the ambient non-Jewish culture in the midst of which they live. True Jews do not assimilate with the majority culture. Nor do they retreat into a closet of anonymity. Except for the State of Israel, where Jews enjoy majority status, they almost always constitute a tiny minority within an overwhelmingly dominant non-Jewish majority. Thus it is often hard to resist the temptation to emulate the lifestyle of the prevailing culture. In many places, Jews found life much less arduous when they assimilated into the surrounding Christian landscape. Some even forsook their inherited faith and converted to one of the majority Christian sects. Adamantly Wiesel objects to assimilation since, in his view, it results in an inevitable debilitation of genuine Jewish values. While acknowledging that minimal adaptation is frequently unavoidable, he recommends that such adaptation occur only within the framework of a faithful adherence to the Jewish faith. One can adapt, but, at the same time, one should remain faithful to the traditions of forefathers: "it is important to adapt, but for the Jew the only way one can fulfill oneself is inside of one's Jewishness."[19] If Jews are not to disappear altogether as a unique people, they must not ape non-Jews. They must adhere to their own values and customs. True, whenever a tiny minority is drowned in the prevailing tide of the majority, a certain degree of assimilation may be unavoidable. But this assimilation ought to be held in check by rigorously aggressive self-discipline.

One way for Jews to remain faithful to their own traditions is for them to celebrate the memory of their late forefathers by engaging in prayers in which their sacrifices on behalf of Jewish continuity are recalled. Through religious ritual (e.g., the Kaddish prayer, the Yizkor service), Jewish history is made to live uninterruptedly. Jews ought also to pray for the coming of the Messiah, and they must never lose patience: "It is given to us to remain faithful to that which we are, that is to say, to live our experience by sharing it, by assuming the truth that is ours by communicating it to our neighbor who proclaims his own truth with as much fervor and faith: one day we shall all welcome into our midst a being who has not yet come, but who will come for we are waiting for him."[20]

Regretting that a significant number of Jews have selected the path of least resistance, assimilation, Wiesel refuses to sit in judgement over them by condemning their lack of fidelity to Judaism. Of a Jew who has converted or assimilated, this is what he once wrote: "perhaps he experienced hardships and tortures in his country of origin: now he seeks a refuge, a bit of peace. How can I judge him? Do I have a right to condemn him? I tried to understand him without approving him. Only I thought that it was a pity."[21]

Jews who by choice remain anchored to their roots are obligated to accept a number of prerequisites, the most important of which requires that they recite prayers exalting and pledging allegiance to their God. Symbolically, Wiesel opened his Oslo address at the Nobel ceremonies with an expression of thanks to the Lord. He began by declaring "Words of appreciation. The first one goes to the Creator of the universe. The tradition which I call my own orders me to do this." Thereupon, he recited the traditional Hebrew prayer thanking his Lord for having carried him to this moment of international recognition by the Nobel Committee.[22]

Another prerequisite requires Jews to pronounce frequent prayers in remembrance of the dead. Since the Holocaust these prayers also mark the memory of the six million and of all other past martyrs.

A third prerequisite, Wiesel opined, is to be willing to share with their non-Jewish neighbors certain quintessentially Jewish virtues, such as respect for justice and the sanctification of human life. In sharing the lessons of Judaism, he asks his fellow Jews never to seek to convert others to Judaism since one must always respect the integrity of other religions. Intrinsically Judaism possesses no superior virtues over other religious movements in the world. While promulgating their own values, Jews must understand that other religious groups also possess similarly lofty virtues: "We are taught [in the Talmud] to discourage candidates to conversion, for the mission of the Jew is not to judaicize the world but to humanize it . . . it is not permissible to utilize one's Jewishness to attack, to diminish, to ridicule, to lower another human being, another tradition, another faith."[23]

Wiesel believes that the one characteristic distinguishing Jews from other religious groups is the solidarity stemming from a commonality of history, traditions, ritual, and ethical values. He stresses that all Jews, both those scattered in the diaspora and those within the borders of Israel, are a single undivided people whose common destiny is forever united. What happens throughout the world to the Jews in one nation concerns Jews in the other nations. Similarly, what occurs in the State of Israel may affect Jews elsewhere. On this point, he once wrote that "What Israel has is the Jewish people. Once again we are one people. Once again we must demonstrate this solidarity, that whatever happens in Jerusalem affects us here [in the United

States], and what we do here must affect Jerusalem and the Golan and Suez."[24]

Despite his enthusiastic affection for his co-religionists, Wiesel admits that as a total people, Jews are far from being infallible or free of faults. Nonetheless, he has deliberately decided to avoid, at least in public forums and the media, criticizing the policies and actions of the Israeli state or of Jewish Diaspora leadership. To express overt criticism, he believes, would be tantamount to exposing a family's most private secrets in public. Moreover, for Wiesel, as a resident of the Jewish Diaspora, to involve himself in expressing his differences with the Israeli government would be an inappropriate act. Only Israeli citizens can resolve Israeli problems. Thus, whenever he feels especially strongly that Israeli authorities have committed a gaffe, he restricts his critical comments to discreet intramural discussions with the Israeli leadership or with those entrusted with Jewish policies outside of that nation. Here is how he explains this position: "My loyalty to my people, to our people, and to Israel comes first and prevents me from saying anything critical of Israel outside of Israel . . . a Jew in New York is as important as a Jew in Israel because we have only one destiny, one history, one past."[25] Even when Jews err he is convinced that ultimately they will rectify their mistakes: "I have confidence in Israel, for I have confidence in the Jewish people."[26] To sum up, no one in today's world more consistently than Elie Wiesel has exhibited a greater degree of Judeophilism. What he does, what he writes, what he says, much of this seems to be based on his love for Judaism and for the people of that faith.

His decision to reside outside of Israel has occasionally placed him in a defensive posture whenever some of his critics have blamed him for living in New York City rather than in Israel, where certain purists believe all good Jews ought to reside. And it is true that the author, feeling himself a bit vulnerable in this case, often becomes defensive about his not having made *aliyah* (immigrating to Israel). But Wiesel insists that one can be a perfectly authentic Jew either as a citizen of the Jewish state or of any other nation. What is essential for him is that all Jews, wherever they happen to reside, ought to accept the oneness of all of the Jewish people, both in time and space. But this sense of oneness mandates the maintenance of the closest ties between the people of Israel and of all of the other countries of the Diaspora.

Occasionally Wiesel betrays uneasiness about his decision not to make *aliyah:* "Yet I do not feel good about living outside of Israel . . ."[27] Compensating for this shortcoming he travels to Israel several times every year. Whenever crises develop, as when Israeli territory became a target for Iraqi SCUD missiles, he flew instantly to Jerusalem and Tel Aviv to make public appearances as a concrete demonstration of his solidarity with the nervous civilian population.

Wiesel first visited Israel in 1949, only one year after the establishment of the Zionist state. Remembering the emotional moment of his first arrival on the shores of his beloved state he wrote as follows: "In 1949, I came to Israel by ship. Of course I was more than excited, I was tense. I hadn't slept all night long in order to be there on the deck of the ship at dawn and to see Israel surging up before me. I remained speechless. It was a boatload of emigrees, and at the time I was a journalist."[28]

What is most worrisome to the author of *Night* is his feeling that when the security of the Jewish people is threatened, the non-Jewish world generally reacts with silence, indifference or with pious but hollow words of regret. Such was certainly the case during the Holocaust, and history repeated itself, prior to the Six-Day War of 1967 when the Egyptians blockaded Israel's southern gateway of the Port of Eilat, threatening to strangle the nation's entire economy. Few non-Jews intervened. Few sought to prevent the systematic destruction of the remnants of Europe's Jews who had survived the Holocaust and had immigrated to Israel. Few sought to force the Egyptians to loosen their stranglehold. France even transformed its foreign policy from one of close cooperation to one of near-hostility. The other nations pretended that the Jewish plight was not their concern. With such a blemished track record, Wiesel had ample justification to believe that at moments of dire crises, the international community could not be depended upon to help secure the Jewish people in their battle to survive. Votes in the United Nations had clearly supported the Arab side, and the General Assembly had even voted to declare that Zionism was a form of racism. Of this controversial resolution, Wiesel wrote: "In terms of propaganda I could not care less what they are saying. One has to be stupid to believe we are racist. No tradition in the history of culture is as generous as the Jewish tradition."[29] Another example of international indifference towards Jews was the silence of the Vatican during the Shoah; with irony and sarcasm Wiesel noted that "the Vatican maintained silence. The world kept quiet. Let the Jews be massacred; they would be mourned later . . . and the so-called Christian nations, civilized and progressive, faithful to their tradition, would watch—

and do nothing."[30] When Israel was attacked during the Yom Kippur War, the exasperated Wiesel observed the indifference of most nations: "Once again, except for the United States, Holland, Norway, and Denmark, the entire world looked cynically, silently on Arab aggression. Again we felt abandoned. And today, too, except for a few voices . . . we are alone. Europe has betrayed us. Africa has betrayed us. We get one betrayal after another."[31]

Given this dismal history of international callousness, Wiesel reminds his Jewish brethren than in the final analysis the only people upon whom they can rely to defend them are the Jewish people themselves. Sadly he is convinced that if in the future the State of Israel were to confront the peril of annihilation, only the Jewish people of the world would provide support to that embattled nation. At the same time, whenever Jews are threatened outside of Israel, he is certain that Israel would come to their defense, as it did in saving the remnants of Ethiopian and Soviet Jewry and in deploying a rescue mission to save the Jewish passengers of a highjacked French airliner in Entebbe, Uganda. In one of his most memorable addresses, directed at the President of the United States, Wiesel declared that "Israel must never feel abandoned. Israel must never feel alone. Israel must never feel expendable, Mr. President. We plead with you because it is the dream of our dreams . . . It is because we remember the solitude of Jews in those times [the Holocaust] that we feel linked to and so proud of the State of Israel today."[32]

Since the beginning of his career, the fate of the Jewish state has been a recurrent theme in Wiesel's writing. For him one of the criteria that defines the authentic Jew is the degree of involvement demonstrated by the latter in the destiny of the State of Israel. Nowhere does Wiesel enunciate his commitment to Zionism more eloquently that in *Paroles d'étranger*, where he made the following confession: "Israel occupies a central place in my life as a man, as a Jew, as a writer. When I was a child, it was a prayer. For me as an adolescent, it was a dream. Now that I am an adult, Israel is a challenge, an obsession."[33]

That he champions the Israeli cause does not, however, prevent him from defending non-Jewish causes affecting the other people of the world. An ardent humanitarian, Wiesel believes it is his mission to work towards the alleviation of all human pain and suffering, among Jews and non-Jews alike. Despite his intense loyalty towards Israel, he has spoken for the diminution of suffering of the Palestinian people, a fact that has created a trying dilemma for him. How can one support the cause of Israel and also simultaneously uphold the cause of legitimate Palestinian rights? Outraged that defenders of the Palestinian cause have compared the exiled Palestinians in the refugee camps of the Gaza strip and on the Lebanese coast with the plight of the Jews in the Nazi concentration camps, he argues that this analogy is patently false. Underlining the fundamental difference between the Jews of the Holocaust and the Palestinians, Wiesel insists that no one has ever threatened or planned the extermination of the latter people, whereas Hitler's Germany, driven by its policy of the Final Solution, had devoted substantial national resources to the perfection of technology to slaughter human beings on a massive basis. Wiesel further stresses that the Israelis did indeed invest significant resources to upgrade the miserable living conditions of the Palestinians and repeatedly indicated their desire to find a solution for the Palestinian question through direct negotiations with the Arab states as part of an overall Middle-East peace agreement.[34]

For the city of Jerusalem, Wiesel maintains an undivided cult. Nevertheless, surprisingly, the ancient city plays an important part in only one of his volumes, *A Beggar in Jerusalem*. With heady joy, the novelist celebrates the almost miraculous victory of the Israeli army as it vanquished the Jordanian defenders and recaptured Israel's holiest site, the Kotel Wall. But it is in *Signes d'exode* that the author reveals his most exuberant passion for Jerusalem: "No city has such a total hold on the visitor. You plunge into it as a poem, you depart from it with reluctance. . . . I love Jerusalem, I have always loved it. I know and I do not know why it has acquired my love. . . . no city in the world inspires in me so many profound and above all lasting feelings. That sounds simplistic, childish? Too bad. In Jerusalem I became a child again."[35] Wiesel's lifelong love affair with Jerusalem and Israel has served him well. During episodes of despondency, he almost always finds consolation in dreaming of Jerusalem and in rejoicing over the impressive achievements of the Jewish State.[36]

From the Holocaust and from Israel's struggle to live and to remain autonomous, Wiesel has learned a painful lesson: to wit, Jews must never allow themselves to become smug; never should they take their survival for granted. In his Nobel address in Oslo, he revealed his underlying uneasiness about the fate the Jewish people faced in the coming years: "Israel itself which, after two thousand years of exile and thirty-eight years of sovereignty traversed by five wars, still is not entitled to peace: for how much time will this people, which is mine, have to live while confronting the hatred of its nearby and distant neighbors?"[37]

Given the perils surrounding the Jewish nation since its inception, Wiesel's trepidations concerning the future of this country are of course understandable. That anti-Semitism still exists after more than fifty years following the defeat of Nazi Germany continues to disturb him profoundly. The discriminatory practices of the former Communist regime in Russia, supported by an ingrained history of pogroms by the local populace in eastern Europe, all of this further fueled Wiesel's natural tendency to worry about the future of the Jewish people. Too well did he remember, from his childhood days in Sighet, the tales of pogroms that took place regularly throughout eastern Europe. Thus, once Wiesel achieved international status as a writer, he decided to take his first trip to the Soviet Union to learn from direct observation the truth about the plight of Russian Jewry. What he saw there was worse than he had expected. He witnessed the slow strangulation of Jewish life under the weight of Communist restrictions. Judaism appeared to be on the verge of disappearance. Here is his assessment of the Jewish question in Russia: "I found the situation to be worse and, at the same time, better than I could have imagined. . . . There is such a fear—among those Jews—that you are silent. You cannot break through it. I tried to speak to people, and they did not answer."[38] At the same time, Wiesel sensed that many Russian Jews, despite the social pressures and legal constraints, were thirsting to remain Jewish, to practice the religion of their ancestors, and to adhere to the traditions of their parents. Despite all of the discriminatory policies of the Soviet regime, Judaism had not been entirely stifled. Once he realized that many Jews were still struggling to maintain their identity and values, he decided to launch a worldwide campaign to work for the liberation of the long silent, suffering Russian Jews. Together with other prominent Jewish leaders, Wiesel worked to persuade world-wide governmental leaders and organizations to bring pressure to bear upon the Soviet authorities until they would permit the emigration of Jews who wished to move to more hospitable countries where they could practice their Judaism and be protected from anti-Semitic outbreaks.

The most tangible result of Wiesel's eye-opening trip to the former Soviet Union was the publication of *The Jews of Silence*. The original edition appearing in Hebrew in 1965 was immediately translated into French and English. On both sides of the Atlantic the work attracted worldwide attention and provoked a great deal of debate. In effect, *The Jews of Silence* may well be regarded as a declaration of war against the anti-Jewish policies of the Soviet Union. A "firsthand report on Jews in Russia" (the subtitle of the work), it focused international attention on the fate of millions of Jews, a fate that, according to Wiesel, could easily deteriorate into the second Holocaust of this century. The title suggests a double meaning: on the one hand, the Russian Jews suffered in silence, fearing repressive treatment if they protested; on the other hand, the title also suggests the silence of the Jews outside of Russia who were reluctant to involve themselves in the internal life of a foreign power.

To date, Wiesel has devoted three entire books to the question of Soviet Jewry. That Wiesel's campaign was not waged in vain has been corroborated by the facts of subsequent history. Soon Jewish communities everywhere, inspired by Wiesel's battlecry, launched aggressive campaigns to save the Jews of the Soviet Union. National governments, especially that of the United States, supported Wiesel in his campaign to permit Russian Jews to emigrate to Israel or elsewhere where they could worship without fear of persecution. For Wiesel the "greatest Jewish problem of the contemporary world" included the security of the Israeli state, the future of Soviet Jewry, and the question of living Jewishly in certain anti-Semitic states.[39]

Wiesel was especially embittered when he visited the site of the infamous Babi Yar massacre, near Kiev in the Ukraine, where tens of thousands of Jews had been savagely killed in a ravine while thousands of Ukrainian onlookers witnessed the tragedy with a mixture of jubilation and indifference. Angrily he denounced the Babi Yar monument for not announcing that *all* of the victims were murdered for being Jewish, and not for being Soviet citizens. The survivor of Birkenau wrote that "Hitler and Eichmann had as their principal goal the annihilation of the Jewish people down to the last child. By being so general, the Soviets aim to universalize the Jewish tragedy, which was nonetheless special and specific—and why not say it— unique in the annals of humanity. In Russia—whenever the men and women in charge of culture and history—and politics—invoke the Jewish dead, it is to offend their memory."[40]

With the coming to power of Chairman Gorbachev, Wiesel was hopeful that a more liberal Soviet leader might at last attenuate the anti-Jewish policies of his predecessors. In the beginning, in spite of glassnost and perestroika, Gorbachev maintained the usual discriminatory restrictions against the Jews. Wiesel complained that the Russian government was moving too slowly, even after the doors of Jewish emigration had opened; for they had opened only partially, allowing only a trickle of Jews to leave. But Wiesel also waged a simultaneous battle to persuade the Russians to halt their overtly anti-Israeli foreign policy, one that did not even allow diplomatic contacts between Israel and the Soviet Union. Eventually, Wiesel's unabating efforts bore fruit: today hundred of thousands of Russian Jews reside in Israel and diplomatic relations have been restored between Russia and Israel.

Wiesel's political offensive continues today. In September, 1991, when the newly autonomous Ukraine decided to rectify the mistakes of its past, he was invited by the new government in Kiev to participate in a special ceremony marking the Holocaust. This provided him with the perfect opportunity to remind the Ukrainian president that the people of the Ukraine, both by their indifference and by their active involvement, shared the guilt of Babi Yar. Wiesel furthermore played an important part in urging the Ukraine to reach out to the State of Israel by establishing diplomatic relations. He also urged the Ukrainians to erect a more fitting monument at Babi Yar, one that would acknowledge at long last the full extent of the Jewish tragedy. It should be noted too that the author of *Night* was instrumental in convincing the Ukrainian government to vote in favor of the revocation by the United Nations of the infamous declaration equating Zionism with racism.[41]

Here let us emphasize Wiesel's particular orientation towards Judaism. Having viewed Judaic religiosity through the prism of Hasidism, he has almost always interpreted the tenets of his faith Hasidically. Under the spell of his maternal grandfather, his intellectual and religious view of life has always been enrooted in Hasidic Judaism. From his grandfather and his first rabbi, a Hasid, Wiesel had learned "how to put one word after another . . ." He confessed that "I try to do what my grandfather taught me: to take words and to make them sing."[42]

The way Wiesel arranges words in a sentence, the way he utilizes questions ceaselessly, the way his sentences and questions form paragraphs, and the way he blends musical tonality with verbal substance—all of this epitomizes the Hasidic approach to expressing oneself through a special kind of religious chanting. Within the texture of his literary style, Wiesel communicates through verbal melody. Many Wieselean sentences might easily be set to music. Wiesel explains himself Hasidically: "A Hasid who does not sing is not a Hasid. Through singing he liberates himself and relocates himself outside of time, in the distance, before the storm, before the fire.[43] But in this instance, the Hasid does not sing for purposes of entertaining himself or others but he really does so in order to connect himself with God.

The term Hasidism needs to be defined here. The Hasidic movement began during the seventeenth century, as the result of a wave of bloody anti-Semitic uprisings throughout eastern Europe. Denied many professional opportunities by the Tsarist regime, many Jews, having few fields of work available to them, were forced to become tax collectors for the government. Notoriously, the least popular governmental employees of all, the tax collectors, easily become the most despised people in their community. During times of adverse economic conditions, the frustrated citizens, especially in eastern Europe, held their Jewish tax collectors responsible for their poverty. Consequently the Jews became the scapegoats for Russian anger. Pogroms exploded at regular intervals, and during the seventeenth century alone some 200,000 Jews were murdered by their Christian neighbors. Jewish morale suffered severely. Recognizing the need to revitalize their demoralized co-religionists, a number of rabbis developed Hasidism as a new, more attractive approach to religion. In lieu of the traditional method of the study and interpretation of the Torah, the Hasid rebbes (a popular term used by the Hasids for "rabbi") added an element of spiritual renewal based on joy, exuberance, and song. The new Hasidic leaders, led by their charismatic founder, Rabbi Israel Balshemtov, stressed the spiritual connections that united the souls of every member of the Jewish community. These interpersonal bonds could be intensified by joyful passion, spontaneity, singing, and dancing, all of which added a healing force to the more ancient Jewish service comprised entirely of enunciated and silent prayer. Now the Hasids could celebrate their holidays, festivals, and the Sabbath with a greater sense of vigor and more active participation in the rituals. Finally, the Hasidic reformers stressed the presence of God in every crevice of human existence. Bordering on pantheism, they preached God's involvement inside of each human act and in every natural phenomenon.

Out of Hasidism there grew the notion that God and godliness were synonymous with emotion, ecstasy, and celebration. Song and dance became the vehicle by which one prayed. Through intense feeling the worshipper became unified with God. This monistic philosophy shapes the core of Elie Wiesel's religious beliefs. It influences the way he writes. Whenever he discusses Judaism, he does so from the perspective of a Hasid. He makes this point in the following citation: "A Hasid does all the things Jews do, but he does them with passion . . . Whatever he says, he is always passionately involved. Hasidism is protest against divine indifference."[44]

For Wiesel the Hasidic movement stands as the "apotheosis of humanism in modern history," since it stresses the "importance and sacredness of man and what makes him human."[45] Out of his Hasidic roots Wiesel has forged his humanistic view of life. Tirelessly he implores us to honor the sanctity of human life and the necessity for us to live so that we respect the lives of all those around us. Through mutual esteem and universal amity, the human race ultimately constructs an international and multicultural environment of peace and harmony. His craving for peace reflects the prayers for peace that permeate all of the Hebrew liturgy. The typical salutation among Jews who greet each other, "Shalom," signifies peace.

Subscribing to the ideal of universal brotherhood, Wiesel believed that human beings must work to create an ambience of interconnectedness. Friendship (interconnectedness) is an even loftier state of existence than love: "The experience of friendship marks a life as profoundly—more profoundly—than that of love," writes Wiesel.[47] Wiesel is totally convinced that it is among Jews that one finds the strongest manifestation of interconnectedness, more so than among any other religious community: "After all, what is Hasidism? It is a movement based on friendship, a protest against indifference and loneliness. One cannot know it [solidarity] unless one belongs."[48]

Two of Wiesel's most admired collections of tales, *Souls on Fire* and *Messengers of God,* are constructed of legends and stories from the Hasidic tradition in Judaism.

Jews seem to have always lived at the precipice of extinction, extinction that comes from persecution, massacre, Holocaust. Yet, they survive. Why? Wiesel believes that their survival grows out of three cardinal lessons Jews have learned from their sacred texts: "You must love your fellow man;" "You must love God;" and "You must love Torah" (a buzzword for education).[49] Judaism has survived the most menacing dangers thanks to its ingrown humanism, monotheism, and learning. Through learning, especially through the study of the sacred texts, Jewish traditions have resisted the corrosive energies of persecution, bigotry, prejudice, anti-Semitism, campaigns of extermination, conversion, intolerance, assimilation. Even the ferocity of the Nazi Holocaust did not eliminate the Jews' will to live and to practice Judaism.

Wiesel sees Jewish survival as one of the real miracles of history. That Jews have not been erased from the face of the earth is a miraculous fact of history in the saga of the human race. Wiesel's oeuvre celebrates this miracle.

9
In Search Of Jewish-Christian Dialogue

During an important interview with Elie Wiesel, the French journalist Brigitte-Fanny Cohen asked him the following question: "How can the Jew have a real exchange with the Christian?" In his response Wiesel not only clarifies his thinking on the subject of Jewish–Christian relations but also expresses his conviction that the two religious groups ought to initiate a meaningful dialogue based on mutual respect: Here is the author's somewhat lengthy reply to Cohen's question:

> If he recognizes my right to be a Jew, and I his right to be a Christian, the exchange of his objective is to convert me. At the time of the presentation of my Nobel Prize, I was obligated, in accordance with the ritual, to go to Stockholm to deliver an address at the cathedral. Lengthily did I speak before thousands of devout [Christians] from the raised pulpit. In all frankness, this is what I told them: "I hope that you did not expect me to leave my memory as a Jew outside. I cannot forget that there was a time when the Jew was invited to enter a cathedral for the sole purpose of leaving from it as a Christian. As a child, I used to stay far from churches, I was afraid of them. Because the cross, which represents for you the symbol of charity and grace, was for us a symbol of fear. I respect you for being Christians, but respect me for being a Jew . . ." I strongly wish to have a sincere discourse, to tell Christians the truth. For, from that vantage point, a veritable dialogue can be undertaken.[1]

Throughout his career Wiesel has promoted the concept of dialogues between these two communities, both of which have lived through tempestuous collisions for almost two thousand years.

As a prominent writer, Wiesel composes his books and the texts of his talks not merely for Jewish audiences but also, but mainly, for his Christian public. Polls of his readers in France and the United States prove conclusively that far more non-Jews read Wiesel than Jews. This is to be expected since in both countries Jews constitute no more than two percent of the total population.

9: IN SEARCH OF JEWISH-CHRISTIAN DIALOGUE

One of Wiesel's major objectives as a writer is to help create an environment of greater mutual respect and understanding between Jews and Christians. But he believes steadfastly that this environment will be possible only if Jews remain true to their own faith, and Christians to theirs. Only from positions of strength and self-confidence can both forge a healthy, ecumenical relationship. Addressing himself "to a Christian in search of prayer," Wiesel writes that "We need to live together in the past [to share the memory of past horrors like the Inquisition, the Crusades, the Holocaust] so that there may be a future. From days of destruction, we would move forward to days of creation."[2]

The childhood universe of Elie Wiesel in Sighet was a thoroughly Jewish one. He grew up in the Jewish sector of the town. His family had almost no dealings with Gentiles. He attended a Jewish school, knew mainly Jewish people, and his parents traded mostly with Jewish clients. For him the only holidays observed were those of the Hebrew calendar. Consequently, as he admitted, he knew almost nothing of the values outside of his thoroughly Jewish world:

> As a child I felt no animosity and surely no hate toward our Christian neighbors. In truth, I was profoundly ignorant not only of things Christian but also of the non-Jewish world in general. I did not know that Christians and Moslems both saw their roots as the history of my people, that the Land of Israel was the spiritual cradle of nearly half the world, that the role Jews played in history and civilization was so out of proportion to their actual numbers. . . . [3]

During his childhood in Sighet, it seems—from everything Wiesel writes about that period of his life—that the Jewish community lived in some isolation from the neighboring Gentile population. The Holocaust catapulted Wiesel and his family into the vortex of Gentile–Jewish relations. From this forced relationship Wiesel learned a cruel lesson: to wit, the Gentiles were the killers, and the Jews their victims. Having discovered the full fury of the anti-Semitic world, he witnessed in the deathcamps the unleashing of the most terrifying example of hostility ever manifested by non-Jewish people of the earth against the children of Abraham in an already long history of persecution and pain. What he saw in the camps made the savagery of the Crusaders and the Inquisition pale by comparison. That he emerged from the harsh world of the Nazis as a man determined to work for the betterment of interfaith amity instead of for vengeance is a most remarkable happening. In lieu of leaving from the camps imbued with a desire for vengeance, he found himself filled with anguish and with the desire to help put an end to anti-Jewish hatred. Ted Estess notes that the future author of *Night* tried not so much to seek revenge against the Gentiles for their violent criminality against the Jews but rather to understand their motives and to analyze the causes of their anti-Semitism.[4]

Wiesel lodges two fundamental complaints against the international Christian community. First, he blames the Christians of Europe for their indifference; after all, they did almost nothing to halt the Nazis in their murderous genocidal campaign. Second, he explains that in its relentless effort to convert Jews to Christianity, the Christian community implicitly suggested that the Jewish faith was inferior to Christianity. Otherwise, why try to convert? That the converters have never stopped trying to convert Jews to Christianity was for Wiesel totally unacceptable behavior. Such behavior can only lead to anti-Semitism. Wiesel points out that when Christians call upon Jews to abandon their faith, they are effectively demonstrating little respect for the values of Judaism.

Wiesel maintains that interfaith harmony can be realized only after all religious groups accept the right of other religions to practice side by side, each one practicing in its own individual fashion. Addressing his fellow Jews he wrote, "If we could find Christians to listen to us—I mean *really* to listen to us—I still hope we have enough arguments, enough reasons, enough intelligence and sensitivity to convince them that they will never succeed in converting us. It's a lost cause. It's silly . . . And we still live in the same world, respecting one another. But I insist: respecting one another."[5] On another occasion he further expounds on his opposition to religious proselytism: "We had enough problems with converts. We do not want converts, we do not want others to convert us, and we do not want to convert others. We want Christians to be good Christians, Buddhists to be good Buddhists, and Jews to be good Jews."[6]

In the preceding chapter we noted that Wiesel opines that the authentic Jew accepts fully the values of his or her ancestral religion and its history. On many occasions, the writer reminds his readers that one of the reasons that Jews have remained relatively small in numbers when compared to the huge populations of Christians and Moslems derives from Jewish rejection of the notion that Jews must promote their faith among non-Jews. With a certain degree of bitterness, Wiesel also attributes the small number of Jews to the fact that for two thousand years Christians have decimated their Jewish brothers through campaigns of killing or through aggressive campaigns to convert them to Christianity. In fact, Wiesel marvels that the Jewish people survived at all, considering the obstacles they have faced in the past. His message is succinct: enough is enough; proselytizing and persecutions have proven to be exercises in futility. It is time that Christians accept Jews, once and for all, but it is time also for Jews to recognize the worth of their Christian neighbors.

The authentic Jew must resist the temptation to incorporate into Jewish worship certain customs inherent to Christianity. Likewise the authentic Christian ought not to incorporate into Christianity the traits peculiar to the other religion, especially if these traits are alien to their own religion.

Wiesel cannot conceal his ire against those who claim that they can be simultaneously Jewish and Christian. Especially does he object to those Christian missionaries who, calling themselves "Jews for Jesus," seek to entice Jews to espouse a kind of bi-religiosity. Wiesel wrote that "In telling their victim that he can be Jewish and Christian at the same time—as if the history of Christianity did not give them the lie—they are laying a trap of trickery and lies. Even more detestable, they play on their victim's vulnerabilities."[7]

Elie Wiesel wrote a review in the French newspaper, *Le Monde*, 4 December 1987, concerning his reactions to a book written by Aron Lustiger, the well-known Catholic Cardinal and Archbishop of Paris, entitled *Le choix de Dieu* [The Choice of God], in which the Jewish author revealed his disappointment with his close friend, the Cardinal. Wiesel confesses his sorrow that the Church prelate had been converted from his inherited religion of Judaism to Catholicism. Wiesel found it difficult to accept the Cardinal's assertion that in adopting Christianity he never renounced his fidelity to Judaism. After Wiesel's review, a heated polemic exploded between the prominent French priest, Riquet, and the author of *Night*. In this polemic, one that reached national notoriety in France, Wiesel argued that one cannot remain faithful to the message of Judaism as transmitted by Abraham, Moses, and the Prophets and still be a disciple of Christ. For the Christian, the Messiah has already arrived; but for the Jew, the Messianic wait still continues. One cannot have it both ways: either the Messiah has arrived or he has not yet done so. Heatedly Wiesel argues that "Judaism is for the Jew what Christianity is for the Christian: the best, if not the only way possible to attain a truth that is destined for him. . . ."[8] But these two truths, the Jewish and the Christian, are irreconcilable. The writer sternly warns us that choices must be made. In such a vital question of faith, compromises are not possible.

In his vigorous arguments for a much more meaningful harmony between Jews and Christians, Wiesel paradoxically maintains that this harmony cannot develop until both religious groups are willing to take cognizance of their past history and to formulate a strategy whereby the tragic mistakes of the past will not be able to be repeated. Before Jews and Christians can improve their conditions of future coexistence they must appreciate their sins of history. They must also accept the significant differences that will always inevitably divide them (e.g., the question of the Messiah, the role of Jesus as the son of God, the immaculate conception, dietary regulations, etc.). Once they accept these differences, they can begin to dialogue about how to diminish their mutual animosities and suspicions. Eventually they will understand that it is preferable to live alongside of each other than to engage in mutually destructive warfare. Once both sides learn to tolerate each other's dissimilarities they will be able to develop positive interrelationships based on mutual respect. Just as Wiesel calls upon Jews to agitate against injustices perpetrated against Christians, he expects the latter to become involved in defending Jews who happen to be treated unjustly.

To illustrate Christian indifference to Jewish suffering, Wiesel uses the Munich Olympic Games as an emblematic example of how the Gentile world failed to appreciate what the massacre of Israeli athletes by Arab terrorists meant to the Jewish worldwide community. To prove his point that the Christian world had still not learned a lesson from the Holocaust, he decries the fact that instead of canceling the remaining games as a tangible act of support for the slain Israelis, the Olympic officials (all of whom were non-Jews) decided to schedule a symbolic conscience-assuaging memorial service (a prolonged moment of silence), after which the scheduled games continued as scheduled and everyone immediately forgot about the massacre. For Wiesel wrote that ". . . when, in the course of the solemn memorial ceremony, the loudspeakers announced that the games would go on, frantic applause shook the earth. After all, the blood was only the blood of Israel . . . Dead or alive, Jews are alone!"[9]

Although history has provided too many examples of Christian indifference and of Jewish aloneness, Wiesel remains optimistic that the Gentile world is ripe for reform and gives every indication that Jewish–Christian relations can really be altered for the better. In the post-Holocaust era, his efforts to combat Christian indifference have borne fruit. Today he is heartened to acknowledge that at long last Christians have begun to comprehend that indifference to the tribulations of one people eventually leads to the suffering of all people, including the Christian majority. No less a Christian leader than the late Joseph Cardinal Bernardin, Archbishop of Chicago, wrote that Wiesel's collaborative volume (with Albert H. Friedlander), *The Six Days of Destruction,* shows that "The Shoah, while it is a unique Jewish event, also belongs to the entire human family. If we Christians are true to ourselves, then we will acknowledge that the pain and horror of the Holocaust are also ours."[10]

Throughout his literature, Wiesel contends that the Holocaust is both a Jewish tragedy and a Christian problem. The Jews were the victims, but for the most part it was the Christians (at least nominal Christians) who were the killers. Until the Christians accept this incontestable fact, Wiesel avers that true dialogue between Jews and Christians is virtually impossible. Shocking though this allegation may be for some Christians, Wiesel even charges that the Holocaust is the logical result of two thousand years of systematic and doctrinal anti-Semitism sponsored wittingly or unwittingly by the Christian churches themselves. After all, didn't Germany, the nation most responsible for the Holocaust, always regard itself, since the early Middle Ages, as a Christian nation? And wasn't Germany the birthplace of Lutheranism and the site where the Protestant Reformation was launched? Didn't most Germans observe Christian rites, either as Catholics or as Lutherans? Wiesel argues, rightly so, that German history was inextricably bound to that of European Christendom. He insists that when the German people subserviently followed the Nazi program to destroy the Jewish population of Europe, their national psyche had already been fashioned not only by German patriotic fervor but also by their Christian heritage. And what about the other national groups who gleefully aided and abetted the Germans in their war to exterminate the Jewish people—the Poles, Lithuanians, Latvians, Ukrainians, Estonians, Croatians, Austrians, and the others? All of these people were part of Europe's Christendom. And of course Wiesel marvels at the public silence of the Vatican during Hitler's genocidal campaign. Few church leaders in Germany and elsewhere raised voices of outrage to decry the liquidation of the Jews, Gypsies, and other "undesirables." How does one explain the taciturnity or the acquiescence of the international Christian world? These troubling questions permeate Wiesel's publications. He knew that international pressure can often be an effective weapon against a nation's misbehavior. Wiesel notes the example of how the Soviet Union, then one of the world's two superpowers, eventually yielded to international pressure and began to permit Jewish emigration. Once Hitler had been convinced that the non-Jewish world would allow him to proceed with impunity, he realized that he had a carte blanche to do whatever he wished.

Profoundly disappointed that the ecclesiastic leaders of world Christendom had demonstrated such callous indifference at the specter of Jewish destruction, Wiesel knew that the indifference vis-à-vis the Jews displayed by Christians throughout past history could conceivably continue for years. With consistency he has maintained "that [the Nazi plan to eradicate the Jews] was inseparable from the past of Christian, civilized Europe . . . the history of Christianity . . . is full of anti-Semitism. More than that—there would have been no Auschwitz if the way had not been prepared by Christian theology."[11] In similar vein he declared that the German concentration camps were the "climax of ten centuries of Christian civilization, of irrational contempt and hatred." In the same passage he voiced his conviction that the greatest humanists of the Christian tradition— Kant, Fichte, Goethe, Voltaire—"are guilty because they aspired to prove that the hatred of the Jews and love of man could be reconciled."[12] The respected Wiesel authority, Abrahamson, concurs with Wiesel's arguments and writes that "Wiesel recognizes, as have many others, that the flames of terror that swept all across Europe were the culmination of two thousand years of Christian civilization. . . ."[13] Pointedly insisting that the Holocaust must be recognized as a Christian problem, the author of *Night* reminds his Christian audience that "all the killers were Christian." To this non-Jewish world he poses the following disturbing rhetorical question and his reply to it:

> Now was it the Christianity in them that made them killers? I hope not. But the fact is that they did not become killers in a vacuum. They were the outgrowth, a result of the 1800 years of a certain civilization, of certain teaching, of a certain tradition—of hate—and they became the example, the living example of what happens to people when they learn to hate. And that's a Christian problem.[14]

Wiesel proposes the interesting theory that as Christians were destroying Jews, they were at the same time destroying their own faith too since their religion, like Judaism, was based on belief in the sanctity of human life and on love for one's fellow men.[15] In his usual lapidary style, the writer summed up his accusation against the Christian world like this: "What mankind did not foresee was that when the world kills Jews, it kills itself."[16]

Given all of the dismal facts handed down to us from history Wiesel believes that true dialogue between Jews and Christians will never take place until Christians accept some degree of responsibility for the Holocaust. He believes also that Christians will have to take concrete steps to suppress anti-Semitism to the extent that its roots can be found in certain Christian doctrines. Fortunately, the Catholic Church, for its part, under the leadership of Pope John XXIII and, to some extent, under that of Pope John Paul II has already taken meaningful and specific measures to eliminate anti-Semitic sentiment in its ritual. This, according to Wiesel, is a long overdue step forward since he believed anti-Semitism to be a clear betrayal of Jesus' teaching of tolerance and love for mankind.

Wiesel's recurrent accusations against Christians who label Jews as "Christ-killers" are filled with irony. In his opinion, it is the Christians who have "crucified [the Jews] by collective madness in the Holocaust."[17] In another passage, Wiesel quotes from Christian theology in which it is stated that "the Jewish people belonged to 'Satan's Synagogue.'"[18] The writer expands his indictment of Christian dogma by wondering aloud if Jesus ought even to be regarded as a messiah: "A messiah," writes Wiesel, "who divides the Jewish people is a false messiah. I often quote this definition when I speak to Christians: Jesus, more than anyone else in history, provoked dissension and division in the world. So many massacres were conducted in his name. Can that be the Messiah?"[19]

Before one can combat anti-Semitism, Wiesel knows that it will be imperative that the origin and meaning of the term "anti-Semitism" be understood. He observed that the earliest seeds of this hatred could already be identified in some of the earliest Christian dogma. But anti-Jewish attitudes really pre-dated the establishment of Christianity. Wiesel believes that much of the world's anti-Semitism stems from ignorance by non-Jews of the true nature of Judaism: "When one does not understand, one hates and wants to erase."[20] In addition, the hatred of Jews may well be based on economic factors. At times of economic duress and high unemployment, non-Jews see Jews as a threat to their economic stability. The author even interpreted the Spanish Inquisition as the outgrowth of economic conditions on the Iberian Peninsula. Christian Spain wished to expropriate the wealth and property of two affluent populations, the Jews and the Moors. Anti-Semitism also arises out of a common human tendency to blame some scapegoat for one's misfortunes. Because, in most nations, Jews represent a small fraction of the population, they become a vulnerable target for blame. Wiesel even explains anti-Semitism from an ethical point of view: Thanks to the exalted ethical standards promulgated by Judaic law, non-Jews perceive Jews as people who claim to occupy a superior stratum within the international community. As such, they represent the conscience of humanity, an unsettling conscience that reminds Gentiles of their previous guilty conduct: "The Jewish people is . . . the conscience of mankind. And because we are the conscience, because we make mankind realize its guilt, we are hated."[21] Wiesel was especially impressed by a statement once made by the French writer, Thierry Maulnier, who, upon analyzing the reasons why some Christians hate Jews, claimed that "the Jewish people is special because it does not let us sleep."[22] So long as Jews reside on this planet, their presence will haunt the Jew-haters; they cannot erase from their conscience the memory of the earlier discriminatory campaigns waged by non-Jews against the tiny and fragile Jewish minority.

In the eyes of Elie Wiesel, the anti-Semites have devised a set of myths and distortions to justify their hatred of the Jewish minority. In the absence of plausible and credible rationales to substantiate their prejudice, the anti-Semite fabricates convenient arguments to support racist behavior. Wiesel states his case like this:

> We have suffered because of myths. Jewish life was destroyed because of baseless, yet dangerous myths spread by enemies who had nothing in common except hatred of the Jewish people. They claimed we killed a God, and for that they murdered us. They claimed we poisoned wells, and for that they drowned us. They claimed we committed ritual murder, and for that they burned us.[23]

In his novel, *Le Crépuscule au loin* [Dawn], Wiesel depicts pogroms inflicted by Poles against the Jews, the very same Jews who had been their neighbors for centuries. Twice a year inebriated Poles would take to the streets, storm Jewish homes, destroy their property, loot their shops and houses, and assault the very people with whom, at other times of the year, they lived side by side in the same villages. Ironically, Wiesel notes that Jews had learned to adapt to the violent Polish behavior by accepting physical abuse as a normal and inescapable price to pay for their right to reside in Polish towns.[24]

9: IN SEARCH OF JEWISH-CHRISTIAN DIALOGUE

The Holocaust ended more than a half century ago. The once-prisoner of Auschwitz/Birkenau wanted to believe that the human race had learned a painful, but necessary lesson about the sins of anti-Semitism and racism. The spilling of blood, the destruction of irreplaceable human resources, the demolition of cities, all of this represented an inestimably costly price for civilization to pay. After the long night of terror of the Holocaust, Wiesel dared to believe that humanity might forge a new era of tolerance and respect for human life. To his astonishment, to his great disappointment, however, he discovered quickly that the hatred of Jews had not vanished. Pockets of anti-Semitism were springing forth here and there out of the ashes of World War II. Hebrew cemeteries and synagogues continued to be desecrated all over Europe and America. In Poland, returning survivors from the death camps were killed by the local populace. Even where no Jews returned or survived in Poland, the local Christian population blamed their bad fortune on the Jews. So a new phenomenon had emerged: anti-Semitism where there were no Jews left to hate and to persecute! Swastikas and hate slogans were scrawled on walls in public places. Myths about Jewish evil and about sinister Jewish plots to seize control of the world continued to float about in the clouds of hatred and racism.

Wiesel's shock concerning the rebirth of anti-Semitism reached its crescendo when books, some written by persons with academic pretensions, began to appear in which their authors claimed that the Holocaust had not even existed, that the six million had not been murdered, that the camps of death were figments of Jewish imagination, and that tales of Nazi atrocities were tales devised by Jews in search of financial reparations or sympathy. With utter contempt, he who had lost almost his entire family at Auschwitz wrote:

> If anyone had told them [the survivors]—or me—one generation ago that there would be American Nazis to stage public demonstrations in our lifetime [referring to a Nazi march in Skokie, Illinois], that they would claim kinship with the worst killers in history and be proud of them, we would have dismissed the idea as implausible ... Sixty-five books [appeared in 1978 alone], in a variety of languages, ... telling readers everywhere that the Final Solution was but a Jewish invention; that the Holocaust never took place; that six million did not vanish....[25]

The worldwide recurrence of anti-Semitism caught Wiesel by surprise. He found himself speechless before the spectacle of anti-Jewish fervor that poisoned the planet from Carpentras, France to Chicago, from Warsaw to Bucharest, from Los Angeles to Moscow.[26]

And yet! Wiesel did not totally lose his optimistic streak. He refused to be completely disheartened. Here and there he discerned a glimmer of hope. The vast majority of the Christian world seemed to reach the conclusion that anti-Semitism, racism, and the hatred of minorities were counterproductive. Even though Wiesel was deeply disappointed by the way the world had returned to some of its criminal conduct, he continued to cling to the opinion that the course of history could still be changed for the better. The writer even believed that for many Christians the Holocaust represented an apocalyptic event, one that shocked Christians into a reevaluation and a reexamination of their conscience. To demonstrate the metamorphosis in Christian attitudes, Wiesel contrasted the attitudes of Pope Pius XII, the reigning Pope during the Nazi era, and Pope John XXIII, the Catholic prelate of the post-World War II era. Whereas the former did not, at least openly, raise his voice to decry Nazi barbarism, the latter removed Jews from the stigma of deicide. Of Pius XII, Wiesel wrote that "Pope Pius XII, who was alive during the Holocaust, did not do his duty. He should have gone to Auschwitz. He should have tried to save Jews then and risk his life. Had the Pope, the father of the Church, done his duty then, I am convinced fewer Jews would have been killed.[27] In Pope John XXIII, however, Wiesel saw a ray of hope. At last there seemed to be a transformation in the Christian outlook towards Judaism. The Holocaust had forced the Church to comprehend the inconsistency between the teachings of Jesus about the brotherhood of man, on the one hand, and the long track record of persecutions by the followers of Jesus, on the other hand. Now that the Pope viewed Auschwitz as a logical result of Christian anti-Semitism, Wiesel hoped that it would finally be possible to establish a meaningful sense of solidarity between Christians and Jews. The Jewish writer wrote that "[John XXIII] understood, also, that Auschwitz represented a failure, a defeat for 2000 years of Christian civilization. Pope John XXIII understood that what happened in Auschwitz marked an end to orthodox Christianity. And therefore he opened the doors and began to liberalize the Church. That explains Vatican II, the ecumenical movement."[28]

With the advent of the current Pope, John Paul II, Wiesel sadly noted a partial reversal in the enlightened policies of his predecessor. Especially irksome to Wiesel was John Paul II's continued refusal, until only recently, to recognize the reality of the State of Israel. Also the writer expressed regret that John Paul II had praised Pope Pius XII's wartime policies during a widely publicized meeting with Jewish leaders in Florida; here is Wiesel's reaction to this praise: "Personally, I found it bizarre and shocking."[29] The latter was particularly incensed when John Paul II celebrated a mass at the site of the infamous death-camp at Birkenau, a site that Wiesel regarded as sacred Jewish soil. Needless to say, Wiesel was dismayed when the Pope granted an audience to Chancellor Kurt Waldheim of Austria, just after he had been accused by Jewish leaders and the United States State Department of having a notorious record of anti-Semitic behavior during World War II.

In the final analysis Wiesel contends that Christians must learn to appreciate the reality of Jewish survival. After millennia of trials and tribulations, especially after the most recent near-genocide of the Holocaust, Jews defy all of the odds and simply refuse to disappear. This survival, Wiesel believes, is one of the most incredible miracles of all human history. Proudly he points out to his friend Saint Cheron that "it is true that of all of the peoples of the Ancient World, we Jews are the only ones to have survived."[30]

Only after the Christian world fully understands the special, indestructible quality of Judaism, and only after Christians accept the fact that they must permit Jews to be "thoroughly Jewish" can there emerge a meaningful dialogue between Christians and Jews. When that happens, mankind will embark upon a new era of mutual understanding and harmonious co-existence between these two great western religions.

Hopeful that such a day may yet arrive, Wiesel applauds the fact that leaders of these two peoples have at long last begun to plant the seeds of Jewish–Christian solidarity. He himself has actively engaged in meaningful dialogue with Catholic prelates, Protestant ministers, and theologians from every branch of Christianity. And so the author of *Night* perceives the first glimmers of light at the end of the long somber tunnel. Wiesel fervently hopes that the human race will successfully reach the other end of that tunnel.

10
The Sanctity of Life

Arguably the most riveting theme in Wieselean literature is the author's insistence upon the sanctity of human life. This theme lies at the heart of his entire philosophy of life. It is particularly ironic that Wiesel, a witness of the Holocaust, who had observed the wholesale destruction of human lives, should proclaim the preciousness of the human being. In Auschwitz and Birkenau, he saw little else but the daily and systematic murder of tens of thousands of men, women, and children. During his lifetime an estimated twenty-five million humans were ruthlessly killed in the camps, in bombings, battles, starvation, and ghastly mistreatment, torture, death-marches. Cities were reduced to rubble, nuclear bombs eradicated whole urban complexes. Considering the events that he saw, one marvels that he could possibly write about the sacredness of human life. Never before in history did life seem so expendable, so valueless.

And yet! He who had seen these bloody atrocities emerged from the abyss of World War II with an absolute conviction that nothing on this earth was more valuable than the lives of its inhabitants. Rooted in the Jewish Bible, he wrote: "The world is worth burning. Yet we Jews decided not to burn it. Why? Because we believe in man . . . We believe that man is ultimately sacred."[1]

As a devout Jew, Wiesel believed in life! Jews have always affirmed that life was sacred because it originated out of the creative action of God.

Probably the single most influential writer to have shaped Wiesel's *Weltanschauung* was Albert Camus. Especially from the latter's *Myth of Sisyphus* he learned a significant lesson: that to live means that we must be engaged in a ceaseless ascent up an unascendable mountain. Despite the steepness of the slope, despite the obstacles along the path towards the summit, the climber must never stop until the peak has been reached—and the peak may never be reached! But the climber must never yield to fatigue. As Wiesel revisited the memories of his own tragic ascent through the Shoah, he learned that even though he had faced so many vicissitudes, so many disappointments, he could not lose his faith in humanity. Even though human history has been marked by disaster after disaster, Wiesel, like Camus's Sisyphus, knew that he could not allow himself to yield to despair. Life required a constant renewal of the affirmation to live, even in the face of seemingly insurmountable odds. To even come close to reaching our ultimate objective of protecting human life and working to build universal peace on earth, we must accept the concept of universal solidarity. Unless individuals accepted responsibility for the welfare of the entire human race, they would be unable to attain the peak towards which they were striving. Each individual must acknowledge the fact that he or she is inextricably bound to the destiny of the entire human family. Consequently Wiesel insisted that "we speak out on behalf of suffering neighbors."[2]

Early in his career, the author of *Night* decided that it was his role to become a spokesperson in behalf of the tormented and persecuted underdogs of the earth, whoever they might be, wherever they might be located. Wiesel knew well the tragic history of his own people and made it his duty to champion the cause of all those who unjustly suffered mistreatment at the hands of their fellow human beings. One of his most compelling messages is his plea for the universal acceptance of the principle that all human beings possess certain fundamental human rights. Despite this he lamented that "There exist in the world so many injustices and sufferings that solicit our attention: victims of hunger, racism, dictatorships—as in Chile and Ethiopia. . . . The rights of man are violated on every continent. The number of oppressed persons surpasses that of free men."[3]

At various moments of his life, Wiesel, the humanist of humanists, confessed his shame at being a member of the human race. How could one not be embarrassed when there exist so many bullies who mistreat the meek and the weak? To an audience of young people, he once admitted that "I am ashamed too. I am older than you . . . but I am ashamed: not as a Jew but as a human being. Believe me or not, often I am simply ashamed of belonging to the human species, of having two eyes and one mouth and a nose."[4]

After his liberation from the camps, he believed that the world had learned a bitter lesson, one that would prevent the repetition of new Holocausts. Since that awful *Hourban*, however, persecutions, exterminations, racism, and hatred continue without abatement. Injustice, racism, and hatred have a pattern of continuing to stay alive around the world. Anti-Semitic manifestations continue. Synagogues, cemeteries, and other sacred places continue to be desecrated. Church burnings, ethnic cleansing, discrimination, skinheadism, hate-crimes and other unsavory events are reported in the media almost daily. The nightmare continues.

In the face of all of the above, Wiesel clings to the conviction that one day human beings will accept the fact of their solidarity and indivisibility. Certain that a better day will come, when all races, ethnic groups, nationalities, and religious sects will come to accept their interdependence, he believes that the scourges that divide us will someday vanish. With his faith in the inevitability of universal brotherhood, Wiesel conducts his passionate campaign against hate. He believes further that of all people it is the Jews who ought to play a pivotal role of leadership. As the premier victims of persecution, Jews have a special responsibility in the battlelines: they must educate the human population about the terrifying price that all of us must pay when we permit hatred to prevail so freely. Since the Diaspora has dispersed Jews in so many scattered corners of the world, they hold a universal place on this planet, and can, therefore exert positive influences in so many countries. As the most persecuted of people, Jews epitomize the scapegoats and the downtrodden of the human condition: "As a Jew," Wiesel writes, "I make no distinction between the Jewish condition and the human condition."[5]

That his concern for all underdogs, for all minorities, is a sincere one is evident from the fact that Elie Wiesel, as a representative of the Jews of the world, has made it his objective to travel frequently to many countries, always positioning himself on the side of all people who happen to be undergoing discrimination and humiliation. The Jew in him requires that he support the cause of the underdog, no matter where. He reminds his readers that "I went to Argentina to help get Jacobo Timmerman, the publisher, released from jail. In Russia the motivation was the same as in Biafra, Bangladesh. Traveling and working for causes—always centered around Jewish consciousness at the center of human consciousness."[6]

Martin Niemoller, the celebrated Lutheran pastor during the Nazi era, is one of those figures to have played a key role in fashioning Wiesel's thinking. By his attack against indifference during the Hitler Holocaust, Niemoller became one of Wiesel's icons. In him the Jewish writer saw the arch example of the righteous Gentile, one who did not fear sacrificing his own life for the principle of human solidarity. His oft-quoted statement in its entirety, along with a similar enuncia-

10: THE SANCTITY OF LIFE

tion by Pope John Paul II, form an integral part of the interreligious church/synagogue ecumenical service composed expressly for *The Six Days of Destruction: Meditations Toward Hope,* written collaboratively by Elie Wiesel and Albert H. Friedlander.[7]

Decades after the *Hourban,* minorities continue to be victimized by more powerful majorities. It always astounds Wiesel that, for the most part, large segments of the international community observe these injustices with indifference and noninvolvement. On behalf of the battered communities, whether they be Jewish or non-Jewish, the writer has assumed the role of unofficial spokesperson for the oppressed. Here is how he chooses to define this role:

> As a member of the human family who must, still today, witness the misery that afflicts Uganda, the starvation that stalks Cambodia, the persecution of Jews and dissidents in the Soviet Union, I am tempted to succumb to a feeling of resignation. But, because I am a Jew, I am able to find the strength to fight against all these things and find a justification for doing so.[8]

In his Oslo address, he expressed jubilation at the fact that former political prisoners like his friends Lech Walesa of Poland and Nelson Mandela of South Africa had been freed and could, in fact, get elected to positions of national leadership in their countries. But to his public in the great Aula of Oslo, he pleaded that they not rejoice excessively; Walesa and Mandela were only isolated examples of righteousness triumphing over injustice. Alas, all too often the unjust manage to prevail. He reminded his audience that at the time of his address fanatical Syrian and Iranian sympathizers were holding Americans and western Europeans as hostages.[9]

When President Jimmy Carter appointed Elie Wiesel to serve as Chairman of the President's Commission on the Holocaust, the latter expanded the responsibilities of his new job so that he could work not only towards the establishment of a memorial to honor the victims of the Holocaust but also to work to honor all persecuted populations, all of those who suffered injustice and mistreatment. Here, for example, is a statement by Wiesel in defense of the human rights of the Vietnamese: ". . . on behalf of the Commission I implore all countries to extend rights of refuge and asylum to the boat people [of southeastern Asia]."[10] In his confrontation with the fate of the Palestinians, Wiesel faced a particularly irksome dilemma: As a Jew he rejoiced at the establishment of a Jewish state; but it was his moral duty also to work for the alleviation of the plight of the Palestinians dispossessed by the creation of Israel. In his work for human solidarity, in its broadest sense, Wiesel realized that he would need to develop a suitable formula to reconcile his concern for both the Israeli and Palestinian causes. As he issued a plea for the international community to accept the post-Holocaust reality of Israel, he sought also some kind of just solution for the Palestinian refugees. But his efforts were exacerbated by the intermittent terrorist tactics perpetrated by groups like Hamas and Hezbollah that had privately been sanctioned by the Palestine Liberation Organization (PLO). Knowing that terrorism would only aggravate the tensions by justifying hardline Israeli policy to retaliate, Wiesel issued statements that betray his uneasiness as he carefully chose his wording. Here is an example:

> After all, these people [the Palestinian Arabs] are suffering. What do I have to tell a Palestinian Arab? . . . What I really try to say there is that I do feel responsible for his pain; I do feel responsible for his suffering. *Everybody's suffering involves me, indicts me in a way* [emphasis mine]. I accept indictment if I don't speak up. And this is true of the Palestinian too . . . . The PLO has used your [the Palestinian people] suffering to kill Jews, from Maalot to Entebbe to Lod, from murder to murder, from massacre to massacre. They are betraying your suffering. And you did not speak up against them.[11]

And thus Wiesel appealed to the Palestinians to transcend their inclination to conduct campaigns of violence against the Israelis by adopting instead a rational policy based on peaceful negotiation with their Israeli neighbors. Only then could an equitable and peaceful solution be developed. But Wiesel makes it crystal clear that, until the Palestinians renounce violence and terrorism, they must be held accountable for at least some of their tragic fate since they do not protest against the excesses of the PLO leadership. Obviously no one rejoiced more than Wiesel when Prime Minister Rabin and Chairman Arafat signed an accord of peace in Oslo.

As someone who had seen more than his share of violence in the concentration camps, Wiesel had become a passionate advocate of international peace. He became convinced that conflicts could only be resolved through negotiation and dialogue based on faith in the solidarity of mankind. Whenever disagreements between nations and disputes between people assert themselves, only one course of action can lead to the avoidance of belligerency: peaceful negotiation, arbitration, mediation. This is a central principle in his overall philosophy of life. An avowed peacemaker, he unabashedly proclaimed his pacifist philosophy: "I am a pacifist, I do not believe in wars, I do not like weapons. Warcraft does not impress me—I know how to write about people, not about tanks."[12]

Nowhere did this Nobel Peace laureate speak more forcefully about his philosophy of peace than in *Paroles d'étranger.* There, in an essay entitled "The Jew and War," written at the end of the Yom Kippur War of 1973, he stressed the basic peacefulness of the Jewish people. Noting that their holiest prayers and their most celebrated sacred texts were little more than the exaltation of peace, he emphasized that as a Jew he had no option but to uphold the cause of peace and of non-violent resolutions of conflict. Violence, he insists, runs counter to the most fundamental principles of Judaism. In his analyses of early Hebrew history, he emphasizes that whenever conflagrations developed, it was always the Jews who were victimized by violence, even when Jews were not directly concerned in the wars between nations: "Whenever two nations fought, it was the Jewish people who lost. . . . Whether it was a war of religion or a war of conquest, we [Jews] were always nabbed by the tempest, always vanquished, on the side of the vanquished—and often victims of the victims."[13] In contrast with Moslems, many of whom glorified the concept of Jihad—a war in the name of Allah—or in contrast with the Christians, who treated the Crusades as a model of man's devotion to their divine mission, Jews have never treated military events as anything else but as a cause for embarrassment. Summing up this point, Wiesel wrote: "There you have one of the beauties of the Jewish tradition. It recognizes no war as holy; war cannot nor must it serve as a means to attain nobility or saintliness. To kill, even if it is for a superior cause, diminishes man. Judaism has never bestowed an aura of sainthood upon its military heroes. A Saint Louis would be, for us, inconceivable."[14]

A committed pacifist, a Jewish pacifist, Elie Wiesel did not find it easy to reconcile his love for the State of Israel with his passion for peace. It troubled him that the Jewish state had created one of the most effective fighting armies in the world, that it had developed one of the most admired air forces of any nation, that it had fought in more wars than almost any other nation during the last fifty years, that it owed much of its existence to the high quality of its defense forces, but he recognized that without this massive force, the people of Israel would have been obliterated. Wiesel argues that for Israel the military buildup was little more than a last resort; Israelis had no alternative if they wished to preserve the lives of the survivors of the Holocaust who had moved to Israel. Since, for the Jew, the most sacred responsibility was the preservation of human life, the defense of the State of Israel did not, therefore, seem to Wiesel to be inconsistent with Jewish values. If Israel did not take preemptive measures to debilitate the massive and heavily armed Arab armies threatening her very existence, enormous numbers of her citizens would have lost their lives. Jews had already lost more than a third of their total population in the Holocaust, and there was no other means of ensuring Jewish survival except to make a heavy investment in military hardware.

The only wars that Wiesel has ever tried to justify were defensive actions that occurred only when no other alternative was available. Note how he voices his support for a militarized (but not militant) State of Israel: "If the world, once again, tries to attack Israel, to deny Israel, to kill Israel, it will be the end of the world. Israel must live in order that the world live. I am against war and in favor of humanism, but, as a Jew, belonging to a traumatized generation such as ours, I stand in total solidarity with what is taking place in Israel. I am with Israel; and what Israel does it does it in my name also."[15] But when Israel wins wars of survival, Wiesel neither rejoices nor gloats. Like the Israelis, who never jubilated after their victories over the Arab states, he felt saddened that human lives had been destroyed, effaced—on both sides of the battlefield, Jewish and Arab. Life is, after all, sacred!

In the aggregate of Wiesel's writings and public addresses, one of those motifs that stands out in salient and constant relief is the theme of human solidarity, peace, and the sacredness of human life. Certainly it made sense for the Nobel selection committee to have singled him out for its Peace Prize in 1986. Appropriately, the most impressive section of his Nobel address, it seems, contains the following statement: ". . . in Judaism, the literature of war is surprising on account of its paucity. On the other hand, that of peace is majestic and flourishing. God would not have created the Torah except to have peace reign among men. Peace is worthy of all blessings, for it contains and justifies all of them. Peace is the supreme duty, the supreme reward, the supreme obligation and the ultimate hope."[16]

11
What Is Literature?

For the writer literature is an almost magical instrument that transforms his or her personal memory into art. Through stories, poems, novels, plays, and essays, the writer communicates to an audience of readers recollections of experiences past and recent, thoughts, feelings, hopes, joys, pain, dreams, aspirations, anticipations for the future. Literature is a tool that empowers the writer to transmit to others his or her innermost and personal impressions of what human life is all about. Before these impressions can be conveyed, however, the writer must devise a way to transfigure the inchoate and often the chaotic elements of memory into some kind of organized system or form. In traversing the divide between formlessness and form, the artist must pass through various stages in the creative process: among which, the selection of the indispensable elements, decisions about those ingredients to eliminate and those to embrace, the arrangement of those bits and pieces that are to be retained, and the assembling or packaging of all of these components into some kind of acceptable (to the artist) schema. Thus, literature may be viewed as a way by which the creative artist transmutes the chaos of memory into an organized, formal text.

In his literary undertaking, Elie Wiesel has always elevated the role of memory to a lofty level; it may even be the primary source of his inspiration. No twentieth-century writer has been more haunted, more continuously obsessed with the importance of memory. His greatest fear is that one day the world may be inclined to forget the memory of the Holocaust, a highly significant tragedy in human history. His most ambitious objective has been to create a body of literature that helps guarantee the preservation of the "Event."

For Wiesel it is shocking that the Germans, of all people, should have been the ones who had engendered and implemented the most savage national crime in recorded history. Were the Germans not among the most highly cultivated and most educated, the most thoroughly literary and literate populations in western civilization? This is one of the truly agonizing questions Wiesel raises again and again. In his Nobel address he expressed this troubling issue once more: "all of those doctors in law or in medicine or in theology [the German officials in the camps], all of those lovers of art and poetry, all of those admirers of Bach and Goethe who, coldly, intelligently had ordered the massacre and had participated in it: what was the meaning of their metamorphosis? How does one explain their loss of ethical, cultural, religious memory?"[1] This problem becomes a virtual leitmotif in Wiesel's collected works. In yet another text he restated the same theme: "many Germans cried when listening to Mozart, when playing Haydn, when quoting Goethe and Schiller—but remained quite unemotional when torturing and shooting children."[2] From this observation of German behavior during the Nazi era he concluded that literature, art, music, sophisticated levels of intellectual life, advanced education, state-of-the-art scientific and technological research—none of this was sufficient to restrain highly cultured human beings from behaving inhumanly:

> To put it differently: all that which they [the Germans] had been able to absorb, in the various schools and institutes of advanced learning, in matters of culture, did not prevent them in any way from assassinating men, women, and children; their education did not serve them as a shield. They could thus admire a master's painting, savor a beautiful poem, appreciate the finesse of a philosophical reflection and at the same time, slaughter thousands and thousands of human beings.[3]

This paradox he articulates in yet another passage: "something must be wrong with culture, if Germans could quote Schiller and Fichte while killing Jews. Something must be wrong with books and language if people who write so impressively and who play music so artistically could become allies of death."[4] His condemnation of culture, the arts, and education swells into an even greater crescendo: "Among them [the Germans] were philosophers and psychologists, doctors and artists, experts in management and specialists in poisoning the mind: all collaborated in this patriotic national mission which consisted in sowing death among the children and their parents."[5]

If the track record of the "cultured" German nation bewildered Wiesel, he was almost equally astonished that the other western nations were no less guilty than the Germans since, by their indifference, they acquiesced to the crimes of the Nazi movement. Even when the victims of Nazism tried to flee to these other countries, almost all of them closed their frontiers to the despondent and desperate Jews: "The wind carried their lamentations to the four corners of the earth, but men and nations, near and far, refused to listen ... Only now the civilized countries—the enlightened, hospitable countries—did not want them to come at all."[6] And so when the German fury unleashed itself, millions died.

Once the advanced civilizations committed or condoned mass murder and genocide, the guilt spread itself almost equally among those who killed and those who passively watched the killing. In Wiesel's view, both the murderers and the spectators conspired in criminality. Out of this international reality, Wiesel formulated his philosophy of literature and of artistic creativity. He concluded that unless the creative arts were inextricably linked to moral and ethical values, they could not possibly function as a force of enrichment for human life. Wiesel decreed that literature and the other arts must be based upon a firmament of morality and human values. His call for the fusion between art and morality forms the spine of his philosophy of literature.

Viewing western (in particular, German) civilization, in its most elitist form, as the firmament underlying the crass destruction of millions of innocent lives, Wiesel refused for many years to set foot on German soil or to travel to those countries where, in his view, intellectual and artistic life had divorced itself from moral considerations. Eventually he came to realize that it was time to help the Germans and other once guilty peoples to acquire a new respectability. He declared that the crimes of yesterday's generations ought not to haunt the younger generations of today, especially when the latter were not even born at the time of the Holocaust. The young must be unshackled from the culpability of their elders and must be given a chance to forge a more humane present and future. Otherwise the contemporary German nation might never liberate itself from the insanity of the Holocaust years. In his positive attitude vis-à-vis today's younger generations in Germany, Wiesel continuously reminded his readers that they must be unforgiving of the German past: "of the entire German people, no more than two hundred risked their lives to free the nation from Hitler. They and they alone deserve to be remembered ... No German chancellor since World War One achieved as much unity in almost every stratum of the population as did Hitler. Documentary films of the Nazi periods show convincingly that the German people idolized Hitler until the last months of the war."[7]

Contrary to those who reject the notion of collective national guilt, Wiesel, for his part, believed that this guilt is indeed legitimate, provided that it is limited to those individuals directly or indirectly involved in crimes against humanity. Those who were either too young to commit savage acts or those who were not even born at the time of the crimes must necessarily be exempt from culpability. He writes that "I believe in collective guilt, unlike many liberals. I believe that the whole German people who were adult and who could commit crimes either actively or passively were guilty. I do not believe that young Germans, who were born after the war or were too young to have committed any crimes, are guilty. I feel a sympathy for these young Germans because their tragedy is tremendous."[8] Before a seminar of Susquehanna University students visiting him at his home in Manhattan, Wiesel, with visible emotion, proclaimed that "only the guilty are guilty!"

Morality, ethical values, the sanctity of human life, the wisdom to distinguish between evil and justice—these are the fundamental principles that shape Wiesel's philosophy of art. From this it follows that art must not be created solely for the sake of art. Passionately the writer maintains that the creative artist must seek to convert his visions, experiences, and dreams into a product that transmits much more than mere esthetic pleasure to his public. He insists that art must embody both the beauty of form and the beauty of the message; and the message ought to contain the beauty found in human life. Art should aim at the enrichment of not only the mind and the senses, but also it should reach out to the human soul. Literature must embody much more than felicitous metaphors and phraseology; it must also contain moral lessons that encourage readers to distinguish between righteous and unjust behavior. Literature must stimulate the reader to pose questions about the nature of justice and evil. Wiesel wrote that "If life, art, or literature are not moral, then there can be no life, art, literature—or anything. If we do not question the camps, then we will not question extermination by H-bomb. If there is any value in man, it is only when he faces up to these questions and answers them honestly."[9]

Moreover, Wiesel believes that literary works must be aimed at improving the human condition; it is not enough to provide readers with pleasureful entertainment: "Remember that culture alone is not enough. Remember knowledge without morality is sterile."[10] In this respect, Wiesel continues the tradition of two of his preferred French authors, Albert Camus and André Malraux, both of whom viewed the upgrading of human values and esthetic standards as being consubstantial and mutually complementary.

But the writer must be committed to more than a merger between morality and artistic finish; it is imperative that he or she lead an exemplary personal life that sets the example others should emulate. The writer ought to be a *mensch*—in the Yiddish sense. A *mensch* is someone endowed with honesty, fairness, justice, integrity, respect for the sanctity of human life, and with compassion for the underdog. Such a writer was Samuel Beckett, one of those French-language writers Wiesel admired immensely and of whom he wrote: "In his presence one feels enriched, uplifted. For he is not just a great writer, he is also a great man."[11] Wiesel hoped that more writers would live a life similar to that of Beckett.

Wiesel believes that the well educated and cultured German Nazis could act as killers in the Holocaust precisely because their education and literary culture reflected little more than the values held by their esthetic and intellectually gifted individuals who could also possess barbaric instincts and thus seek the destruction of other fellow men and women. In such an environment art became little more than an attractive patina devoid of human values. In the following statement, Wiesel justifies his conviction that art and morality belong together:

> Some of the killers, to our great shame, had degrees in philosophy, sociology, biology, medicine, psychiatry, and the fine arts. There were even jurists among them and—may God have mercy upon us—theologians. Products of old European culture, theirs was a culture which proved to be a thin veneer . . . It became clear that the degradation of the individual is unrelated to his cultural or social background. One can shoot at living targets and nonetheless appreciate the cadence of a poem, the composition of a painting . . . Ah, if only the killers had been savage brutes, lunatics, unhinged sadists . . . but they were not . . . While innumerable victims toppled into the pits and the flames, the princes of culture discussed culture.[12]

Literature soars far beyond the frontiers of pure art; it really captures the totality of human existence. It encompasses all sorts of human experiences: history, religion, jurisprudence, ethics, politics. Literature becomes an all-inclusive interdisciplinary domain, the ultimate objective of which is the advancement of justice and the improvement of the quality of human life. Alexander Solszenitsin, another one of Wiesel's ideal writers, exemplifies what, in his view, an author ought to be. Even though the Jewish writer laments that Solszenitsin neglected in his depiction of life in the former Soviet Union the plight of Jews there, at least the Russian writer was "a conscience, a man obsessed with justice and truth, a missionary who took seriously his spoken word, a messenger who expressed himself in the name of countless victims that the official executioner had rendered mute."[13]

Saint Cheron, one of the most perceptive authorities of Elie Wiesel's work characterized the writer's literature as "so much more than a literary oeuvre." Saint Cheron contends that "it was situated within the domain of a spiritual overture."[14] This seems to be the case since whenever a new Wieselean book appears on the market, it is treated by the reviewers as much more than a literary event; it is also, even mainly, a human and spiritual experience. Estess, for his part, lists three interrelated aspects in Wiesel's works: ethical, esthetic, and religious, adding that "Wiesel rejects the idea of the pure life. For him, art and life are dramas of good and evil, of time and eternity, of history and imagination."[15]

Although Wiesel provides us with lavish quantities of comments on his own conception of literary art, he does not as a rule make theoretical and generic statements concerning the writing professional in general. Wiesel does not like to pontificate, to enunciate broad theories and rules. It would be pretentious for him to assume the role of a Boileau-like formulator of literary law. Instead he prefers to delineate his own personal notions of his own literary art and his own craft of writing. Brigitte-Fanny Cohen calls him "more of a story-teller than a theoretician." Concurring with this modest appellation, he declared that "I distrust theories. Perhaps there was a lack, in my education, of a certain intellectual discipline to have the capacity, or to experience the need to elaborate on theories. Whatever the case, I have always preferred stories."[16] Imbued with such Judaic texts as the *Haggadah,* the sacred text recited by Jews during the Passover seder (Wiesel has even edited his own version of this work), he believes that the role of literature is almost synonymous with the art of storytelling. By his own admission, "it behooves us not to judge; only to relate stories."[17]

In so many respects, the author of *Souls on Fire* is not unlike the vagabond storytellers, beggars, and madmen who visited Sighet and the other small towns in eastern and central Europe during his boyhood days, entertaining their enthralled audiences with their tales about episodes from the Talmud and other works of Judaic folklore. Wiesel confesses his affinity for these roving bards:

> I am a teller of tales. The only claim I make for myself. Therefore, I feel close to the *maggidim,* those anonymous wandering preachers and storytellers who went from town to town, from village to village, telling tales—always the same and never the same—thus creating links between people and communities, Jews and their destinies, sometimes embodying their very destinies.[18]

Much more than an entertainer, the storyteller was also a vital link who brought together communities, people, and diverse publics from many countries in Europe. His stories served as messages flowing from storyteller to listener, from one venue to another, from one moment in time to another. Thus, through the *maggid*'s stories, past, present, and future merged into each other, national boundaries evaporated, one social class coalesced with another, and authors and readers were bonded together into a unified continental community. Sighet, Vilna, Jerusalem, New York, Paris, Riga, Minsk, hamlets and cities, large and small, throughout the world coalesced into an entity that one may label "the Jewish world."

Literature thus has the magical power of cementing factions of humanity into a common family. Wiesel once wrote that "The storyteller brings people and words together. The aim of every book, of every tale is to initiate as many encounters on as many levels as possible: between writer and reader, speaker and listener, fact and fiction, imagination and reality, present and past."[19] In this community the listener and the reader play as active a role as the storyteller. The words in the story serve as a crossroads at which the one who creates meets the one who reads or listens. The text (oral or printed) serves as a verbal tapestry within which an indivisible bond is formed between the originator and the recipient of the work(s) in question: "If a teller tells you tales, listen to them. . . . When one tells a tale, one relives it. One does not talk to the listener. One talks *with* [emphasis mine] the listener. To listen is as important as to talk, sometimes more so."[20] This interactive relationship between teller and listener constitutes what Wiesel believes to be the literary experience.

Through his tales, the storyteller may help to ameliorate the human condition. In his tales the narrator illustrates some of the human follies to be avoided and some of the positive virtues that one may desire to emulate. Narrated language often possesses a corrective, a curative power. In his effort to improve the human lot, Wiesel wrote that "My goal in my storytelling is to make Jews better Jews, Christians better Christians, and men a little bit warmer so they will not feel crushed by their solitude."[21]

Through storytelling, Wiesel hopes to unite people, places, and time; he hopes also to elevate the quality of life for all who will take the time to read his texts. But there exists yet another dimension in storytelling: by writing stories, the author delves deeply into the experiences of his life, selecting those events worthy of sharing with others. This involves the participation of memory. Memory is the writer's tool for combating the all-too-human tendency to forget the past. Through memory people resist the erosive forces of the present moment, forces that disintegrate the threads of the past. Once the reader or listener has been exposed to the author's tale (his memory), that reader or listener has the potential of becoming a storyteller: He or she may choose to prolong the memory of the original writer by retelling it to future generations.

In perpetuating themselves from generation to generation, the original tales assume the characteristics of a myth. Through his text the writer thus transmits his memory into eras of human history yet to unfurl. Once a writer has produced a text that lives beyond the duration of his existence, the mission of that writer has been accomplished. Wiesel knows that a well-written, successful text has the capability of prolonging his personal past (his memory) well beyond the natural limits of his span of personal existence. This is what he seemed to be suggesting when he wrote that, "I have no message—only tales. Some are nostalgic; others call for exaltation . . . Yet I claim them all as mine. I choose them retroactively, so as to speak, as being part of my memory, which is my entire being, which is what I am."[22]

Wiesel, like most literary artists, is aware that he needs a reading public if he is to survive for any length of time. Unless he can attract interested readers to read his texts, these texts will be doomed to extinction. As they evaporate into oblivion, for lack of a public, the writer's memories will perish with them. Without an appreciative audience, the writer and his message have no afterlife. But a reading audience plays more than the role of prolonging the writer's memory. Once a number of individual readers form an audience, each person lends to the text a personal interpretation. As these interpretations multiply, the literary text assumes new dimensions of meaning, even multiple meanings, the net result of which is that the original text will have a rich afterlife. The moment this cumulative afterlife radiates in many directions, affecting additional people and new generations, the original text has the power of exerting much impact on the world. This is what Wiesel seems to have had in mind when he wrote that "A book that is being read gets something from the reader. That is the mystical quality of art, of literature, and of history."[23]

In addition to serving as a medium by which the author transmits a part of himself or herself to others; it is also a chronicle, a compilation of memory, a record of history. In French, his adopted language, the term "histoire" means both a story and a history. In fact, Wiesel once defined the writer as a historian: "What is a writer? A writer is a messenger, a messenger between the reader and his theme, between word and word, between one era and another. A writer is, therefore, a historian."[24]

Within a writer's oeuvre, the professional critics can almost always identify a set of recurrent themes, settings, references, and character-types. During the course of a lifetime, a prolific author may produce as many as a hundred different books, but within the range of those volumes one generally finds only a handful of dominant and recurrent themes. It is this particular menu of themes that distinguishes the writer's works from those of others. Elie Wiesel is no exception. The more familiar we become with his books, the more we realize that, despite the vast quantity of titles, they represent variations of the same few themes that have always haunted Wiesel's soul. There are limits to a writer's imagination. There also limits to the range of experiences in a writer's life. Wiesel is open to criticism—and occasionally he has been criticized—for having created a relatively restricted variety of character-types and for the fairly small number of themes in his novels. In some ways, his novels seem to be built around the Holocaust, how it affected one of its witnesses (himself), how survivors of the Holocaust rebuilt their lives, and how the children of these survivors were shaped by the memories of the Holocaust transmitted to them by their parents. Also, Wiesel has not been able or willing to create especially important feminine characters. All of this is true, to a degree. With predictable regularity, Wiesel's readers return to the Holocaust, to the survivors and their offspring, to the author's dream of lost childhood, to the question of indifference to evil, to his love of the State of Israel, the City of Jerusalem, and the Jewish people, and to his call for human solidarity. Repeatedly, faithful Wiesel readers encounter the same cast of characters: the madman, the storytellers, the Hasidic and Biblical figures.

Wiesel calls his personal arsenal of themes and characters "obsessions." Without them, his writing might lose its uniqueness; it might even seem shallow. These obsessions ought to be viewed as the building blocks of his craft, the girders that hold it all together. He admitted that "Literature to me is a sum of obsessions. If you are not obsessed with your own topic and with your own characters you cannot write. I believe writing is a kind of fanatical commitment."[25] A propos of his play, *Zalmen or the Madness of God*, he expressed the same idea, but in slightly different words: "The play is a tale. Like most of my tales, it deals with certain of my obsessions. Literature is an accumulation of obsessions. And mine are madness, fear, silence, solidarity, or lack of solidarity."[26] That his books are constructed around a limited number of themes and character-types is a fact that he is not ashamed to acknowledge: "one encounters a *hasid* in all of my novels. And a child. And an old man. And a beggar. And a madman. They are a part of my inner landscape."[27] This "inner landscape" shapes the contours of the Wieselean literary universe. But he is scarcely different from other writers, each of whom has tried to create a personal "comédie humaine," in the Balsacian sense of the term, a human comedy with a special collection of characters, settings, situations, and themes. Almost all writers possess their special world. In this world one finds a web of intertwining themes, venues, personalities, prevailing moods. From this web, there leaps forth a kind of mythology. This was Wiesel's point when he wrote that "Every writer tries to create a universe of his own . . . permeated with myths and symbols and forces, so of course I have a mythology; the same people reoccur in all of my books. The same tale is being told in different spheres."[28] Using this "tale" as a basic tool with which to explore his inner life, he believed that through literary creation he could reach self-understanding. Introspectively he could penetrate deeply into his soul. In a revealing statement on the subject of the purpose of literature, a statement inserted in the recently published second volume of his *Mémoires*, he confesses that "I still have so many stories to tell, so many subjects to explore, so many characters to invent or to reveal. It's always the same anguish that torments me: in spite of the books that I have written, I haven't yet begun. But then, why did I write them? To understand as much as to make myself understood."[29] At the outset of his career he had also mentioned literature as a means of self-understanding: "I do not believe in catharsis. Catharsis is much too easy. I believe in inner exploration—to explore your own inner universe. Every writer has only one universe. He should not have more. I do not want to get relief from this universe. On the contrary, I want to explore it . . . What you need is your own garden, your own room, your own city; it is always the same world you write about."[30]

Who are the people who populate Wiesel's special world of characters? It was natural for him to create types whom he knew most intimately and/or with whom he could empathize. He preferred underdogs and victims, people like those innocent souls rounded up by the Nazis or packed tightly in cattle cars, starving people struggling to survive in the death camps. For these meek souls Wiesel became the spokesperson: "I distrust those who win, I love those who lose."[31] He holds a predilection for children. In the heartless world in which he spent the most unforgettable years of his life, he learned that it was the children who suffered the most. Along with children we find in his novels the ailing elderly, many of whose spirits have been frayed by their dismal days in the Holocaust. By juxtaposing young and old, Wiesel dramatizes the unremitting flow of time, from generation to generation.

While many women populate Wiesel's literary universe, few stand out in bold, three-dimensional relief. To date, Wiesel has not been successful at creating unforgettable, impressive feminine characters. His most memorable creations are his male figures. When one of his most avid readers confronted him with this fact, he admitted that, in effect, his strongest figures were men. But he offered a credible explanation, stating that he had grown up and was educated in a largely masculine world, that of the *heder*. In the concentration camps, men were segregated from women, and he lived necessarily in men's barracks. His mother and sisters had been separated from him at the very outset of his imprisonment in Auschwitz. When finally he got married, he was already forty-one years old. In his memoirs he confesses to a sense of insecurity or shyness with women throughout his life. With his greater familiarity with male characters, he felt more comfortable depicting them in his novels than women. Nevertheless, most of his novels do contain episodic references to amorous relationships between his male protagonists and various lady friends. To correct this imbalance, Wiesel assures us that in the future, he hopes to create feminine personalities who will play more central roles in his novels.[32]

In many respects, the texts of Elie Wiesel resemble musical compositions. They seem to be constructed around themes and variations of these themes. Those who study closely the structure in his books will almost certainly be impressed with the musical quality that floats throughout most of them. Acknowledging this musicality, Wiesel refers to his texts as songs: "If I have attempted to do something with my words, it is to make them sing, and with them to make you dream, and that is all."[33]

Wiesel-watchers know that this author has always been strongly attracted to music. This predilection seems to have originated in the *heder* where as a child he initially learned to chant the ancient Hebraic prayers and the hymns interpreted by the synagogue cantor. After his release from the camps, he found himself in Paris earning his livelihood by leading a religious choir in singing Jewish songs and *nigunds* (Jewish melodies). Even Gabrielle Cohen, a witness of the early years in Wiesel's career, attests to his talent for music.[34] Fifty years after the camps, whenever he is alone he amuses himself by humming ancient Jewish tunes and by chanting prayers of worship. So it is unsurprising that music spills over into the composition of his literary works. For him a piece of writing is little more than a textual expression of some deeply rooted melody buried inside of his soul. As the melody exteriorizes itself, it helps shape the contours of his written text. This is what he means when he states that "literature is not words but a voice, a melody. If you do not have your melody, you may have ten books, but not literature."[35] Through music Wiesel comes close to transforming his prose into poetry; for what is poetry if not a kind of musical version of language? Like music, Wiesel's texts are marred by rhythmic and sonorous effects, melodic cadences, and haunting themes (themes not unlike the leitmotifs found in certain operatic works).

In addition to the musicality in his work, Wiesel has injected into his sentences the elements of prayer—poetic prayer. Whole pages of his prose read and sound like poetry, or rather like liturgical chanting or musical prayer. One is tempted to draw parallels between Wiesel's approach to writing and the thinking of the eminent French-Catholic literary critic, Abbé Bremond, whose well-known book *De la prière à la poésie* [From Prayer to Poetry] makes a point of stressing the intimate rapports between prayer and poetry. Whereas for Bremond poetry issues out of prayer, for Wiesel, prayer grows out of poetry. It is not impossible that Wiesel came into contact with Bremond's theories during his Paris period. Friedlander noted this phenomenon in Wiesel when he wrote that "Poetry [in Wiesel's prose] becomes prayer and fiction becomes fact."[36] Wiesel himself believes in the indivisibility of prayer and literature:

11: WHAT IS LITERATURE?

> Between prayer and literature, between the creative act and the act of accepting, there exists then a most apparent link. Prayer and literature, both of them, take hold of daily words, and bestow upon both of them a different sense; both call out to that which in the human being is the most personal and the most elevated of his needs. And both are enrooted in the most obscure and mysterious zone of our being. . . . The writer and the religious man dig into the same collective source, that is to say, there where sound becomes language, and language becomes prayer, and prayer changes into offertory.[37]

As in the case of Jewish liturgy, the most felicitous pages of Elie Wiesel are a convincing manifestation of the true convergence among poetry, music, prayer and prose. In this convergence one senses something of the synagogue service itself. One almost hears there the chant of the cantor, the prayers sung by the congregants, and the entreaties of the rabbinical leader.

For the author of *Célébration hassidique*, poetry and Judaism come close to becoming a single entity. Unsurprisingly, he wrote that "To be Jewish means to be a poet. There is poetry in Jewish existence, and we are commanded to see its Jewish dimension. We are to write it down in order to share it with as many people as possible; every Jew is commanded to read the Torah, to write it, and thus to transmit it."[38] In at least one respect, one may read texts by Wiesel as one reads from the scrolls of the Torah: Just as the Torah may be regarded as a history of the ongoing heritage of the Jewish people, Wiesel's books add to this history by describing the drama of the Jewish experience during the period of the Holocaust. To the chain of texts in Jewish history then, one day researchers may wish to add some of the finest texts by Wiesel—for they represent the annals of the middle decades and the second half of our century. Thus Wiesel's literary work has the potential of becoming one of the links in the ever vibrant flow of Jewish history.

Whenever a new book by Wiesel appears, critics do not deal with it with levity. They understand that a Wiesel work merits serious attention. Nor does Wiesel himself treat his writings with levity. We have already pointed out that *La Nuit* appeared only after a ten-year period of gestation. Writing has never been an easy task for this author. On the contrary he reveals that it has always been an arduous, almost breathtaking labor for him, requiring his most penetrating attention, his most undivided concentration. Whenever words flow too easily from his pen, he becomes suspicious and rereads his text several times with almost painful self-criticism. Wiesel has always feared facility.

When he first arrived in Paris in 1945, Wiesel developed an intimate familiarity with seventeenth-century French classicism. From the Classical tradition he learned the virtues of writing with clarity, precision, and conciseness. He learned too that it was important to say as much as possible in the fewest number of words possible. Since the days when François Mauriac recommended to him that he reduce an eight-hundred page manuscript to scarcely a fifth of its original size, Wiesel has championed the art of reductionism or minimalism. During his compositional stages, he devotes enormous amounts of time to the elimination from his text of unnecessary verbiage and superfluous imagery. He tries always to simplify and reduce complex and lengthy sentences. Despite his Jewish/Hungarian/Rumanian background, he has become thoroughly imbued with the French Classical models of Racine, Boileau, Corneille, La Fontaine, and Molière. Most of his novels and stories are quite brief, even when the message there is dense.

For Wiesel the art of writing resembles the art of sculpture. Like the sculptor, he generally begins his creative process with a large mass of content. Then, like the sculptor, he spends much of his time feverishly chiseling away the excessive material. What remains is the skeletal essential. Thus he differs from the painter whose work most often consists of adding layers of color and detail to the layers of paint already on the canvas. Wiesel described his sculptural process like this:

> How does one write? *Night,* my first tale, had eight hundred pages in the beginning. But then I felt this theme required a certain attitude. I did not want to paint a picture on the canvas but to carve a sculpture on stone. I wanted to work in depth, not horizontally. Therefore I cut it down to a hundred and sixty pages. I cannot write differently. To bring back a certain fragment of the truth the writer becomes responsible not only for the words but for the white space between the words, not only for the language but also for the silence. Therefore, the less you write, the more true the message. . . . One useless word and the whole structure falls apart and becomes a lie.[39]

From eight hundred pages to a hundred and sixty pages! This process of reductionism has become the guiding principle in Wiesel's writing methodology. Part of his success derives from his deliberate elimination of verbiage, and his frequent use of silence and ellipses to replace the language already eliminated. By using that which is unsaid he can hint at or suggest much that is pregnant with meaning. As for the words that he considers to be indispensable within the space of his silence, his aim is to make them as electrically charged as possible.

Another salient trait in his literary art is his manner of opening and closing his works. He believes that the first and last sentences ought to be the most vital portion of the text. With his initial sentence he tries to capture the attention of the reader and establish the mood for the rest of the text. With the final sentence he wishes to create a lingering impression, one that will endure in the reader's mind for a long time and will bring dramatic closure to the work. Wiesel wrote that "But the beginning and the end—that is very important, because the first page must catch your attention, and the last page must hold it together, after you have left."[40]

Writing books has always been an exhausting and intensive experience for him. Laboriously he produces at least three drafts for each of his books. With each rereading, he suppresses what he regards as excessive sentimentality and wording. His goal is to write with straightforwardness, directness, and with a certain degree of austerity. Following is his revelation of this method:

> I write every book three times. The first draft is handwritten. The second and third I type myself. I always say, "If I take this chapter out, will there still be a book? Will the chapter still be a chapter, if I take this out? The main thing is never to fall into sentimentality or mellowness. Writing must be stark, austere.[41]

"Stark, austere"—these are the adjectives that best denote how he views his own literary style.

Although his objective is to construct an art that is at once minimalist and devoid of decorativeness, his style is far from being dry or bland. On the contrary, whenever he wishes to stimulate more intensively the interest of his readers, he indulges in word-play, paradoxical images, alliterations and musical references. The following samples illustrate his stylistic "tricks." (Because I am discussing style here, I prefer to cite the original French, to which I add my own translations in English.) In the first sample, Wiesel creates word-play by interchanging "victims" and "Jews:"

> En racontant le martyre de mon peuple, j'évoque la souffrance de tous les peuples privés de liberté en Europe occupée. Je l'ai dit, je le répète:

toutes les victimes n'étaient pas juives, mais tous les juifs étaient victimes, tous étaient destinés à l'anéantissement.

[In relating the martyrdom of my people, I evoke the suffering of all the peoples deprived of freedom in occupied Europe. I have stated it, I repeat it: All the victims were not Jews, but all the Jews were victims, all were destined for extinction.] [42]

In the next example, he defines the word "exile" by moving in gradations of reductionism, starting with the broad space of "country," then comes the narrower space of "train," and eventually the abstract notion of "exile."

La guerre est l'exil et surtout notre guerre, je veux dire la guerre contre les Juifs. C'était l'exil ultime, parce qu'il y eut un processus de réduction. Le pays est devenu une ville, la ville est devenue une rue, la rue est devenue une maison, la maison un abri, l'abri un train et puis plus rien . . . la fumée. C'est cela l'exil.

[War is exile and especially our war, I mean the war against the Jews. It was the ultimate exile, because there was a process of reduction. The country became a city, the city became a street, the street became a house, the house a shelter, the shelter a train and then nothing more . . . smoke. That is what exile is.] [43]

In the last sample we note more than simple word play; one also senses how Wiesel creates a growing sense of terror, doom, and panic as the Nazis close in on their prey.

Purposefully Wiesel selects simple, everyday language into which he injects a special electrical charge that issues from his strongly felt personal sentiments. Placed side by side with each other, these otherwise commonplace terms assume a certain incandescence that ignites what would otherwise be standard prose, transforming it into poetry. This verbal alchemy converts ordinary language into poetic sparks. Wiesel describes his process as follows: "What is a writer? I take words from everywhere, your words, my words, we all have the same source, and I simply put them together. Then I try to send a certain current, a certain electric current through them."[44] In similar vein, he stresses the poetry in his prose: "What is art, after all? Art is tension, ambiguity, telling and not telling. When a thousand words are pressed into a single line, a poem is born."[45]

During the creative process, writers naturally wonder about the kind of reception their finished product (the book) will receive on the part of the critics, and how their work will affect the public for

11: WHAT IS LITERATURE?

which it was intended. A writer's readership generally consists of two principal clienteles: the professional reviewers or specialists, and also the public-at-large that reads mainly for personal pleasure or intellectual edification. During his process of writing and rewriting, Wiesel must surely reflect upon the reactions his future text will provoke. Overtly Wiesel (like so many writers) claims that he remains indifferent to the kind of reception his readers will give his latest title. It is impossible to ascertain the extent to which he really is indifferent to public response, his disclaimers notwithstanding. When asked about his interest in knowing how his audience might react to an as-yet-unpublished work, he replied that "I couldn't care less, when the work is true and is what I want to say. I do not try to please the reader . . . I write for the dead."[46] Always he insists that the primary purpose of his writing is to preserve the memory of the departed victims. He also claims that he assiduously avoids reading reviews and critiques by the professional critics out of fear of contamination by their judgments. Convinced that a writer must listen only to the voice of his inner self, he confided that "I don't read the reviews. I made it a point when I began writing not to read many reviews. Once you give in to that weakness, you are so vulnerable that you will be stopped, you will be paralyzed. So I don't hear, I don't listen. Those whose judgment I respect are almost invisible people, or sometimes dead people. I write for them, and I hear them."[47]

The number of readers matters less to Wiesel than the quality of those who read him. Directing his texts to those who may be most sensitive or responsive to his special message, he always hopes that his readers will be open-minded enough to permit his words to enrich their view of the world. Paraphrasing the poet, Paul Valéry, he averred that "Rather than to be read by a thousand people, I wish to be read by one person a thousand times."[48]

If Wiesel claims that he places relatively little stock in the verdicts of the professional critics, many newspapers and publishers continuously besiege him with requests for reviews of the works of other writers. Here he admits to a bias in favor or writing positive critiques and a reluctance to write destructive evaluations of someone else's works. Systematically Wiesel restricts his critical efforts to reviews of books that he can praise, in all sincerity. But he refuses to comment upon books that he would feel compelled to disparage. Here is his blunt statement on his personal policy of critiquing other authors: "If I cannot be elogious about them, I keep quiet."[49]

One of the rare occasions when Wiesel voiced a harshly negative judgment was after the presentation of the NBC mini-series "The

Holocaust;" there he opined that NBC, despite its good intentions, had really trivialized, even distorted the most tragic moment in human history.[50] Also, in his memoirs, he reveals some fairly negative views concerning two or three authors with whom he had engaged in some fairly stressful relationships. Even there it is not their publications that he finds offensive but rather their personal dealings with him. Especially does Wiesel praise those writers who contributed to the formation of his own philosophy of literature. In his responses to several provocative questions posed by Saint Cheron, Wiesel identifies those writers who played the most pivotal role in helping him to shape his own literary views: Dostoievski, Kafka, Mann, Malraux, Mauriac, Camus, Unamuno, Bernanos, the Hebrew Bible, the Babylonian Talmud, Maimonides, Saul Lieberman, Levinas, and even the anti-Semitic novelist, Céline.[51]

Why does someone like Elie Wiesel decide to become a literary artist, one who hopes that he will continue in the tradition of Camus, Malraux, and Kafka? To respond to such a question, we must first understand the connections between Elie Wiesel the human being and Elie Wiesel the professional writer. First, he feels driven to write because he has never been able to rid himself of the obsessive nightmare of the Holocaust. This riveting experience underlies all that he has written, even when his subject is not ostensibly linked to the Shoah. Through his writing Wiesel hopes to understand the motives of the killers and the responses of the victims to their unjust treatment. He tries to understand how human beings can inflict such unprecedented pain upon other human beings. Additionally, by writing texts he aspires to honor the memory of the dead and to describe how they were able to confront the nightmare of their existence before their death.

Wiesel is not content to remain within the declarative and narrative mode. Incessantly he asks questions. Why did the Holocaust take place? How could it have taken place? Why did he and a few others survive, while so many others perished? What were the reasons behind the German genocidal behavior? Why the Germans? Why the Jews? Why were most of the others so indifferent? Why do seemingly rational people indulge in irrationality? Where was God? In short, Wiesel's literature came into fruition largely out of an unquenchable thirst by a survivor for answers to some compelling, troubling questions.

Wiesel also writes because he yearns for that golden childhood that vanished in the smoke of the Holocaust. By writing about his early years, he seeks to reconstruct the happiest moments of his life. He writes too because he wishes to perpetuate the memory of his slain parents and his beloved youngest sister. In a word, he composes literature because he hopes through his texts to persuade humanity to live a better, more humane life.

Brigitte-Fanny Cohen has distilled the hundreds, if not thousands, of questions posed by Wiesel in his cumulative writings and divided them into the following four categories:

1. How could a civilized and advanced nation like Germany seek the extermination of a whole people?
2. How can one possibly explain the silence of the entire world while such a heinous act was taking place?
3. How can human beings still believe in God after Auschwitz, and how can they not believe in God?
4. How can human beings continue to believe in mankind, and how is it possible to build a better world upon the ashes of the Holocaust?[52]

In her four categories, Cohen is surely on target for she seems to have covered the entire expanse of Wiesel's endless flow of interrogations.

Wiesel's primary purpose in writing books is to raise vital questions. His second purpose is to protest against the brutalities and injustices rampant throughout the world. By protesting against injustice, he hopes to appeal to that part of the human conscience that instinctively rejects barbarism, cruelty, and hate. Although during the more than five decades since the closing of the death camps, the world contains lingering vestiges of Nazism, ethnic hatred, discrimination, and prejudice, he refuses to yield to despair. In effect, his literary activities have become a source of comfort for him, shielding him from despondency and cynicism. Literature thus provides for him a defense mechanism against absolute pessimism.

In the final analysis, Elie Wiesel believes that the underlying raison d'être for literature is self-knowledge, self-understanding. For him literature leads him towards a fuller and more accurate appreciation of the person he had been in the past, the person he really is today, and the person he will become in the days ahead. Through writing Wiesel hopes to discover the revelation of his innermost soul: "A mystery?" he writes, "Really for an artist, for a writer, for a creator, there is nothing more mysterious than the very moment when something, inside of himself or herself, begins to express itself, to reveal itself, in painting as well as in music or in language."[53]

Despite his celebration of literary art, Wiesel sees certain limitations in literary creativity. In reality, the writer cannot fully create anything out of a void. His powers of creativity are severely limited. Literary creation is only a form of re-creativity. A religious Jew, Elie Wiesel maintains that only God the Creator of the universe holds the power to create something out of a vacuum. In Wiesel's eyes, the writer merely transforms into artistic form that which he already witnessed. The writer's language is little more than a document or a record of an event, an experience that needs to be preserved. The author of *Night* best sums up his purpose as a literary artist in the following passage:

> My purpose and aspirations as a writer are not to build but to try to rebuild a vanished universe [Sighet, youth, the Holocaust, etc.]; instead of creating characters and situations, I try to re-create them book by book, story by story, tale by tale—be they Biblical, Talmudic, Hasidic, or modern. My goal is always the same; to bring back, at least for a while, some of the men and women the killers robbed of their lives and their names. My goal is always the same: to invoke the past as a shield for the future; to show the invisible world of yesterday and through it, perhaps on it to erect a moral world where men and women are not victims and children never starve or run in fear.[54]

Literature, specifically Wiesel's literature, can be likened to a Kaddish chanted by himself and subsequently by his readers in which are memorialized the six million who perished in the Holocaust as well as those who died in the other criminal events of our century. But Wiesel's literature, like the original Kaddish in the Hebrew prayer service, is more than a memorial prayer in honor of the dead. It is also the glorification, the exaltation of the Almighty. Thus, in its most poignant passages, Wieselean literature contains inside of its soul an impressive measure of religious fervor.

12
A Portrait of the Writer as Teacher and Scholar

VISIT WIESEL'S SPACIOUS APARTMENT IN A MODERN HIGH-RISE TOWER on Manhattan's upper East Side. Instantly you find yourself engulfed by books staring at you from all directions. Most often your host will invite you to install yourself in a comfortable contemporary sofa in his crammed library where you will be surrounded by floor-to-ceiling bookcases, overflowing with volumes of all sizes and in many languages. Books lie on the floor. Others are stacked up on the desk. Elie Wiesel is someone who lives inside of a vortex of books—those that he has written, those written by other authors that he is reading, has read, or will read, and those that he is in the process of composing.

Books have always been the sine qua non of Elie Wiesel's life as a writer, speaker, and teacher. Books are his tools of research and his source for ideas. Like all serious teachers, Wiesel continues to regard himself as a lifelong student. More than a student, he is also a scholar, in the fullest sense of the term. Extensive portions of his daily schedule are devoted to his serious, dedicated, and voracious study and reading of texts, his own and those of other writers.

Wiesel has always viewed life with the attitude of a scholar. He has always studied both sacred and secular texts. He enjoys working in archival collections of libraries. Without this reverence for learning, he would probably not have been able to compose works like *Célébration hassidique* and *Célébration talmudique*. In his love for books Wiesel incarnates a certain spirit of Judaism. Jews like to call themselves the people of the book. They often exhort each other that "Thou shalt teach thy children?"! And Wiesel reminds us that Judaism could not have survived for thousands of years of perilous existence were it not for the fact that Jews have never ceased to study the Torah and all of the other holy texts of their faith. It is the adoration of texts that has given Jews the courage to resist the many attempts by non-Jews to eradicate their religious traditions. Whenever Jews accidentally drop their *siddurim* (prayer books), they instantly pick them up and kiss the binding. When the Torah is carried through the synagogue, the congregants rush forth to kiss the silken sheath covering it. When a Jewish book deteriorates after decades of use, it is sinful for Jews to discard or burn it; instead it is buried with the same solemnity manifest at the burial of a cherished human being. The most agonizing pain the Gentile community can inflict on Jews is to hold public book burnings of Jewish books and scrolls. The happiest memories in Wiesel's life, the memories that he recalls with the most pleasureful nostalgia are those of the time he spent studying in his boyhood *heder*. There he learned to read Biblical Hebrew and studied the appropriate texts as he prepared for his Bar Mitzvah. Even today he continues to reread many of these same literary passages. After his release from the death camps where books were not available for the prisoners to read, Wiesel rediscovered the joys of reading in postwar Paris. Elderly Parisians, who today still remember Wiesel as an undernourished, skeleton-like survivor of the concentration camp nightmare wondrously describes his enthusiasm for both the traditional Hebrew texts and the newly discovered French books that he devoured enthusiastically once he could read the language of Molière and Racine. This boundless love affair with books colors much of the author's life even today.

For the teacher the first objective in professional life is to impart knowledge to disciples. But the genuine teacher also realizes that no accumulation of knowledge, no matter how intensive or comprehensive, is ever complete. In every discipline the scope of knowledge continues to expand at varying degrees of speed and in differing quantities. The seasoned teacher is thus resigned to accept the fact that he or she will always have to pose questions for which there are often no easy answers. Wiesel is the first to acknowledge that neither he nor any other mortal can unravel every mystery in life. Teachers are doomed to acquire only a partial knowledge of all that remains to be learned in a given field. All mortals always yearn for omniscience; none obtains it. This being the case, Wiesel stresses that teachers have no choice but to continue indefatigably to search for additional information and to go on endlessly to learn from others and to pose questions that hopefully will bring them new knowledge. For Wiesel, to teach, to be a scholar, signifies that one must be always engaged in asking questions.

All of Wiesel's books are saturated with rhetorical questions. His literary style distinguishes him from many authors by the quantity of questions, riddles, and dilemmas that permeate his texts. Aware that this is one of the salient traits of his writing, he wrote: ". . . do not believe anyone who tells you he has the answers to the questions. There are no answers to true questions. There are only good questions, sometimes painful, sometimes exuberant. All I have learned in my life is questions . . ."[1]

In Wiesel's view, being Jewish means to live with an unending fascination with questions: "Well I think that to be a Jew is not to give answers. To be a Jew is to ask questions and to live these questions. And the questions are tough, strong."[2] So many of Judaism's vital literary documents consist of efforts by the rabbis of old to formulate responses to the perplexing and eternal enigmas faced by the human race. As rabbis seek explanations they refer to the interpretations of other rabbis who preceded them. The rabbis of today interpret, confirm, reinforce, or contradict the earlier responses of their antecedents. This ongoing process of dealing with previous responses, often referred to as "responsa" in Judaism, underscores the complexity, indeed the drama of human existence. There exist no facile, glib solutions for the mysteries of human existence.

In *Célébration talmudique* Wiesel has compiled an anthological collection of legends and portraits of some of the early rabbis who lived, preached, and wrote during the first three centuries of the common era. He describes there the methodology used by these early scholars as they sought to penetrate the troubling dilemmas of man's life on this planet. Wiesel demonstrates how these rabbis often replied to the same question from three or more different, even sometimes contradictory, vantage points. The obvious message here is this: There are no simplistic, all-encompassing answers. Life is much too complex to be easily explained. Little in human existence is absolutely black or white, true or false, right or wrong. The genuine Jewish scholar is someone who never tires of searching for plausible explanations for ambiguous problems. In searching for answers and solutions, the scholar wades through ancient texts heavily laden with conflicting, vague, and hazy language. Allusions, paraphrases, and parenthetical statements must be deciphered, decoded, interpreted. Each of the multiple meanings of words must be analyzed with meticulous attention to detail. But there exists no other way of understanding the intricacies of these texts as they pass on to us from generation to generation.

Like the Talmudic scholars of the past, so lovingly described in

Célébration talmudique, Wiesel utilizes his own writing as an instrument by which he conducts his own meandering inquiries into the recondite crevices of human life. On the verge of clarifying some of the complexities, he lets himself to be drawn, almost irresistibly, into other inquiries of related topics, inquiries that lead him into more extended investigations and sometimes steer him into unpredictable directions. Estess emphasizes Wiesel's unending interrogations: "Wiesel's questioning is religious in the narrow sense that it asks about God, evil, suffering, and the future of Judaism. But it is religious in a broader sense as well, if by *religious* we mean 'asking passionately the meaning of our existence and being willing to receive answers . . . ' "[3]

In reality, even when the writer recounts his Hasidic or Talmudic tales, he implicitly encourages his readers to pose their own questions and to find their own answers in the unresolved dilemmas hinted at by Wiesel's legends and stories. The questions raised by this author are fundamental ones, dealing with some of the major concerns of life: the role or non-role of God in our daily existence; the meaning of interpersonal relationships; the impact of such behavioral patterns as tolerance, charity, love, prejudice, hatred, compassion, cruelty; the rapport between nations, religious groups, and ethnic populations; the purpose of life; the meaning of death; the need to remember; the difference between madness and sanity, right and wrong, morality and immorality. And, in fact, as Wiesel discusses these phenomena, we confront the principal themes both in his literature and in the courses he teaches at the University.

Obviously these topics do not lend themselves to glib responses. Some defy dispassionate discussion. Nonetheless, there is something of the spirit of the true teacher that seems to reside in Wiesel's breast, and it inspires him ever onward in his pursuit of solutions, no matter how elusive these solutions can be. Elie Wiesel has faith in the efficacy of the Socratic method of instructing students. Thus, as a writer and as a teacher, he endeavors to awaken in his disciples a heightened curiosity and to help them develop a more critical acumen in problem-solving. He knows too that by intensifying their curiosity for knowledge, they will move more closely towards the development of their own answers. Eventually they will come to understand that complex subject matter requires the investigation and analysis of the multilayered, variegated strata of often contradictory data.

For his students and readers his strategy of teaching at first may seem frustrating; people are seldom satisfied with anything less than comfortable, comforting, and lucid answers. It behooves us now to illustrate Wiesel's pedagogical methodology. First he challenges his readers or students to help him find answers to one of the troubling problems he would like to resolve: the Middle East tensions between Israel and the surrounding Arab peoples, for example. Here is the question Wiesel raises: How can the Palestinians be dissuaded from harboring animosity against the Israelis who had established their state in a land once belonging to these same Palestinians? Instead of answering his own question, he confesses that he too is baffled by this problem: "How does one survive this era of hatred? One must disarm this hatred. It is urgent that it be disarmed, but I do not know how."[4] Realizing that he has supplied no answer, he briskly shifts to another issue, leaving it up to his interlocutors to develop one or more responses to his question. But already Wiesel has sown seeds of doubt or curiosity that he hopes will help his students to search for solutions. Another example: On replying to his own question about whether God had abandoned the Jews during the Shoah, Wiesel declares that "there is no answer. It is very clear, for me the Shoah has no answer. There is no answer to Auschwitz. Whether it be theological or human, any answer is a bad answer."[5] In his response to another question raised by him concerning the meaning of death, he replies by posing yet another question: "Who am I to respond to this question?" Immediately afterwards, as Wiesel grapples with a way to formulate a satisfactory reply, he concludes that evasiveness is the only available remedy for a problem that cannot ever be resolved by the human intellect: "This question is so serious, so weighty . . . I must reflect upon it deeply, lengthily, for weeks and months, before being able to respond to it, otherwise it would be irresponsible on my part."[6]

Thus Wiesel's technique of teaching (both in his books and in the classroom) is to answer questions by asking more questions. The method is similar to that of most Talmudic scholars: To wit, they develop commentaries on other commentaries, leaving it up to still other specialists to make commentaries on their own commentaries on earlier commentaries. As all of these commentaries accumulate on top of each other, they blend together and gradually provide the information needed by people to come to grips with complicated questions. The methodology favored by Wiesel seems to imply that we can achieve clarity only after wading through layers of ambiguity.

In Wiesel's judgment, the pedagogue ought never to be embarrassed at being unable to formulate convincing answers. For some questions there are simply no answers. Nevertheless, even if the teacher cannot provide the answers, there is no reason why these questions should not be raised. To raise questions is for the author of *Night* a perfectly acceptable means of imparting knowledge. Of course, Wiesel did not originate this pedagogical approach. Others have used it for centuries after Socrates. The young Wiesel observed this approach in the *heder*, within his immediate family, and in the synagogue. In several of his texts the writer expresses his indebtedness to all those who had taught him, that is to say, the very people who became his spiritual and intellectual guides during his journey through life.

Wiesel opens *Célébration talmudique* with a statement identifying those who played dominant roles in his educational and moral background. First, he lists several unnamed teachers and tutors of Sighet who first exposed him to the sacred pages of Jewish scriptures. After his liberation from the camps, he met in Paris Rav Mordechai Shoshani who exposed him to the magical universe of the Talmud. Later, in New York, he fell under the spell of Rabbi Saul Lieberman who imbued him (even more profoundly than Shoshani) with the lessons in the Talmud. After Lieberman's death Wiesel pursued his studies with Haras Menashe Hakatan, a respected Hasid from Brooklyn, as well as with a childhood friend, David Weiss-Halivni of Columbia University, to whom he dedicated *Célébration talmudique*. This book may well be regarded as Wiesel's expression of appreciation for the masters who had helped fashion his philosophy of life.

What does Wiesel owe to his teachers? Here is how he explains this indebtedness: upon learning of the death of Rav Mordechai Shoshani of Paris, he wrote that "For three years, in Paris, I was his disciple. Alongside of him, I learned much concerning the perils of reason and language, concerning the ecstasies of the wise man and the madman, concerning the mysterious evolution of a thought through the centuries . . . The rapports between master and disciple are, on a certain level, more dramatic than those linking father and son. And certainly more complex."[7] In a somewhat longer statement Wiesel details his rapports with Shoshani:

> Also, my teacher after the tempest, in the postwar years, was Mordechai Shoshani . . . he was the man who made me become what I am, who left an imprint on my thought, on my feelings, on my language. I took him as a prototype for many of my messengers, for many of my teachers, in many

of my tales . . . he taught me philosophy . . . He prepared me for the Sorbonne. Whatever I knew, I got from him."[8]

Concerning Saul Lieberman, under whom Wiesel studied regularly in New York for seventeen years, he wrote an equally rapturous passage: "I think that he was the greatest Jewish learned man of these last centuries . . . All that I know, I owe him. Our rapports were not only rapports between master and disciple. We were close to each other. Since he had no child, he considered me to be his child."[9] Wiesel discloses that before sending any of his manuscripts to his French publisher, he would frequently encourage Lieberman to critique his work first. Interestingly, Wiesel always marveled at Lieberman's mastery of the French language. The author of *Night* even predicts, with a certain hyperbolic degree of modesty, that Lieberman's "works will remain long after mine are forgotten."[10] In a delightful, story-like vignette in the manner of the seventeenth-century writer of portraits La Bruyère, Wiesel paints a charming picture of one of the most fascinating teachers he had ever known, David Karliner, a man whom he admired above all for his fierce independence and his nonconformism. From Karliner he learned much about the miraculous survival of the Jewish people during their millennia of torment.[11] And how could Wiesel not also remember one of the great Jewish teachers of his lifetime, Abraham Heschel? Here is a capsulized comment on this celebrated teacher: "Common sense, a thirst for justice, a profound understanding: these are the traits that characterize Rabbi Abraham Yeoshoua Heschel."[12] The supreme lesson Heschel taught Wiesel was that mankind must never forget the ultimate sacrifice made by the six million Jews exterminated solely because they were Jews.

Wiesel speculates that the continuity of civilization depends more on the effectiveness of the educational process than on any other factor. Jewish life itself has always depended upon the interrelatedness of teaching and learning. The writer stresses that "The Jewish tradition is a tradition of learning. We are teachers because we are disciples. We are disciples because we know how to listen. We know how to accept. The knowledge of how to accept is as important as the knowledge of how to give."[13] What teachers of today have learned from teachers of yesteryear they communicate to their disciples who one day will become, in turn, the teachers of tomorrow. And so through this process of teaching/learning and learning/teaching, knowledge flows uninterruptedly from century to century, from parents to offspring, from teacher to disciple, from author to reader, from lecturer to listener. Elie Wiesel considers the educational regimen as the defining bond holding together the multiple components forming civilization.

To those about to graduate from their formal university education, the author once offered this advice:

> May I share with you one of the principles that govern my life? It is the realization that what I receive I must pass on to others. The knowledge that I must pass on to others. The knowledge that I have acquired must not remain imprisoned in my brain. I owe it to many men and women to do something with it, I feel the need to pay back what was given to me. Call it gratitude. Isn't this what education is all about?[14]

Periodically, Elie Wiesel the writer transforms himself into Elie Wiesel the teacher, who always behaves as Elie Wiesel the learner!

Familiar with the environment of the university campus, Wiesel has taught for years on at least two campuses. Currently holder of the Andrew Mellon Chair in the Humanities at Boston University, he had served previously as professor at the City University of New York's main campus. Recognizing his accomplishments as one of the distinguished teachers of our time, scores of universities around the world have bestowed upon him their honorary doctorates, not only because of his distinguished career as a teacher but also because of his remarkable achievement as a writer of international renown. At times the author prefers teaching over writing. With candor he avows that "There is something beautiful in teaching. Nothing is as uplifting to me as seeing some of my students grow, develop and ask the right kind of questions."[15]

Just as this author holds the conviction that there exists no great literature unless it is intimately linked to ethical values, he holds that there is no great teaching—particularly Jewish teaching—unless the teacher sets the highest moral example for his or her disciples:

> The difference between a Jewish teacher and a Hellenistic one was the matter of personal example. In Judaism, a teacher had to be the example of his teaching. Today, for instance, we say that literature excuses many things. We forgive Beethoven's foibles because he wrote such beautiful music; we close our eyes to Dostoievsky's anti-Semitism because of his great novels. But in Jewish tradition a man who is evil cannot be a teacher

> ... The purpose of knowledge in our tradition is not to humiliate but to lift up the listener, the student, the one who transmits.[16]

The celebration of the teacher—this theme constitutes one of the most prominent points of focus in all Wieselean literature. Throughout his writing Wiesel betrays his obsession with the educational process. Many of the characters in his novels and his stories are career teachers. Sometimes he disguises them as messengers who visit young people, beguiling their souls with the magic of their message. Sometimes Wiesel's teachers are masked as madmen who tell their entranced listeners that they must remember history, that they must remember not only the lofty achievements of humankind but also the rotting abysses of evil into which men and women have descended.

For Wiesel teachers are the buttresses linking past and present, present and future. They serve humanity as the agents who ensure the continuity of civilization. As a respected writer and teacher, Elie Wiesel has become one of today's most sought-after commencement speakers. In 1992 he told one of the graduating classes that "The books that I have read were composed by generations of fathers and sons, mothers and daughters, teachers and disciples. I am the sum total of their experiences, their guest. And so are you."[17] He knows that those who hear his many graduation addresses will one day become the leaders of tomorrow. That is why he almost always accepts invitations to speak to graduating seniors.

13

The French Connection

MANY INTERNATIONAL WRITERS HAVE ADOPTED FRENCH AS THEIR primary medium of literary expression. In the seventeenth and eighteenth centuries, when French was the lingua franca of the western world, foreign heads of state like Frederick the Great of Prussia, Catherine the Great of Russia, and monarchs of the Hapsburg Dynasty in the Austro-Hungarian Empire used French extensively, even in their daily lives. The German author Grimm corresponded with Diderot in French; the correspondence between Voltaire and the intellectual leaders of his age scattered around the world was all in French. American founding fathers Thomas Jefferson and Benjamin Franklin developed proficiency in French. Since the Middle Ages the City of Light has been a magnet for musicians, intellectuals, writers, and painters from throughout the western world. Mary Cassatt, James Whistler, Alexander Calder, Marc Chagall, Pablo Picasso, Joán Miro, Rubén Dario, Jorge Luis Borges, George Gershwin, Ernest Hemingway, F. Scott Fitzgerald, James Joyce, Frederic Chopin, Franz Liszt, Georges Enesco, Henry James, Gertrude Stein, Vincent Van Gogh, Pushkin, came to the French capital at an important moment in their lives and all, having fallen under the spell of the French cultural spirit there, were fluent in French. During the German occupation of France, many expatriates fled Paris and took their talents with them principally to New York City. However, since the end of World War II, Paris has regained much of her cultural glitter. The allure of this city is indeed noteworthy. Even in more recent times, Paris has attracted such well-known writers as Eugène Ionesco from Romania, Arthur Adamov from Russia, Samuel Beckett from Ireland, Julien Green from America, Fernando Arrabal from Spain. All did their best writing in French.

Elie Wiesel continues this remarkable tradition. His literary language of choice is French. But for him French is more than a literary

13: THE FRENCH CONNECTION

tool; it serves also as a medium for many of his daily relationships and activities.

It would be inaccurate to classify Wiesel as a purely French author; he is neither French by birth nor by citizenship; nor is he truly French in his outlook on life; nor is the French language his exclusive medium of expression. Although most of his books and many of his articles were originally written in French, he has also composed a few volumes and many articles in English, Yiddish, and Hebrew.

Wiesel is truly *the* archetypal example of cosmopolitanism in western civilization. Born in the Carpathian border region skirting Hungary, Romania, and the former Soviet Union, he has visited almost every corner of the earth. Although he lives in Manhattan, he feels equally at home in Paris and in Israel. During much of the Mitterrand presidency, he was a familiar habitué of the Elysée Palace, the official residence of French presidents. The President and writer maintained close relationships and even collaborated in a number of projects, including an international conference at the Elysée Palace at which most of the living Nobel laureates were brought together to discuss some of the capital problems of the world. However, Wiesel's friendship with Mitterrand came to an abrupt end, shortly before the latter's death. When the Jewish writer learned that Mitterrand had once worked with Nazi collaborators during the Occupation, especially with the accused collaborator René Bousquet, and when he discovered that the President had given speeches in Germany and Russia during which he appeared to have some admiration for Hitler's *Wehrmacht,* Wiesel asked his friend to make a public statement of regret for past mistakes, but the proud Mitterrand refused. This refusal caused the rupture of relations between the two. Despite this Wiesel, in his memoirs, following an old Talmudic dictum not to speak ill of a dead man, since death effaces all sins, decided in his public comment to express himself in the following diplomatic manner: "Mitterrand has left his mark on an era . . . Many praise his European spirit, others his political genius, still others will not forget his passion for the freedom of man."[1]

In response to a questioner who asked Elie Wiesel to identify his nationality, Wiesel emphasized the extent to which he believed himself to be a true cosmopolitan:

> Personally I consider myself at the same time a Jew and an American, and nonetheless I love Israel with all of my heart, and nonetheless I write in French. I am close to all of these countries. It is the Jew in me that is

American, it is the Jew in me who loves France and the Jew in me, who with all of his heart and all of his soul loves Israel. Perhaps at one time we needed to make these geographical choices. Today geography has disappeared.[2]

In the age of supersonic travel and state-of-the-art telecommunications it is of course much easier for a writer like Wiesel to adopt the attributes of world citizenry. His very existence is divided among three cities: New York, Paris, and Jerusalem. When prodded by another questioner to name which of these three cities he really preferred, he replied tactfully and somewhat evasively: "It depends for what. New York is the best place to work because the isolation in New York is better than anywhere else. Paris is good because it is beautiful and because you cannot work in Paris if you try. As for Israel, it responds to a need. I need to be there. Whenever I need to feel gratitude, I go to Israel."[3]

Some have referred to Wiesel as a citizen of the world. He has traveled so extensively and played such a visible role in so many places that this multinational label is understandable. Nonetheless, the term "citizen" suggests an affiliation with a political or geographical place and does not fully do justice to his worldwide span of activities. His place of birth on the Hungarian–Romanian border, his imprisonment in Poland, his post-war years in the Paris basin, his journalistic work in India, Israel, America, and elsewhere, his unending movement from locus to locus, all of these peripatetic sojourns make him seem more like a world-personality than a "citizen." When given the opportunity to move back to his hometown of Sighet, he could not go back to a place where the local residents refused, even symbolically, to help their Jewish neighbors at their supreme hour of need. Even in Paris, where he spent some ten years, he initially felt like a "stateless" person. At the time, he could not move to British-mandated Palestine since the hostile Arab residents there and the British authorities both did all they could to prevent Jews like him from emigrating to what was their traditional Jewish homeland. Eloquently he explains his feelings of stateless anguish in his memoirs, *Tous les fleuves vont à la mer*. Despite his residence in New York City, he spends part of the week in Boston and, in fact, because of his endless travels, he is absent from his home much of the time.

In Paris he did manage to develop some degree of "belonging" to a specific place. He gradually mastered French. He imbued himself with French culture, read assiduously countless texts from France's superb literary tradition. He made many lasting friendships in Paris. It was not until 1956 that he went to New York and—following a serious accident—decided to remain there on a more or less permanent basis. But he continued to be employed during his early New York days by an Israeli paper and flew to Tel Aviv on a fairly regular basis. That is why it is so difficult to classify Wiesel within a single nationality.

Although he writes in French, he transcends the rubric of being a "French writer." Brigitte-Fanny Cohen makes sense when she argues that before all else, Wiesel is a Jew, a product of Hasidic and Biblical humanism more than that of the western-European/American cultural tradition. Cohen insists that despite his indebtedness to authors like Camus, Sartre, Malraux, Mauriac, Kafka, Dostoievski, his real loyalty belongs to the Judaic tradition.[4] While her theory is convincing, one cannot overlook the prominent place in his literary thinking occupied by western European writers, especially French authors.

In essence, Wiesel amalgamates two major cultural currents: the French (western) intellectual influences and his inherited Jewish sensibility. The latter seems to permeate the former, but the former also seems to reshape the latter. Much more than a Jewish spokesman or a French-language author, Wiesel really stands at the crossroads where elements of linguistic and cultural pluralism are intertwined; furthermore, he incorporates within himself the values of universal humanism. He sees each individual human being, regardless of national or linguistic origin, as a member of the *whole* human brotherhood. In his view, no ethnicity, no patriotic zeal, no national citizenship, no religious adherence should be allowed to interfere with the general concern all human beings ought to have for each other. Wiesel sees himself as a man who incarnates the concern for universal mankind: "My true self belongs neither to France, not to America, nor to any other place; it belongs to a world that is not here [with those who perished in the Shoah]."[5]

As he recaptures that nearly vanished world of eastern European Jewry, we must constantly remember that his message to us is transmitted in French. This reality must not be ignored; it must be taken into consideration as we consider the entire equation of Wieselean literature. The language deliberately selected by a writer, especially when this language is not an inherited mother tongue, becomes the vehicle by which that writer expresses his innermost thoughts, dreams, emotions, and visions. Wiesel stresses this fact in a conversation with Saint Cheron:

> My generation spoke several languages. We were born in countries where nationalities, religions, traditions intermingled. I remember that the Christians spoke Yiddish as fluently as we did. At home, in Sighet, they spoke Romanian, Hungarian, German, Yiddish of course, Czech, Russian, Ukrainian—and on the Sabbath, we spoke Hebrew. Today, of all of these languages, I have retained only four or five along with French and English, in addition.[6]

Why did Wiesel select the language of Racine, Molière, and Hugo as his tool for literary expression? He once explained his decision in a lengthy and important statement that must be cited here in its entirety:

> After the war, I had adopted this language with a real feeling of love. But this language, as a matter of principle, ought not to have been mine for it does not always suit the themes that I treat in my books [Hasidism, Jewish doctrine]. For example, on mysticism. Well it so happens that French does not cope well with mysticism. Furthermore, French denies mysticism; it is the most Cartesian language in the world! Mysticism is evoked more readily by German or Hebrew. Choosing French grew out of a challenge, I believe. I had been searching for a different language: Hebrew, Yiddish, or Hungarian symbolized all of my childhood. On returning from my deportation, at the age of sixteen, I developed a horror for my native language, the Hungarians having shown themselves so cruel towards the Jews. And I wanted to demonstrate that I had entered into a new era, to prove to myself that I had survived. I was anxious to remain the same, but in a new landscape. And the French language constituted this new landscape.[7]

The writer amplifies even more fully than above his rationale for selecting French. Responding to perplexed Americans who wondered why someone residing in America should continue to compose his most significant books in a language other than English, he made the following three statements:

> Why I chose French, I don't know; maybe because it was harder. I'm sure that symbolically it meant something to me; it meant a new home. The language became a haven, a new beginning, a new possibility, a new world. To start expressing oneself in a new language was a defiance [a defiance against those who had robbed him of much of his childhood and of his family].[8]

> It [French] is my working language. I do not know English that well. I think in French. Why? Because I chose that language or maybe because it

chose me. When I came to France in 1945, I needed something. I needed a country. And the language became my country. I needed something different, something new, something strange—something so new that I would be allowed to believe in its possibilities, and French was totally new to me. Before the war I did not know a country named France existed. And here I was in a new country. I had to communicate experiences, themes, obsessions, which are contrary to French culture and expression, which, as far as you know, is Cartesian. Everything must be clear, reasonable, rational. And what I had to communicate was an irrational event and a mystical perception of that irrational event.[9]

My English is not that good. I write my books in French because that is the language I acquired immediately after the war, as a protest. I know Hungarian, but I hated it and made a physical effort to forget it, to eradicate it from my brain. I never knew German that well, and the little that I did know I didn't like. Yiddish for me was always connected with my study of Talmud and so forth. So there I was without a working knowledge of any language. I chose French as a refuge, and whatever I read later in literature or philosophy was in French. I really do not know English as well as I should. I am trying not to hurt my French. That is why I do not write in English.[10]

Upon careful analysis of the above several pronouncements, we note that French filled for him not only a practical need for a "working language," but it also represented a solution to a disturbing psychological problem that festered in his soul after Auschwitz. Wiesel makes several important revelations here: In the first place, he notes that immediately after his release from the nightmare of the camps he needed to escape from the tragic memories of his recent past (among which the indifference of his neighbors in Sighet, the languages and cultures of his native region, the anti-Semitism of the Hungarians, and the German language that symbolized for him the brutality of the death-camps). He longed for a new life, a new land, a new vision of the world, a new beginning, a future without persecution, torture, and starvation. Compared to what he had seen at Auschwitz, France represented a total escape. It represented newness, unfamiliarity. France offered him a new home, a new hope, a new life, new values, a new linguistic system, one that was unlike anything he had known before. The French authorities welcomed him warmly. They impressed him with their humaneness. They provided him with nourishment, compassion, hospitality, shelter, and medical care. French thus symbolized a much-needed evasion from the terror of the past.

Second point: for someone like Wiesel, who seems to have been endowed with a natural facility for languages (already in his childhood he was multilingual), learning French proved to be a relatively painless, even a joyful experience. Moreover, at the time of his arrival in Paris, when he first discovered this new language, French literature was traversing one of its most glorious moments in an already rich history: Camus, Sartre, Malraux, Gide, Mauriac, Saint-Exupéry, Maurois, Valéry, Giraudoux, these and so many other French writers were viewed as the literary giants of the western world. Existentialism, French-style, enjoyed a place of honor as the most respected school of philosophy; better than through any other intellectual movement of the time, intellectuals could comprehend the most agonizing problems of the day. Existentialist philosophy facilitated Wiesel's appreciation of the ordeal he had just experienced.

But if the French language and literature helped him to analyze some of the Holocaust horrors, Wiesel found that the characteristic clarity, logic, and orderly structure of this language did not lend itself easily to his descriptions of an irrational event like the Shoah. Nor was it the ideal medium for the transmission of such spiritual and abstract concepts as Hasidism and Jewish mysticism. Thus, Wiesel believed at first that he would have to rely upon his Yiddish and Hebrew whenever he wished to deal with mystical topics. His disclaimers to the contrary, he did indeed learn to deal with the vagaries of Judaism and Hasidism in French. With aplomb and success he seems to have found a formula for adapting this language to his needs. His most successful books, like *Célébration hassidique, Ani Maamin, Célébration biblique,* and *Célébration talmudique* prove that French can indeed do justice to Jewish mysticism and Hasidism, especially when placed in the hands of a talented literary artist. By the time he composed these major works on Jewish themes, Wiesel was already so adept in French that he could bend and twist this otherwise precise and somewhat rigid language until it yielded to his personal requirements.

In the foregoing citations, Wiesel makes a third point. In his attempt to justify his choice of French, he underscores the psychological implications of his decision. French represented for the eighteen-year-old Wiesel a refuge, an outlet, a liberation from that anxious moment in life during which he had lost his parents, his youngest sister, and most of his closest relatives. At the time, he even assumed that his two older sisters had been murdered by the Germans (only later on did he learn that they too had survived miraculously). As a defense mechanism against his recent tragedies, and out of a desire to place upon himself a self-imposed challenge to remake himself and to adopt a different cultural outlook and a brand new literary tradition.

Today, many of his hundreds of thousands of Anglophone readers wonder why Wiesel, an American resident, did not select English. American readers ought to remind themselves that after Auschwitz Wiesel was sent not to America or the United Kingdom, but rather to France. There is even some question as to whether he could easily have immigrated to the United States or England, at that moment in history. By the time that he moved to the United States and learned English, his reputation as a respected writer of French had already been established. There seemed then to be no point in switching languages, especially since he felt so secure in writing in French.

One last point. We cannot overestimate the fact that Wiesel *chose* to write in French just as a convert chooses a new religion. Converts most frequently become model practitioners of their newly acquired faith and adhere to its principles much more devoutly than those born into the religion. This truism surely applies to Wiesel's conversion to the French tongue. To this day, he has never regretted his decision, and his enthusiasm for French remains unabated.

During all of his life, Elie Wiesel has demonstrated a reverential attitude towards language in general, and French in particular. Anyone who, like this author, devoted a part of his life to the study of Torah instinctively reveres language for the sake of language. The typical scholar of Torah enjoys the analysis or words, phrases, idiomatic expressions, grammar, metaphors, and the other verbal paraphernalia that comprise a literary composition. Frequently, in his own writing, Wiesel likes to comment on the usage of language by other writers. For example, in his discussion of the literary prose of Nelly Sachs, he deals with the linguistic question of her choice of German. He wonders why, as a Jewish author, she continues to use a language polluted by the Nazi murders, even after residing in Sweden for years: Sachs, in her reply to Wiesel answers that she could not write sufficiently well in Swedish, and could only write in the language in which she was raised, German. Accepting her answer, Wiesel comments that "She wrote in German long before the murder of the six million." He then vigorously contrasts Nelly Sachs' inability to master Swedish after moving to Stockholm with his own success in learning French, once he went to Paris.[11]

If Wiesel had compelling reasons to use French, one wonders whether he also appreciated the culture and civilization of the

French people. What were his initial reactions to his newly adopted country? A half century after his arrival there, have his views towards France changed in any way? Often he expresses his gratitude to the French for their willingness to extend hospitality to him and to the tens of thousands of other survivors. Having originally been scheduled to be transferred from his concentration camp to Belgium, he speculates on the reasons for his train being rerouted to Paris. Here is what he believes: "France? Why did we go to France? De Gaulle heard about them. He heard about 400 Jewish children in Buchenwald who did not know where to go. As prime minister, president, and provisional governor, he rerouted a train to take us to France."[12] Immediately upon arrival in Paris, a French officer offered him the opportunity to become a French citizen. Because his ability to decipher spoken French was non-existent, Wiesel did not understand what the officer said to him, and he declined his proposal. This *malentendu* was to change his entire life because, for the entirety of his ten-year sojourn in France, he led his life there not as a French national but rather as an alien resident. And so many work opportunities were unavailable to him, and he lived under somewhat dire financial circumstances, as a result. When, in 1964, the hallowed Académie Française presented an award to Wiesel for his four earliest novels, President de Gaulle wrote him an effusive, congratulatory letter, reminding him that it was he, de Gaulle, who had once been responsible for extracting him from the Kingdom of Night, as Wiesel often calls the Holocaust.

After their arrival in the French capital, the adolescent Wiesel and his group of 400 young camp survivors were assigned to live in a somewhat sumptuous but fading chateau in Normandy. There they were asked to select one of two lifestyles: secular or religious. Wiesel and his closest friend opted for the latter. They immediately petitioned the authorities to supply them with kosher food and certain Jewish ritual necessities: e.g., a prayer shawl, prayer books, a skullcap. To Wiesel's surprise, the authorities yielded to this request with alacrity. What a contrast between these accommodating officials and those who ruled over him in the deathcamps!

Wiesel's first decision was to learn the host language, French. His teacher, a non-Jewish young man named Stefan, eventually ended up swapping language lessons: Elie learned French and Stefan, Hebrew. One of the most influential persons in the future author's life was a young Jewish woman, Gabrielle (Gaby) Cohen, who had been employed by the Jewish charitable agencies entrusted with the care of the young survivors. For many years, Gaby Cohen and Elie Wiesel remained friends. She recalls that he stood out from the other adolescents in his group because of his extraordinary intelligence, his driving desire to learn about French culture, and his irrepressible love for music. One of the treasured relics that she still guards with loving care is a notebook given to her by her Jewish pupils. Her favorite page in it contains a delightful poem composed for her in French by the future writer. Already his literary talents asserted themselves![13]

To meet his daily expenses, Wiesel assumed various jobs. Gifted in music, he soon became a choral director in a girl's school in Versailles. Off and on he also taught Hebrew. Once he had gained sufficient competency in French, the young man moved to Paris, where he could pursue a university degree at the Sorbonne. Selecting mainly courses in philosophy and literature, he fell under the spell of his philosophy teacher, Wahl, who seems to have exerted much influence on his intellectual formation. An almost instant convert to the Parisian lifestyle, Wiesel frequented the left-bank cafés where as his favorite pastime he enjoyed playing chess. He still finds pleasure in this game and plays with his son, Elisha.[14]

Vis-à-vis his early benefactor, President Charles de Gaulle, Elie Wiesel has betrayed ambivalent sentiments. Always ready to express his appreciation to the man most responsible for his having gone to Paris, Wiesel later revealed disillusionment with his former protector, especially after de Gaulle, once an ardent ally of the State of Israel, abruptly abandoned his Middle East partner during the Six Day War of 1967, precisely at an hour when his support was most sorely needed. When de Gaulle abandoned the Jewish state, declaring an embargo on critically needed jet aircraft that Israel had already purchased from France, Wiesel wrote the following words of disappointment:

> De Gaulle was a strange character. I owe him much. As I already explained, he was the one who brought me to France; he was the one, you could almost say, who gave me my tools, gave me my language, the French language. Yet in 1967 I broke with de Gaulle as I broke with many people who then abandoned Israel.[15]

Despite his misgivings about the latter's foreign policy in the Middle East, Wiesel passionately defends the late French President against those who claim that he was an anti-Semite. Instead, the Jewish author explains the sudden about-face by the President as an understandable, but unfortunate, act of *realpolitik:* Israel, such a tiny country, had no oil. The Arab countries controlled most of the world's oil supplies, and de Gaulle knew that oil-deprived France could not survive economically without importing petroleum from the Middle East. Thus Wiesel concluded that de Gaulle chose fiscal realities over moral values.

De Gaulle's successor, Georges Pompidou, continued to disappoint the otherwise Francophile Wiesel. Noting that Pompidou had been given his earliest professional opportunities when he worked for the Rothschilds, one of France's leading Jewish families, Wiesel expressed surprise that Pompidou never manifested the slightest shred of gratitude towards his benefactors once he became President of the French Republic. Instead of attenuating France's hard-line policies towards Israel, Wiesel complained that Pompidou extended the cycle of France's pro-Arab position after the 1967 rupture between de Gaulle and Israel. And, consequently, Wiesel never concealed his coldness towards Pompidou.

The survivor of Auschwitz, who once had admired France so reverentially, also revealed disillusionment with the French government during the residency of Valery Giscard D'Estaing. Angered that France had bowed to Arab pressure by releasing the notorious terrorist, Abu Daoud, Elie Wiesel addressed a full-page open letter to President Giscard D'Estaing, published in *The New York Times,* in which he exposed his mixed feelings towards the French Republic. On the one hand, he stated his outrage at its one-sided policies. In his open letter Wiesel reveals his sentiments towards France with such clarity that we should cite it here almost in entirety:

> It is because of my love for France and my respect for its people that I feel compelled to express to you my sadness and indignation—shared by many Americans—over your [Giscard D'Estaing] handling of the Abu Daoud affair. Although born in eastern Europe, I owe France my secular education, my language, and my career as a writer. Liberated from Buchenwald, it was in France that I found compassion and humanity. It was in France that I found generosity and friendship. It was in France that I discovered the other side, the brighter side of mankind. I was proud of France. France, to me, represented humanity's highest values in a sterile and cynical society. It evoked Rousseau and Bergson, Proust and Zola, Camus and Mauriac. It symbolized an inspiring quest for justice and brotherhood. France, the birthplace of revolutions against tyranny. France, the herald of human rights. France, haven for the persecuted. France and its freedom fighters . . . No nations had so much prestige. No

culture was so readily accepted . . . Then why did your government free Abu Daoud?[16]

When François Mitterrand was elected President of the French Republic, Wiesel rejoiced heartily. It was gratifying for him to note that almost immediately after his inauguration, Mitterrand became the first French head of state to pay a state visit to Israel, where he was warmly received by the people of that besieged nation. More heartened was Wiesel to discern in Mitterrand's policies a genuine lessening in France's previously overt support of the Arab cause and a visibly improved atmosphere in Franco-Israeli relations. Wiesel's warm association with Mitterrand lasted throughout the fourteen years of this president's two terms. However, the two men experienced a dramatic rupture in their friendship, just prior to Mitterrand's death (discussed earlier in this study).

During his frequent trips to France, Wiesel enjoys the most amicable rapports with the top leadership of the government, with officials of the French university system, with Cardinal Lustiger, Archbishop of Paris, and with the major figures in the Jewish secular and religious communities. Honored numerous times by the France's universities, literary juries, and academies, Wiesel's face is as familiar on French television and in the lecture halls of French universities as in the United States and Israel. The love affair between France and her adopted son has been a fact of literary life in that nation since the publication of *La Nuit* in 1958.

The French personalities who really played compelling roles in the career of Elie Wiesel were the authors whose works he read avidly during his decade-long sojourn in Paris. Surely they influenced the development of his literary style and his view of the world. In many respects, Wiesel ought to be viewed as a writer who coalesces with and fits into the French literary scene of the sixties, seventies, eighties, and well into the nineties. Thus he is included in almost every contemporary literary anthology on the French literary tradition of the twentieth century.

Wiesel likes to quote those French writers whose values coincide with his own. Those whom he frequently cites are precisely the popular authors who dominated his Parisian period. This is indeed understandable since it was then that he was extraordinarily impressionable and when he seemed highly receptive to their approach to literary art: Malraux, Mauriac, Sartre, and Camus. That these writers occupy a special niche in his career is apparent from his reply to the following question: "What other major secular figures . . . influenced you?" Here is his answer:

> Camus, Sartre, and Mauriac. Mauriac played a very important role in my life. We were very close. He prefaced my first book and brought it to the publisher. Whenever I was at the crossroad, he was there . . . But the strong influences are the existentialist philosophers and writers. When I studied at the Sorbonne, they were *the* masters."[17]

At first Wiesel found it difficult to imagine that an eminent Catholic like Mauriac could become one of his closest friends. His orthodox upbringing in the quaint, provincial milieu of the Jewish community of Sighet did not prepare him well for ecumenical friendships. Wiesel acknowledges that " . . . it took me some time before I accepted friendship with a Catholic, but once accepted, that Catholic, François Mauriac, a great writer, became one of my most intimate friends and allies. He became my patron in literature, but it took me some time to break down the walls. The child in me could not imagine that a non-Jew could be my friend."[18] Without Mauriac's advice that Wiesel shorten the manuscript of *La Nuit*, and without Mauriac's willingness to intervene in Wiesel's behalf with the publishing house, Les Editions de Minuit, it is doubtful that this first opus, by an unknown author, would receive such immediate acceptance in the finicky French publishing world and such instant acclaim among the French and international reading public. Besides, the fact that Mauriac wrote an important preface for the book must have been a significant factor in Wiesel's early success.

As for Jean-Paul Sartre, Wiesel has often made reference in his discussions of Nazism, bigotry, and racial hatred to this philosopher's ideas about existential nausea. But Wiesel notes, not without surprise, that Sartre, who had devoted so much attention to the cause of all abused people (especially the Algerian Arabs) had not spoken out in indignation against the deportation of French Jews. Also Wiesel takes issue with the existentialist philosopher for calling man "a useless passion." A champion of humanism, Wiesel is unable to accept any attempt to denigrate human beings. The Jewish writer adds that "In the Jewish tradition, man's life and fate are never useless."[19] At the same time, Wiesel does concur with Sartre's emphasis on the need for humans to be sufficiently free so that they can make authentic choices in their lives and take responsibility for these choices. Despite certain reservations, Wiesel truly believes that Sartre exerted an overall salutary influence on the modern world; here is his general evaluation of the Existentialist philosopher:

> Sartre on the contrary [compared with Karl Marx] seems to me to be a man of courage, a man of vision, especially in his novels and plays. Sartre is a great novelist, a novelist who missed the boat for he did not complete anything. He himself recognized this . . . But what an exceptional visionary. He is undoubtedly one of the personalities who have marked this century."[20]

Of all of the great French writers of his lifetime, it is Albert Camus who struck the most responsive chord in the soul of Elie Wiesel. Especially did he admire Camus's notion that man must never allow himself to be vanquished by cynicism or pessimism, that human solidarity requires that all people work together to improve the universal lot, and that it is a basic responsibility for mankind to add some kind of meaning to an otherwise meaningless and absurd universe. The one statement that seems to have affected Wiesel most deeply was this one: "In a universe of misfortune, one must create happiness." To which Wiesel adds: "this is what I am trying to do—to create a meaning in a universe that has no meaning."[21] As a Jewish writer Wiesel also finds especially appealing the tendency for Camus's characters to laugh through tears; this has always been a typically Jewish response to the incessant tragedies of Jewish history. Below are Wiesel's thoughts on this subject:

> The future? I think of the striking formula of Albert Camus: 'In our times, there remains for man but one choice: to be an optimist who cries or a pessimist who laughs.' I think of 1967 [the Israeli victory in the Six-Day War] and I am sad. I recall 1937 [the era of Hitler's persecution of the Jews] and I laugh. At least our history teaches us that anything is possible."[22]

Yes, there were joyous moments in Israel's almost unbelievable victories over immense Arab odds, but there were also so many casualties on both sides! Yes, the Holocaust was conceivably the greatest tragedy in history, but after the tragedy there emerged at long last the State of Israel. Besides, Judaism survives even after Hitler's atrocious plans for the Final Solution.

Elie Wiesel's literature may well be viewed as an appendage, as a part, or maybe an extension of twentieth-century French literature. In his novel, *Le crépuscule au loin,* whole pages are reminiscent of

André Gide's most rhapsodic celebrations of fervor and the simple delight of merely being alive, rhapsodies that comprise the heart of Gide's *Les nourritures terrestres* [The Fruits of the Earth]. Other pages in Wiesel's novel carry resonances of the ambient atmosphere in Camus's *La peste* [The Plague].[23] As Wiesel vaults without transition from present to past to future time, we are reminded of some of the chronological experimentation found in some of the novels of France's innovative New Novelists of the late fifties and sixties. Moreover, in his more than thirty published volumes, Wiesel leaps from references to and quotations from Pascal, Rousseau, Balzac, Flaubert, Victor Hugo, Arthur Rimbaud, André Malraux, Samuel Beckett and so many other French writers who form the ongoing legacy of French literature. At one moment, Wiesel quotes Pascal: "Pascal said there is a love affair between Israel and God. A love affair has its moments of exaltation and quarrels."[24] At another moment, Wiesel cites Rimbaud's statement that "a poet is a 'thief of fire.'" Wiesel then adds that "We [writers] steal the fire, but our fire does not destroy. Our fire burns and burns and burns—and we burn forever."[25] There is no denying that the thought patterns that flow through Wiesel's texts have, to a considerable degree, been fashioned by his readings of some of the major authors in the French literary tradition.

One of Elie Wiesel's favorite French writers is André Schwarz-Bart, the author of the best-seller, *Le dernier des justes* [The Last of the Just], a best-seller in both the United States and France. In fact, Wiesel and Schwarz-Bart have often been confused with each other; there is a strong physical resemblance between the two, and both deal with Jewish perspectives of the Shoah. The author of *Night* once recounted the following anecdotal incident concerning a conversation he had had with a fellow passenger sitting next to him during an El Al flight to Jerusalem. All through their conversation, the passenger believed that he had been talking to Schwarz-Bart, to which Wiesel reacted in the following way:

> Listen, I know why you make that mistake. Number one, I am also a writer. Number two, I am also Jewish. Number three, I also write in French. Number four, we have the same themes—the Holocaust, Jewishness. Number five, we have the same publisher in Paris. Number six, we have the same publisher in New York. Number seven, we are very close friends. Number eight, there is even a physical resemblance, which even my wife admitted to when she met André Schwarz-Bart.[26]

13: THE FRENCH CONNECTION

Those who have written histories of twentieth-century French literature always—and rightly so—include a chapter on Elie Wiesel. Probably future histories of modern French literature will continue to have a prominent Wiesel chapter. Why not? After all, his literary language is almost always French; his references are to French writers and thinkers; his perspectives or literature reflect a French perspective.

Et pourtant! (And yet—Wiesel's favorite words; in fact, the final chapter in his last volume of memoirs is entitled "Et Pourtant"). *And yet,* deeply submerged in his electrically charged soul, even within the melody of his French words, the reader discerns something indefinably Jewish. With his typical concision Wiesel sums up this duality of "Frenchness" and "Jewishness" in *Ani Maamin:* "*Ani Maamin,* which means 'I believe,' is a poem written for the Messiah. It was written in French, but the theme is Jewish, the inspiration is Jewish, and the waiting it Jewish."[27]

Jewish and French! That sums it all up!

14
And Yet—A Conclusion That Does Not Conclude

As I evaluate the massif of Wiesel's lifelong accomplishments to date—his books, lectures, essays, and worldwide activities of public service—I search for terminology to sum up what he has achieved and what he represents for us today. Before all else he stands out for his *passion for humanity*. Who can argue with his reputation for being one of the century's most effective humanitarians? Surely this is the role he has chosen to play. At the summit of his most cherished values he places the sanctity of human life, the preciousness of each human being. This lofty notion of human life derives from the central tenets of his personal religious belief—Judaism. What a paradox it is that Wiesel, the witness of unprecedented slaughter and atrocities committed against human beings, should even cling to the conviction that life is valuable, that it must be preserved at all costs!

Although there exists in the total Wieselean oeuvre an overarching philosophy, it has hardly ever been presented to us as a coherent, organic system. It is a fact that no single work by Wiesel contains all of his philosophic thinking in a unified package. Instead, his thoughts have been diffused in tiny fragments throughout all that he has written, done, and said. His thoughts glisten through his sentences in recurrent sparks of incandescence. From his maxims, aphorisms, and lapidary pronouncements it is not impossible to assemble a consistent body of philosophic views of human kind. Elie Wiesel does not appear to have undergone any evolutionary modifications in his thinking from 1958, when he wrote his first book, until today, as he continues to compose books not yet published.

At the outset of his life, Wiesel viewed the world through a narrow prism, that of a Jewish lad raised within the protective enclosure of a caring and tightly knit Jewish family. Educated within the restrictive confines of a traditional Jewish parochial school (his *heder*) in a re-

14: AND YET—A CONCLUSION THAT DOES NOT CONCLUDE 189

mote hinterland of eastern Europe, he abruptly witnessed the obliteration of this peaceful insularity when he, his family, and virtually all of Europe's Jews were rounded up, herded in cattle cars, and deported to the dreadful entrails of the German concentration camps where almost all of them were killed.

These camps, designed to carry out Hitler's plan for a "Final Solution" of the "Jewish Problem," formed for the adolescent Wiesel the setting within which he gradually acquired a serious and broad understanding of what it meant to be a human being in a world-at-large that was not always humane. The *univers concentrationnaire* had forcibly and forcefully transmuted Elie Wiesel from a protected individual into someone exposed to the perils of the outside world. Standing in the space between life and death, Wiesel began to contemplate the human condition from a broader, universal point of view. After his release from the camps he began to identify himself with the destiny of all mankind. Looking outward, Wiesel the survivor now saw the world from a holistic and societal perspective. His tragic journey through the nocturnal kingdom of the Holocaust shattered forever the security he had once felt within the membranes of Jewish provincialism. In his confrontation with the harsh post-Auschwitz realities of the world, he discovered a Europe rampant with anti-Semitic hate. He saw a Europe dominated by Christian indifference and, at times, hostility. Now he understood that human history had been poisoned by an unending string of atrocities committed by man against man and by centuries of warfare waged by nation against nation. Between the world he read about in the Jewish Bible and in the Torah, where one of the most common words is shalom (peace), and the world that he had just experienced in the death camps there existed a terrifying contrast.

Once liberated, Wiesel had every reason to be filled with bitterness, pessimism, and nihilism. Had he not lost almost his entire family? Had he not lost most of his dearest friends and relatives? Had he not witnessed the mass murders of innocent children and helpless elderly people? Had he not himself endured indescribably cruel torture?

But Wiesel's innate nature did not allow him to slide completely down the slope towards utter pessimism. In his Jewish education he had learned to search for an essential core of goodness inside of man. He simply could not espouse a cynical position concerning the human race. Although in the Shoah he saw how the force of evil could transform human beings into killers, haters, torturers, he knew that somewhere in human nature there resided the instinct to do good. An optimist by nature, Wiesel believed that mankind's potential for good would ultimately win out against the malevolence he had just witnessed in the camps.

Out of the infernal cinders of Auschwitz the adolescent Elie Wiesel emerged as someone who actually faced his uncertain future not with bitterness but rather with hope and a belief in the worth of human beings. Out of these cinders he looked for flames of hope that might leap forward and save mankind. Haunted by nightmarish memories, he dedicated himself to the creation of a new life. Henceforth he decided to play a constructive role in helping the human race to avoid the repetition of the tragic history through which he and so many others had just passed. In lieu of a desire for vengeance against the killers, he was driven by a determination to work for the uplifting of the human condition. And so he became a genuine humanitarian.

Earlier I discussed the cardinal themes in Wiesel's philosophy of life and art. In my conclusion, I would like to sum up these themes in as succinct a way as possible. Like most novelists, Wiesel has his own repertoire of characters, venues, and major themes. Below are the dominant themes that lend a special flavor to Wiesel's texts and distinguish his work from that of the other writers of his century.

First, there is the theme of an adult who longs to return to a once-blissful boyhood in his hometown (in Wiesel's case, Sighet). This theme reasserts itself in so many of this author's works, even in some of the most recent ones written during his seventieth decade of life. In the concluding pages of his memoirs (published in 1996), he still confesses that he dreams about his childhood days. After recounting a dream about his late father, he admits that "I dream also of my mother, my little sister, I weep in my sleep."[1] So much did he love his own childhood that he later loved the innocence of *all* children, for they always reminded him of his own youth. And so much did he adore his grandparents that he loved *all* elderly people. In the same memoirs he wrote: "To save the life of a single child, no effort is superfluous. To bring a smile to the face of an elderly person, one who is tired of working and struggling, is to accomplish an essential task."[2] No atrocity committed by the Nazis in their deathcamps outraged Wiesel more than the brutalization or killing of children or the elderly.

The second salient theme in Wiesel's literature is that of the Holocaust, a theme that reverberates—both overtly and covertly—

on almost each of his published pages. Although Wiesel does not like to be limited to the label of "Holocaust writer," his disclaimers do not convince me that he ought not to be categorized with those writers who featured the Holocaust in their published work. Almost nothing that Wiesel has written fails in some way to reflect back upon this infernal event, either discreetly or overtly. It is virtually impossible to deal with the Holocaust without including Wiesel's pivotal role in bringing this tragic moment in human history to the forefront of contemporary civilization. Indeed, he is *the* leading Holocaust survivor of our times. No one more than Elie Wiesel reminds us of our obligation to honor the memory of the six million Jews and the millions of non-Jews destroyed in the Shoah. Moreover, in his judgment, what he calls "the Event" must be regarded as a sacred and unique happening in human history, one to which we must accord the most reverential respect.

A third theme commands our attention: the absurdity of hate and prejudice. In effect, one of Wiesel's most significant accomplishments has been his sensitive, anatomical analysis of the phenomenon of hate. In his study of the causes of the Holocaust, Wiesel points an accusatory finger at the 2,000 years of Christian anti-Semitism out of which he sees the Holocaust as a logical end-game. Wiesel emphasizes that most of the killers were at least nominal Christians, and most of the others who watched passively as the slaughter took place share some of the guilt by their indifference, silence, or cowardice. Convinced that the Holocaust would have been aborted had the Gentile world vociferously expressed disapproval of the Nazi credo, Wiesel resoundingly proclaims that "Indifference to evil is evil," a statement that has become his most eloquent slogan of life. This slogan has even been engraved on the face of his Congressional gold medal of honor.

We come now to the fourth theme: Wiesel's exaltation of the Jewish people, their traditions, their ethical, moral, and religious values, and their history. To his co-religionists, Wiesel recommends that they manifest their Judaism overtly and proudly, that they avoid excessive assimilation or embarrassment about belonging to a minority population. Otherwise the non-Jewish world will not extend to them the respect that Jews rightly merit. Despite Wiesel's powerful Jewish pride, he combats religious and ethnic chauvinism. On the contrary, tirelessly and repeatedly he pleads for Christian–Jewish dialogue, for mutual understanding, tolerance, and acceptance. He summons all people, regardless of their race, religion, ethnicity, or nationality to work together in order to achieve a sense of universal brotherhood and solidarity.

A fifth theme: Wiesel's conviction that human beings must develop a more dynamic, engaged relationship with their God. Before the Holocaust, the young Wiesel never doubted God's readiness to defend the Jewish people at moments of critical need. In the camps, however, this confidence in God's divine protection had been shattered. Given God's silence and non-intervention in Auschwitz, he began to believe that it is a Jewish duty to challenge God and to demand explanations for this silence and non-intervention. But his disillusionment with the Almighty did not prevent him from worshipping and from remaining within the parameters of the religious faith he had inherited from his ancestors.

The sixth theme in Wieselean literature stems from this author's cult of education. In consonance with Jewish tradition, Wiesel celebrates the importance of education in human life. The collected works of Elie Wiesel, indeed his personal lifestyle constitute an uninterrupted ode to learning and scholarship. Wiesel is convinced that were it not for his people's respect for scholarship and books, they would have vanished from the face of the earth a long time ago. Learning guarantees the survival of culture from generation to generation.

The importance of the interconnections between past, present, and future time is the last great theme I should like to underscore here. A passionate advocate of memory, Wiesel realizes that human beings must, nonetheless, not allow themselves to become prisoners of their past. In remembering the past, they must also concern themselves with the quality of life in the present and the quality of life that must be passed on to offspring in the future. Above all, however, we must remember. It is a fact that Wiesel has never taught a course at the university in which the theme of memory has not been the pivotal component of the material studied by his disciples.

Wiesel's life has evolved on a worldwide stage where he has worn many masks and played an assortment of roles. In the literary world he has been a novelist, playwright, critic, essayist, and storyteller. In the academic world he has been a teacher, commencement speaker, lecturer, and scholar. In public life he has appeared on television and radio, advised presidents and prime ministers, addressed parliaments, served on prestigious commissions. In the print media he has been a reporter, journalist, editorialist. In the religious world he has

14: AND YET—A CONCLUSION THAT DOES NOT CONCLUDE 193

served as a commentator of the Bible, a confidant of cardinals, rabbis, ministers, and an ecumenical unifier. In international society he has for a long time been the voice of the meek, the weak, the downtrodden, the persecuted. A short while ago the *New York Times* heralded him on its front page as "An Unofficial but Very Public Bearer of Pain, Peace and Human Dignity."[3] In short, Elie Wiesel is universally recognized as an international personality!

At the present moment in time, one may confidently predict that the name of Elie Wiesel will occupy some kind of place in the histories of modern literature, in the chronicles about the Holocaust, and in the accounts of personalities who have played prominent parts in the history of the second half of the twentieth century.

Elie Wiesel is an extraordinary example of tragedy and achievement. Almost miraculously he climbed out of the abyss of Auschwitz, Birkenau, and Buchenwald and scaled the hilltops of Nobel glory, literary and academic success, and international renown. Out of his broad range of experiences, both painful and joyful, he has crafted a message of cautious optimism. In the wake of vestigial racism in the United States, tribal conflict in Africa, religious dissension in northern Ireland, ethnic cleansing in the former Yugoslavia, terrorism and tension in the Middle East, Ku Klux Klan marches in Skokie, Illinois, denial of the Holocaust by historical revisionists, and a rash of synagogue and church burnings and cemetery desecrations in the United States and elsewhere, Elie Wiesel believes that all is not lost. He rejoices over the rebirth of the Jewish state in Israel, the emigration of Soviet Jews from their captivity in the former Soviet Union, airlifts that rescued the endangered Jews of Ethiopia, reconciliation between formerly implacable foes like France and Germany, Israel and Jordan, Israel and Egypt, the collapse of totalitarianism in the former Soviet sphere, handshakes on the White House lawn, the beginning of pacification in the Balkan peninsula, the end of apartheid in South Africa, and the popular success of the national museum of the Holocaust in Washington, DC. As he observes the many points of progress around the world, he rejects the inevitability of despair.

Certainly in his personal and domestic life, Wiesel has much for which he is thankful. Wiesel considers it a miracle that he survived the death camps and could live long enough to enjoy what appears to be a happy marital life, and above all to become the father of a son whose birth will allow the family name to survive in the future. The miracle of his survival and the birth of his son he sees as a symbol of the perseverance of the Jewish people. Thus his cautious optimism. He once confessed that "Today I oscillate between pessimism and extreme hope. I cannot believe that a history of three thousand years can come to an end. I was brought up in a milieu where the words *Netsah Yisrael*, the eternity of Israel, meant something."[4] In another passage, he paraphrases Albert Camus: "My leitmotifs are madness, laughter, saintliness. Can one be a saint in an unsaintly world? How do you reconcile divine justice with human injustice? And the other way around, human justice with divine injustice?"[5] Elsewhere he continued to demonstrate his indebtedness to the author of *The Plague* when he wrote the following: "As Albert Camus used to say, for modern man there are two options: one can be either a smiling pessimist or a weeping optimist. We study and we are both."[6]

In his unremitting battle between hope and despair, Wiesel has confidence that hope will be the victor over despair, especially if human beings learn at last that they must renounce indifference as a mode of reacting to the surrounding world. And so he admonishes his public always to *care* about what is happening to brothers and sisters of the human race. Caring is the antidote to indifference. In his commencement address before the graduating seniors of Susquehanna University he urged them to combat the "plague of indifference":

> Don't people understand that indifference is probably the worse plague that exists in life? It is worse than despair. Despair is a beginning. Despair can inspire you to create great works of art, music, literature, philosophy, theology. Despair evokes compassion, but indifference is an end. There is nothing beyond . . . [7]

The opposite of indifference is love, compassion, sympathy, above all fervor, passion, and feeling. In the same commencement address Wiesel posed and then responded to his own rhetorical questions:

> What is education, what is life, what is friendship, what is love, what is beauty, what is joy, if not our own impulse, our own pulsation, our own protest against an indifferent society, against an indifferent world that you now are called upon to conquer, not with violence but with words; not with cruelty, but with compassion; and surely not with hatred, but with a sense of exultation.[8]

As a writer, a teacher, and public speaker, he uses words and sentences as his most potent weapon against indifference and hate.

14: AND YET—A CONCLUSION THAT DOES NOT CONCLUDE

Language has the power of demolishing indifference. With words a writer or speaker may ignite his audience, making them recall the sins of the past. With words the writer or speaker can recall the memory of the millions killed so savagely in the Holocaust, the Shoahs or the *Hourbans*.

In the literature of this humanitarian witness, we encounter flaming words. We also encounter thousands of screaming silences. Elie Wiesel's literature contains both the explicit (words) and the implicit (silence). During a visit to Birkenau, that site where he spent many terrifying days and nights, the writer was so profoundly affected by the silence of that infernal place that, with his usual gift of poetry, he wrote the following passage of prose:

> Silence. The silence of Birkenau. The silence of Birkenau is similar to no other. It contains the cries of fright, the strangled prayers of thousands and thousands of communities, uprooted by the enemy, condemned by him to engulf themselves into the darkness of an endless and nameless night. Human silence within the heart of the inhuman. Silence of death in the heart of death. It penetrates the conscience without traversing it. It deposits there a secret that no force will be capable of piercing. Eternal silence under a dying sky.[9]

And so through his symphony of words and silences, Wiesel asks us not to turn an unseeing eye or an unhearing ear to those who plead for help. He asks that we not fall prey to the all too comfortable luxury of indifference to evil.

How does one terminate an essay about a (thankfully) still-living author and international personality, one who is still actively engaged in his writing, speaking, and teaching? In general, I, obviously, very much admire Elie Wiesel and his work. But I know that he is not at all infallible. He has his weaknesses. Within the sea of favorable, even adulating critics, a few commentators have tried to identify what they believe to be flaws. Two or three commentators have told me that they believe that Elie Wiesel has made too much of a career out of the Holocaust, that he has capitalized on the tragedy of the six million. Personally, whenever I read his personal accounts of how he felt when his mother and sisters had been separated from him at Auschwitz and how he watched his father gradually yield to starvation, humiliation, and physical weakness, I cannot imagine how anyone can make these charges against him. I am unable to comprehend how anyone can question his sincerity as he pleads with us to remember the victims. One or two of Wiesel's disparagers have told me that they believe that he campaigned too aggressively for the Nobel Prize. As one of those who wrote supportive statements each year at the request of the Nobel Jury, I can attest to the fact that never once did Monsieur Wiesel discuss his candidacy for the Nobel with me, and never once did he suggest that I write letters in his behalf. Besides, when one evaluates Wiesel's work for peace, tolerance, understanding and his work against hate and prejudice, it seems to me (and to most scholars) that no one more than he met the criteria for the Nobel Peace Prize. One or two critics have disparaged the literary merit of Wiesel's novels, claiming that he has not successfully created strong, three-dimensional characters. I acknowledge that Wiesel's female characters tend to be flat and not especially memorable. I acknowledge also that some of his male characters could have been delineated with more forceful relief. But, in my view, Wiesel's literature is not so much a world of people as it is a world of ideas and ideals. Emotions, concepts, symbolic viewpoints, and thoughts are much more important in Wieselean literature than his cast of characters. Wiesel's books are works about important ideas and human values more than about memorable characters. Besides, who can deny that the adolescent protagonist in *Night* is one of the most moving characters in modern literature? One or two critics have even told me that they see Elie Wiesel as a celebrity who truly enjoys ego-gratification. Yes, Wiesel is a celebrity of our times. That is undeniable. But if he does enjoy ego-gratification (and most people do enjoy a bit of this!), he is at the same time an exceedingly modest, even self-deprecatory, and humble human being. All one needs to do is to read both volumes of his memoirs to appreciate the extent of his self-disparagement.

The tiny minority of critics who find fault with Elie Wiesel have various motives for their negative criticism. I shall not question these motives or their sincerity. They have every right to hold their opinions. As for me, in lieu of fault-finding, I prefer to speak about the positive elements in Elie Wiesel, the man and the writer. His achievements far outweigh his defects, to the extent that the latter exist.

One cannot conclude in a decisive fashion when it is a question about a writer who is alive, well, active, and who still writes plentifully. Wiesel may still have much to tell us, more books to share with us, more lectures to deliver around the world. And so we await his forthcoming message(s).

Notes

Note: Most of Wiesel's public addresses, interviews, and assorted short articles prior to 1985 were collected by Irving Abrahamson and published in a three-volume collection entitled *Against Silence: The Voice and Vision of Elie Wiesel*. I have drawn heavily from this work since Wiesel's statements in it contain the quintessence of his thoughts and themes. In my endnotes, I identify my quotations from this work by simply listing "Abrahamson I, II, or III." The Roman numerals indicate the volumes from which I have drawn my citations. Some of the texts by or about Wiesel, published in France, are unavailable in English translation. Since I made the decision to use mainly English-language citations, I have translated the original French into English myself. These translations are identified below by (trans. J. Kolbert). EW is, of course, my abbreviation for Elie Wiesel.

Preface

1. EW, *Tous les fleuves vont à la mer*, (Paris: Seuil, 1994), 434.

Chapter 1: Elie Wiesel — A Life and a Career

1. Irving Abrahamson, *Against Silence: The Voice and Vision of Elie Wiesel* (New York: Holocaust Publications, 1985), III, 238.
2. Ted Estess, *Elie Wiesel* (New York: Frederick Ungar, 1980), See Introductory Chapter.
3. Abrahamson, I, 23.
4. Abrahamson, I, 3.
5. Abrahamson, III, 8.
6. Abrahamson, I, 269.
7. Abrahamson, I, 249.
8. Ibid, 249
9. Abrahamson, II, 23.
10. EW: "Hasidism and Man's Love of Man," *Jewish Heritage* (Fall/Winter 1972), quoted in Abrahamson II, 255.
11. Abrahamson, III, 53.
12. Ibid., 269.

13. Abrahamson, I, 369.
14. Ibid., 269.
15. Abrahamson, II, 146–47.
16. Abrahamson, III, 230.
17. Abrahamson, II, 117.
18. Ibid., 118.
19. EW: *The Jews of Silence* (New York: New American Library, 1966), vii.
20. Abrahamson, I, 195.
21. Abrahamson, III, 276.
22. Abrahamson, I, 290.
23. Abrahamson, II, 236.
24. EW: *From the Kingdom of Memory* (New York: Summit Books, 1990), 232.
25. Jack Kolbert, "Elie Wiesel," in *Dictionary of Literary Biography: French Novelists since 1960* (Detroit: Gale Research Inc., 1989), 329.

Chapter 2: Yearning for Childhood: Sighet

1. Abrahamson, I, 1.
2. Ibid.
3. Estess, 7.
4. EW: *Paroles d'étranger* (Paris: Editions du Seuil, 1982), 155 (trans. J. Kolbert).
5. Ibid., 181.
6. Abrahamson, I, 338.
7. Abrahamson, III, 1.
8. Abrahamson, I, 129.
9. Abrahamson, II, 150.
10. EW, *Signes d'exode* (Paris: Bernard Grasset, 1985), 9–10.
11. Abrahamson, I, 383.
12. EW, *Signes d'exode* 37.
13. Abrahamson, I, 245.
14. Abrahamson, II, 17.
15. EW, *Paroles d'étranger* 71.
16. Brigitte-Fanny Cohen, *Elie Wiesel: Qui êtes-vous?* (Paris: La Manufacture, 1987), 23 and 101. (trans. J. Kolbert).
17. EW, *Le Crépuscule au loin* (Paris: Bernard Grasset, 1987), see 148–49.
18. Abrahamson, I, 20.
19. Ibid., 23.
20. EW, *Paroles d'étranger* 189.

Chapter 3: Remembering the Holocaust

1. Abrahamson, I, 3.
2. Ibid., 211.
3. Abrahamson, II, 56.
4. Ibid., 305.

5. Abrahamson, I, 44.
6. EW, *Paroles d'étranger*, 15.
7. Estess, 63.
8. EW, *Paroles d'étranger*, 9.
9. B-F Cohen, 23–24.
10. Saint Cheron, Philippe-Michael, *Rencontre avec Elie Wiesel: Le mal et l'exil* (Paris: Nouvelle Cité, 1988), 197. (trans. J. Kolbert).
11. EW, *Signes d'exode*, 18–19.
12. Abrahamson, II, 366.
13. Ibid., 269.
14. Abrahamson, I, 14.
15. Ibid., 157.
16. Saint Cheron, 71.
17. EW, *Paroles d'étranger*, 80–81.
18. Ibid., 87.
19. Abrahamson, III, 146.
20. EW and Albert H. Friedlander, *The Six Days of Destruction* (New York/ Mahwah, 1988), 25.
21. Abrahamson, I, 90.
22. Abrahamson, II, 3.
23. Saint Cheron, 86–87.
24. Ibid., 112–113.
25. EW, *Discours d'Oslo* (Paris: Grasset, 1987), 17. (trans. J. Kolbert).
26. EW, *Paroles d'étranger*, 187–88.
27. EW and Friedlander, 33.
28. Ibid., 43.
29. EW, *Paroles d'étranger*, 10–11.
30. Ibid., 45.
31. B-F Cohen, 10–11.
32. Abrahamson, I, 148.
33. Ibid., 127.
34. Henry Kamm, "Anti-Semitic Taunt at Wiesel in Romania," *The New York Times*, 3 July 1991.
35. Abrahamson, I, 92.

Chapter 4: "Indifference to Evil Is Evil"

1. EW, *Signes d'exode*, 95.
2. Abrahamson, I, 90.
3. EW, *Discours d'Oslo*, 13.
4. B-F Cohen, 74.
5. Saint Cheron, 161.
6. See EW, *Signes d'exode*, 41 et seq. Also EW, "The Most Important Lesson of All," *Parade Magazine, The Sunbury (PA) Daily Item*, (24 May 1992) The statement comes also from an unpublished commencement address before graduating seniors of Susquehanna University, Selinsgrove, PA, 17 May 1992.
7. Abrahamson, II, 253.

8. Ibid., 156.
9. For more complete discussion of this topic, see Ibid., II, 175–86 passim.
10. Abrahamson, III, 16.
11. Abrahamson, II, 63.
12. Abrahamson, I, 198.
13. Estess, 60–61.
14. Abrahamson, I, 120.
15. Abrahamson, III, 176.
16. Abrahamson, I, 230.
17. Abrahamson, II, 137.
18. Abrahamson, I, 203.
19. Ibid., 53.
20. Abrahamson, II, 180.
21. Ibid., 268.
22. Ibid., 42.
23. See EW, *Discours d'Oslo*, especially p. 14.
24. EW, *Paroles d'étranger*, 104.

Chapter 5: The Rhetoric of Silence

1. EW, *Paroles d'étranger*, 7.
2. B-F Cohen, 69.
3. EW, *Signes d'exode*, 12.
4. Abrahamson, II, 53.
5. Saint Cheron, 20.
6. Ibid., 268.
7. EW, *Signes d'exode*, 7.
8. Abrahamson, I, 54.
9. EW, *Paroles d'étranger*, 14.
10. EW, *Le Crépuscule au loin*, 230.
11. Abrahamson, I, 56.
12. EW, *Paroles d'étranger*, 14.
13. Abrahamson, II, 83.

Chapter 6: In Remembrance of History

1. EW, *Et la mer n'est pas remplie: Mémoires* 2 (Paris: Editions du Seuil, 1996), 57.
2. EW and Friedlander, 85.
3. Abrahamson, I, 330.
4. Ibid., 336.
5. Ibid., 275.
6. Ibid., 168.
7. Ibid., 229.
8. Ibid., 12–13.

9. Saint Cheron, 22.
10. B-F Cohen, 127.
11. Abrahamson, I, 13.
12. EW, *Le Crépuscule au loin,* 162.
13. EW, *Signes d'exode,* 122.
14. EW and Friedlander, 70.
15. EW, *Discours d'Oslo,* 42.
16. EW, *Signes d'exode,* 92–93.
17. Abrahamson, II, 385.
18. EW, *Night* (New York: Bantam Books, 1989), 32.

CHAPTER 7: AND WHERE WAS GOD?

1. Michael Berenbaum, *The Vision of the Void—Theological Reflections on the Works of Elie Wiesel* (Middletown, CT: Wesleyan University Press, 1979), 6.
2. Saint Cheron, 24.
3. EW, *Et la mer n'est pas remplie,* 93.
4. Richard Rubenstein, interview by author, Tallahassee, FL, 31 July 1991.
5. EW, *Night,* See 31–32, also 63–67.
6. Abrahamson, II, 140.
7. Ibid., 139.
8. Abrahamson, III, 309.
9. Abrahamson, II, 139.
10. Ibid., 142.
11. Saint Cheron, 162.
12. Abrahamson, I, 243.
13. Ibid., 207.
14. EW, *Night,* 65.
15. EW, *Discours d'Oslo,* 24.
16. Berenbaum, 20.
17. Saint Cheron, 53.
18. Abrahamson, III, 244.
19. B-F Cohen, 87.
20. Ibid., 83.
21. Quoted in Estess, 63.
22. Quoted in Estess, 40.
23. EW and Friedlander, 69.
24. Saint Cheron, 64.
25. Ibid., 115.
26. Abrahamson, I, 142.
27. John K. Roth and Michael Berenbaum, *Holocaust: Religious and Philosophical Implications* (New York: Paragon House, 1989), 364.
28. Abrahamson, II, 62.
29. Rubenstein, interview.
30. Ibid.
31. Saint Cheron, 40.

Chapter 8: Hear Oh Israel: The Jewish People Are One

1. B-F Cohen, 44–45.
2. Abrahamson, I, 349.
3. Ibid., 277.
4. Ibid., 281.
5. Ibid., 278.
6. B-F Cohen, 112.
7. Abrahamson, I, 246–50 passim.
8. Ibid., 390.
9. Ibid., 20.
10. EW, *Signes d'exode*, 48.
11. Ibid., 54.
12. EW, *Paroles d'étranger*, 135.
13. Abrahamson, III, 306.
14. EW, *Signes d'exode*, 10.
15. Estess, 66.
16. EW, *Le Crépuscule au loin*, 221.
17. EW, *Paroles d'étranger*, 146.
18. Cohen, B-F. 103.
19. Saint Cheron, 55–56.
20. EW, *Paroles d'étranger*, 153.
21. Ibid., 50–51.
22. EW, *Discours d'Oslo*, 11.
23. EW, *Paroles d'étranger*, 141.
24. Abrahamson, II, 198.
25. Abrahamson, I, 130.
26. EW, *Discours d'Oslo*, 14.
27. Abrahamson, III, 41.
28. Saint Cheron, 207–8. (trans. J. Kolbert).
29. Abrahamson, III, 141.
30. Abrahamson, II, 193.
31. Abrahamson, I, 305.
32. Abrahamson, III, 175.
33. EW, *Paroles d'étranger*, 82–83.
34. Saint Cheron, 65.
35. EW, *Signes d'exode*, 139–40.
36. Abrahamson, I, 316.
37. EW, *Discours d'Oslo*, 37.
38. Abrahamson, I, 231.
39. Abrahamson, II, 221.
40. Ibid., 339.
41. See "Holocaust Challenge," *USA Today*, 13 September 1991.
42. Abrahamson, II, 258.
43. EW, *Paroles d'étranger*, 154.
44. Abrahamson, II, 253.
45. Estess, 5.
46. Abrahamson, III, 77.

47. EW, *Paroles d'étranger,* 66.
48. Abrahamson, II, 254.
49. Ibid., 261.

Chapter 9: In Search of Jewish-Christian Dialogue

1. B-F Cohen, 117.
2. EW and Friedlander, 69.
3. Abrahamson, I, 153.
4. Estess, 71.
5. Abrahamson, III, 110.
6. Abrahamson, II, 22.
7. Ibid., 165.
8. Saint Cheron, 279–81 passim.
9. Abrahamson, II, 328.
10. Quoted in EW and Friedlander, 3.
11. Abrahamson, I, 33.
12. Abrahamson, II, 69.
13. Abrahamson, I, 29.
14. Ibid., 33.
15. Ibid, 134, for more detailed discussion of the subject.
16. Ibid., 35.
17. Quoted in Estess, 76–77.
18. Abrahamson, III, 224.
19. Abrahamson, I, 131.
20. Ibid., 161.
21. Abrahamson, II, 136.
22. Abrahamson, I, 377.
23. Ibid., 361.
24. For exact details of how EW discusses this subject see his novel, *Le Crépuscule au loin,* 19 and 37.
25. Abrahamson, I, 160.
26. For more detailed discussion see EW's *Paroles d'étranger,* 103.
27. Abrahamson, I, 165.
28. Ibid., 272.
29. Saint Cheron, 219.
30. Ibid., 75.

Chapter 10: Sanctity of Life

1. Abrahamson, I, 139.
2. EW and Friedlander, 90.
3. EW, *Discours d'Oslo,* 15.
4. Elie Wiesel, interview with Susquehanna University students, New York, New York, 13 November 1998.

5. Abrahamson, I, 187.
6. Ibid., 188.
7. EW and Friedlander, 93–94.
8. Abrahamson, II, 211.
9. See EW, "The Nobel Address," in *From the Kingdom of Memory*, 233–34.
10. Abrahamson, III, 158.
11. Ibid., 107.
12. Abrahamson, II, 213.
13. EW, *Paroles d'étranger*, 115.
14. Ibid., 118.
15. Ibid., 132.
16. EW, *Discours d'Oslo*, 29–30.

Chapter 11: What Is Literature?

1. EW, *Discours d'Oslo*, 26.
2. Abrahamson, I, 204.
3. EW, *Signes d'exode*, 105.
4. Abrahamson, I, 235.
5. EW and Friedlander, 34.
6. Ibid., 20.
7. Abrahamson, I, 27.
8. Abrahamson, II, 134.
9. Ibid., 47.
10. Ibid., 166.
11. Ibid., 54.
12. Ibid., 69.
13. EW, *Paroles d'étranger*, 76.
14. Saint Cheron, 26.
15. Estess, 109.
16. B-F Cohen, 106.
17. EW, *Paroles d'étranger*, 13.
18. Abrahamson, III, 40.
19. Abrahamson, I, 310.
20. Abrahamson, II, 57.
21. Ibid., 152.
22. Abrahamson, I, 11.
23. Ibid., 19.
24. Abrahamson, II, 106.
25. Ibid.
26. Abrahamson, III, 96.
27. EW, *Paroles d'étranger*, 13.
28. Abrahamson, II, 61.
29. Ibid., 62–64 passim.
30. EW, *Et la mer n'est pas remplie*, 481.
31. B-F Cohen, 103.
32. Ibid., see 103–4.

33. Abrahamson, I, 18.
34. Gabrielle Cohen, interview by author, Paris, France, 10 July 1988.
35. Abrahamson, I, 57.
36. EW and Friedlander, 9.
37. EW, *Paroles d'étranger,* 166–67.
38. Abrahamson, I, 341–42.
39. Abrahamson, II, 65.
40. Abrahamson, I, 320.
41. Abrahamson, III, 291.
42. EW, *Discours d'Oslo,* 38.
43. Saint Cheron, 152.
44. Abrahamson, I, 40.
45. Ibid., 21.
46. Abrahamson, II, 120.
47. Abrahamson, III, 234.
48. Abrahamson, II, 33.
49. B-F Cohen, 50–51.
50. Ibid., see 50–52.
51. Saint Cheron, 133; on Unamuno, see 134; on Kafka, see 138; on Malraux, see 141; on Maimonides and other great Jewish writers, see 141; on Céline, see 143; on Saul Lieberman, see 144; on Camus and Malraux, see 218; on Bernanos, see 208.
52. B-F Cohen, see 25–26.
53. Saint Cheron, 174.
54. Abrahamson, I, 370.

Chapter 12: A Portrait of the Writer as Teacher and Scholar

1. Abrahamson, II, 151. See also Abrahamson, I, 151–52.
2. Abrahamson, I, 261.
3. Estess, 34–35.
4. B-F Cohen, 79–80.
5. Saint Cheron, 224.
6. Ibid., 267.
7. EW, "Have you learned the most important lesson of all," *Parade Magazine, The Sunbury (PA) Daily Item,* 24 May 1992.
8. Abrahamson, II, 23.
9. B-F Cohen, 95.
10. Abrahamson, II, 43.
11. EW, *Paroles d'étranger,* see 48–49.
12. EW, *Signes d'exode,* 77.
13. Abrahamson, II, 23.
14. EW, "Have you learned the most important lesson of all."
15. Abrahamson, III, 256.
16. Abrahamson, I, 344.
17. EW, "Have you learned the most important lesson of all."

Chapter 13: The French Connection

1. EW, *Et la mer n'est pas remplie*, 467.
2. Saint Cheron, 215.
3. Abrahamson, III, 197.
4. B-F Cohen, see page 31 for complete discussion of this question.
5. Abrahamson, II, 77.
6. Saint Cheron, 271.
7. B-F Cohen, 72–73.
8. Estess, 10.
9. Abrahamson, II, 111.
10. Abrahamson, III, 198.
11. Abrahamson, II, 49.
12. Abrahamson, III, 217.
13. Cohen, interview.
14. See EW, *Signes d'exode*, 61.
15. Abrahamson, III, 218.
16. Ibid., 170–71 passim.
17. Abrahamson, II, 112.
18. Ibid., 152.
19. Abrahamson, I, 52.
20. B-F Cohen, 111.
21. Abrahamson, III, 213.
22. EW, *Paroles d'étranger*, 83.
23. EW, *Le Crépuscule au loin*, see 226 for Gide; see 27, 33, and 35 for Camus.
24. Abrahamson, I, 351.
25. Ibid., 318.
26. Abrahamson, III, 73.
27. Ibid., 93.

Chapter 14: And Yet: A Conclusion That Does Not Conclude

1. EW, *Et la mer n'est pas remplie*, 528.
2. Ibid., 527.
3. Clyde Haberman, "An Unofficial but Very Public Bearer of Pain, Peace and Human Dignity," *New York Times*, 5 March 1997.
4. Abrahamson, I, 295.
5. Ibid., 194.
6. Ibid., 151.
7. EW, "Mélange: Commencements 1992, Fostering Grown-Up Citizens; The Danger of Indifference, etc." *The Chronicle of Higher Education*, 17 June 1992.
8. Ibid.
9. EW, "Le Silence de Birkenau," in Adam Buzav, Ed. *Auschwitz, Birkenau* (Freiburg, Germany: Herder Verlag, 1989), unnumbered page.

Select Bibliography

WORKS BY ELIE WIESEL, IN CHRONOLOGICAL ORDER (ORIGINAL FRENCH VERSIONS AND, WHENEVER TRANSLATED, ENGLISH TITLES)

Un Die Velt Hat Geshwigen. Buenos Aires, Argentina: Tsentral Verband Foon Poilishe Yiden in Argentina [Central Association of Polish Jews in Argentina], 1956. (Written in Yiddish).
La Nuit. Paris: Les Editions de Minuit, 1958. Translated by Stella Rodway as *Night.* New York: Farrar, Strauss and Giroux, 1960; also published by Bantam Books in 1982.
L'Aube. Paris: Editions du Seuil, 1960. Translated by Anne Borchardt as *Dawn.* New York: Hill and Wang, 1961.
Le Jour. Paris: Editions du Seuil, 1961. Translated by Anne Borchardt as *The Accident.* New York: Hill and Wang, 1962.
La Ville de la chance. Paris: Editions du Seuil, 1962. Translated by Steven Becker as The Town Beyond the Wall. New York: Atheneum, 1964.
Le Testament d'un poète juif assassiné. Paris: Editions du Seuil, 1980. Translated by Marion Wiesel as *The Testament.* New York: Summit, 1981.
Five Biblical Portraits. Notre Dame, IN: University of Notre Dame Press, 1981.
Contre la mélancolie: Célébration Hassidique II. Paris: Editions du Seuil, 1981. Translated by Marion Wiesel as *Somewhere a Master: Further Hasidic Portraits and Legends.* New York: Summit, 1982.
Paroles d'étranger. Paris: Editions du Seuil, 1982.
The Golem: The Story of a Legend Told by Elie Wiesel. New York: Summit, 1983.
Le Cinquième fils. Paris: Grasset, 1983. Translated by Marion Wiesel as *The Fifth Son.* New York: Summit, 1985.
Against Silence: The Voice and Vision of Elie Wiesel. 3 volumes. Edited and Co-authored by Irving Abrahamson. New York: Holocaust Library, 1985.
Signes d'exode. Paris: Grasset et Fasquelle, 1987.
Job ou Dieu dans la tempête. Paris: Grasset et Fasquelle, 1987.
Le Crépuscule au loin. Paris: Grasset, 1987. Translated by Marion Wiesel as *Twilight.* New York: Summit, 1988.
The Six Days of Destruction. Co-authored by Albert Friedlander. New York: Paulist Press, 1988.
Discours d'Olso. Paris: Grasset et Fasquelle, 1987.

L'Oublié. Paris: Editions du Seuil, 1989. Translated by Marion Wiesel as *The Forgotten.* New York: Summit, 1992.
From the Kingdom of Memory. New York: Summit, 1990.
Célébration talmudique. Paris: Editions du Seuil, 1991.
Tous les fleuves vont à la mer: Mémoires. Paris: Editions du Seuil, 1994. Translated by Marion Wiesel as *Memoirs: All Rivers Run to the Sea.* New York: Alfred A. Knopf, 1995.
Et la mer n'est pas remplie: Mémoires 2. Paris: Editions du Seuil, 1996. Translated into English by Marion Wiesel as *And the Sea is Never Full: Memoirs 1969–* and published in New York by Alfred A. Knopf, 1999.
Célébration prophétique. Paris: Editions du Seuil, 1998.
Les Juges. Paris: Editions du Seuil, 1999.

Selected Secondary Sources (Limited to English- and French-language works)

Berenbaum, Michael. *The Vision of the Void: Theological Reflections on the Works of Elie Wiesel.* Middletown, CT: Wesleyan University Press, 1979.

Brown, Robert McAffee. *Elie Wiesel: Messenger to All Humanity.* Rev. ed. Notre Dame, IN: University of Notre Dame Press, 1989.

Cargas, Harry J. *Conversations with Elie Wiesel.* New York: Paulist Press. 1976.

———. *Responses to Elie Wiesel: Critical Essays by Major Jewish and Christian Scholars.* New York: Persea Books, 1978.

———, ed. *Telling the Tale: A Tribute to Elie Wiesel on the Occasion of his 65th Birthday: Essays, Reflections, and Poems.* Saint Louis, MO: Time Being Books, 1993.

Cohen, Brigitte-Fanny. *Elie Wiesel: Qui êtes-vous?.* Lyon, France: La Manufacture, 1987.

Cohen, Myriam B. *Elie Wiesel: Variations sur le Silence.* (avec texte inédit d'Elie Wiesel: "Then and Now.") La Rochelle, France: Rumeur des Ages, 1988.

Davis, Colin. *Elie Wiesel's Secretive Texts.* Gainesville: Florida University Press, 1994.

Estess, Ted L. *Elie Wiesel.* New York: Frederick Ungar, 1980.

Engel, Vincent. *Fou de Dieu ou Dieu des Fous: L'Oeuvre tragique d'Elie Wiesel.* Paris: Editions Universitaires, and Brussels: De Boeck, 1989.

Fine, Ellen S. *Legacy of Night: The Literary Universe of Elie Wiesel.* Albany: State University of New York Press, 1982.

Friedlander, Albert H. and Elie Wiesel. *The Six Days of Destruction: Meditations Towards Hope.* New York and Oxford: Pergamon Press, 1988.

Friedman, Maurice S. *Abraham Joshua Heschel and Elie Wiesel, You Are My Witnesses.* New York: Farrar, Strauss, Giroux, 1987.

Friedman, John S. "The Art of Fiction LXXIX: Elie Wiesel." *Paris Review* 26:130–78.

Friedman, Joe. *Le Rire dans l'univers tragique d'Elie Wiesel.* Paris: Nizet, 1981.

Frost, Christopher J. *Religious Melancholy or Psychological Depression? Some Issues Involved in Relating Psychology and Religion as Illustrated in a Study of Elie Wiesel.* Lanham, MD: University Press of America, 1985.

Fumia, Molly. *A Child at Dawn: The Healing of a Memory.* Notre Dame, IN: Ave Maria Press, 1989.

Greene, Carol. *Elie Wiesel, Messenger from the Holocaust.* Chicago: Children's Press, 1987.
Haggadah Shel Pessach, The. Commented upon by Elie Wiesel in bilingual Hebrew and English. English Translated by Marion Wiesel. Illustrations by Mark Podwal. New York: Simon and Schuster, 1993.
Kafka, Ariane and Michel Philippe-Michael de Saint Cheron. *Elie Wiesel: En Hommage.* Paris: Les Editions du Cerf, 1998.
Koppel, Gene and Henry Kaufmann. *Elie Wiesel: A Small Measure of Victory; An Interview.* Tucson: University of Arizona Press, 1974.
Langer, Lawrence. *The Holocaust and the Literary Imagination.* New Haven: Yale University Press, 1975.
Lazo, Caroline Evensen. *Elie Wiesel.* New York: Dillon Press and Toronto: Maxwell Macmillan Canada, 1994.
Malka, Salomon: *Monsieur Choucahni: l'énigme d'un maître du vingtième siècle— Entretiens avec Elie Wiesel, suivis d'une enquête.* Paris: J. C. Lattaes, 1994.
McCain, N. "The Struggle to Reconcile the Reality of Evil with Faith in God." *The Chronicle of Higher Education,* 13 April 1983, 75–89.
Medical and Psychological Effects of Concentration Camps on Holocaust Survivors. Edited by Robert Krell and Marc I. Sherman. Introduction by Elie Wiesel. New Brunswick, New Jersey: Transaction Publishers, 1997.
Mitterrand, François. *Mémoires à deux voix: François Mitterrand et Elie Wiesel.* Translated by Richard Seaver and Timothy Bent as *Memoir in Two Voices.* New York: Arcade Publishers and Boston: Little Brown, 1996.
O'Connor, John Cardinal and Elie Wiesel. *A Journey of Faith.* New York: Donald I. Fine, 1990.
Pariser, Michael. *Elie Wiesel: Bearing Witness.* Brookfield, CT: Millbrook Press, 1994.
Rittner, Carol. R. S. M., editor. *Elie Wiesel: Between Memory and Hope.* New York: New York University Press, 1990.
Rosen, Alan, ed. *Celebrating Elie Wiesel: Stories, Essays, Reflections.* Notre Dame, IN: University of Notre Dame Press, 1998.
Rosenfelt, Alvin and Irving Greenbert. *Confronting the Holocaust: The Impact of Elie Wiesel.* Bloomington: Indiana University Press, 1979.
Roth, John K. *A Consuming Fire: Encounters with Elie Wiesel.* Atlanta: John Knox Press, 1979.
Saint Cheron, Philippe Michael de. *Le Mal et l'exil: Rencontre avec Elie Wiesel.* Paris: Nouvelle Cité, 1988. Translated by Jon Rothchild as *Evil and Exile.* Notre Dame, Indiana: University of Notre Dame Press, 1990.
———. Elie Wiesel: *Pèlerin de la memoire.* Paris: Plon, 1994.
———, ed. *Autour de Elie Wiesel: Une Parole pour l'avenir.* Colloque de Cerisy. Paris: Odile Jacob, 1996.
Schuman, Michael. *Elie Wiesel: Voice from the Holocaust.* Hillside, NJ: Enslow Publishers, 1994.
Semprun, Jorge. *Wiesel: Se Taire est impossible.* Paris: Arte Editions; Editions Mille et Une Nuits, 1995.
Sibelman, Simon P. *Silence in the Novels of Elie Wiesel.* New York: Saint Martin's Press, 1995.
Stern, Ellen Norman. *Elie Wiesel: Witness for Life.* New York: KTAV Publishing, 1982.
Walker, Graham B. *Elie Wiesel: A Challenge to Theology.* Jefferson, NC: McFarland, 1988.

Miscellaneous Items, Audio-Visual Media, Collaborations, Etc.

Wiesel, Elie et al. *Dimensions of the Holocaust:* Lectures. Evanston, IL: Northwestern University Press, 1977.

Elie Wiesel's Jerusalem. Videocassette, 25 min. John McGreevy Productions and Nielsen-Ferns Inc. New York: 1978 and 1980.

Images from the Bible: The Paintings of Shalom of Safed. The Words of Elie Wiesel. Introduction by Daniel Doron. Woodstock, New York: Overlock Press, 1980.

Swados, Elizabeth. *The Haggadah Libretto,* adapted and composed by Elizabeth Swados. Translated from Hebrew into English by Elie Wiesel. New York: S. French, 1982.

To Bear Witness. Videocassette edited by Larry E. Rubin and Henry Strolier. Produced by John J. Prescott and Associates for the U. S. Memorial Holocaust Council. 42 minutes. National Audiovisual Center, 1983.

Index

Abraham (biblical patriarch), 39, 42, 110
Abrahamson, Irving, 11, 12, 51, 20, 16, 59, 89, 130
Académie française, 180
Adam (biblical figure), 39
Adamov, Arthur, 172
Aikman, David, 9
American-Israel Public Affairs Committee (AIPAC), 76
Arche, L', (Paris-based Jewish periodical), 27, 28
Arena Theater, the (Washington DC), 37
Arrabal, Fernando, 172
Auschwitz, 13, 24, 25, 29, 33, 50, 52, 54, 58, 91, 62, 64, 83, 84, 91, 94, 95, 97, 98, 100, 101, 106, 133, 134, 136, 167, 177, 179, 182, 189, 190, 192, 193

Babi Yar (Near Kiev, Ukraine), 65, 119–20
Bach, Johann-Sebastian, 144
Balzac, Honoré de, 152, 186
Barbie, Klaus, 46
Bar Ilan University, 47
Beckett, Samuel, 30, 82, 147, 172, 186
Bellow, Saul, 14
Ben Tradyon, Hanina (Rabbi), 91
Berenbaum, Michael, 12, 15, 95, 104
Bergen-Belsen (concentration camp), 22, 107
Bergson, 182
Bernanos, Georges, 160
Bernard, Tristan, 17
Bernardin, Joseph Cardinal (archbishop of Chicago), 129

Birkenau (concentration camp), 13, 25, 66, 75, 91, 94, 119, 136, 193, 195
Boileau, Nicolas-Déspréaux, 156
Borges, Luis, 172
Boston University, 46, 47, 170
Bousquet, René, 173
Bremond, Henri (Abbé), 85, 154
Buchenwald (concentration camp), 25, 28, 29, 35, 53, 57, 62, 95, 101, 103, 180, 182, 193
Bundestag (German parliament), 46
Butor, Michel, 30
Butz, Arthur, 70

Cain (biblical figure), 42
Calder, Alexander, 172
Camus, Albert, 37, 39, 71, 73, 136, 147, 160, 175, 178, 182, 183, 184, 185, 186, 194
Cargas, Harry, 12
Carpathian Mountains (Hungary/Romania), 20, 23, 51, 52, 54, 57, 173
Carter, Jimmy (president), 44, 65, 139
Cassatt, Mary, 172
Catherine the Great (empress of Russia), 172
Catholic Church and the Vatican, 59, 77, 127, 129, 131
Céline, Louis-Ferdinand, 160
Cérisy-la-Salle, Château de, 9, 15, 49
Chagall, Marc, 50, 172
Chirac, Jacques (French president), 49
Chopin, Frédéric, 172
Churchill, Winston (British prime minister), 75
City University of New York, the, 46, 170
Clinton, Bill (president), 48

211

212 INDEX

Cohen, Brigitte-Fanny, 12, 15, 47, 56, 62, 73, 80–81, 90, 124, 148, 161, 175
Cohen, Gabrielle (Gaby), 154, 180–81
Columbia University, 168
Corneille, Pierre, 15

Daoud, Abu, 182
Darió, Rubén, 172
David (biblical king of the Jews), 56, 108
Davis, Colin, 9
de Gaulle, Charles (general and French president), 26, 180, 181–82
Diderot, Denis, 172
Diderot, Denis, 17
Dorfman, Ariel, 14
Dostoievski, Fyodor Mikhailovich, 160, 175
Dreyfus, Colonel Alfred, 46

Editions de Minuit, Les (Paris), 30, 184
Egal, Aarvik, 43
Eichmann, Adolph, 23, 74, 119
Eisenberg, Josey (rabbi), 15
Enesco, Georges, 172
Estess, Ted, 12, 20, 51, 75, 111, 126, 148, 166

Feig, Dodye, 22, 23, 37, 52
Fichte, Johann Gottlieb, 130, 144
Fine, Ellen, 12
Fitzgerald, F. Scott, 172
Flaubert, Gustave, 32, 186
Frank, Anne, 30
Franklin, Benjamin, 172
Frederick the Great (king of Prussia), 172
Friedlander, Albert H., 10, 68–69, 129, 139
Friedman, John, 15, 47

Gershwin, George, 172
Gide, André, 73, 178, 186
Giraudoux, Jean, 178
Giscard, Valery d'Estaing (French president), 182
Goethe, Johann, Wolfgang, 21, 130, 144
Gorbachev, Mikhail (Soviet head of state), 119
Graham, Billy (reverend), 9

Green, Julien, 172
Grimm, Friedrich-Melchior, 172

Hakaton, Haras Menashe, 168
Haydn, Joseph, 144
Hebrew Union College (Cincinatti), 47
Heifetz, Jascha, 22
Hemingway, Ernst, 172
Heschel, Abraham Yeshoua (rabbi), 169
Hitler, Adolph, 22, 23, 24, 66, 77–78, 91, 119, 145–146, 185
Hofstra University, 47
Hugo, Victor, 50, 176, 186

Ionesco, Eugène, 172
Isaac (biblical patriarch), 39

James, Henry, 172
Jefferson, Thomas (president), 172
Jeremiah (biblical prophet), 100
Jewish Daily Forward, the (New York), York), 28
Jewish Theological Seminary, the (New York), 47
Job (biblical prophet), 15, 39, 97, 100, 101, 102
John XXIII (pope), 62, 131, 134
John Paul II (pope), 9, 59, 131, 134, 135, 139
Jonah (biblical figure), 100
Jonathan (biblical figure), 56
Joyce, James, 172

Kafka, Franz, 96, 160, 175
Kant, Immanuel, 130
Karliner, David, 169
Kazin, Alfred, 10
Ku Klux Klan (the march in Skokie, Il), 133, 193

La Bruyère, Jean de, 169
La Fontaine, Jean de, 156
Lazar, Moshe (professor), 26
Lévinas, Emmanuel, 160
Lieberman, Saul (rabbi), 160, 168, 169
Lindon, Jerome, 30
Liszt, Franz, 172
Lustiger, Aron (cardinal of Paris), 127
Luther, Martin, 62

index

Maeterlinck, Maurice, 67
Maimonides, Moses ben Maimon (rabbi), 160
Mallarmé, Stéphane, 50
Malraux, André, 147, 160, 175, 178, 183, 186
Mandela, Nelson (head of state in South Africa), 9, 139
Mann, Thomas, 160
Marquette University, 47
Marx, Karl, 185
Maulnier, Thierry, 132
Mauriac, François, 29, 30, 156, 160, 175, 178, 182, 183, 184
Maurois, André, 10, 178
Mendès-France, Pierre (French prime minister), 29
Milhaud, Darius, 38
Miró, Joán, 172
Mitterrand, François (French president), 10, 48, 49, 173, 183
Molière, Jean-Baptiste Poquelin, 156, 164, 176
Monde, Le (Paris newspaper), 127
Monet, Claude, 50
Munich Olympic Games, the, 128

NBC (National Broadcasting Company), 64, 159–60
New York Times, the, 76, 182, 193
Niemoller, Martin (pastor), 138
Notre Dame, the University of, 47

Oeuvres du Secours aux Enfants (French charitable foundation), 26
Ozick, Cynthia, 14

Palestine Liberation Organization (PLO), 140
Paris Review, the, 15
Pascal, Blaise, 186
Picasso, Pablo, 172
Pittsburgh, the University of, 16
Pius XII (pope), 134, 135
Pompidou, Georges (French president), 182
Protestantism: and the Lutheran Church, 130
Proust, Marcel, 53, 182
Pushkin, Alexander, 172

Racine, Jean, 156, 164, 176
Reagan, Ronald (president), 14, 48, 74
Rimbaud, Arthur, 186
Rittner, Carol (RSM), 12
Rodway, Stella, 30
Roosevelt, Franklin Delano (president), 75–76
Rose, Marion Erster (Wiesel), 35, 43
Roth, John, 12, 95
Rothschild Family, the, 182
Rousseau, Jean-Jacques, 182, 186
Rubenstein, Richard (president, the University of Bridgeport), 16, 95, 97, 104

Sachs, Nelly, 179
Saint Cheron, Philippe-Michaël de, 9, 12, 15, 47, 49, 63, 64, 82–83, 90, 96, 99, 105, 135, 148, 160
Saint-Exupéry, Antoine de, 178
Sartre, Jean-Paul, 73, 96, 175, 178, 183, 184–85
Schiller, Johann Christophe Friedrich, 21, 144
Schwarz-Bart, André, 186
Shoshani, Mordechai (Rav), 168
Sibelman, Simon B., 9, 83
Sighet (Hungary/Romania), 20, 21, 22, 23, 24, 25, 32–33, 34, 50–58, 96, 111, 125, 174, 190
Silber, John (former president of Boston University), 14
Socrates, 168
Solomon (biblical king of the Jews), 108
Solzhenitsyn, Alexander Isayevich, 9, 64–65, 148
Sorbonne (University of Paris), 26, 27, 181, 184
Southern California, the University of, 26
Stein, Gertrude, 172
Susquehanna University, 46, 47, 194

Theresa, Mother, 9
Timmerman, Jacobo, 138
Treblinka (concentration camp), 63, 70, 71, 84, 107

Unamuno, Miguel de, 160
United Nations, the, 27, 115

214 INDEX

United States National Holocaust Commission and Museum, 44, 48, 193

Valéry, Paul, 61, 159, 178
Van Gogh, Vincent, 50, 172
Voltaire, François-Marie Arouet de, 130, 172

Wahl, Gustave, 27, 181
Walesa, Lech (Polish Premier), 139
Waldheim, Kurt (Austrian Chancellor and United Nations Secretary), 135
Warsaw Ghetto, the, 78, 79
Weiss-Halivni, David, 168
Westling, Jon (Boston University President), 14
Whistler, James, 172

Wiesel, Béatrice (Batya), 21, 24
Wiesel, Hilda, 21, 24
Wiesel, Sara Feig, 21
Wiesel, Shlomo, 21, 24
Wiesel, Shlomo-Elisha, 35, 41, 61, 181
Wiesel, Tsipora, 21, 24, 69
Wiesenthal, Simon, 10
Williamsburg (district in Brooklyn, NY), 51
Wise, Stephen (Rabbi), 76

Yale University, 47
Yedioth Ahronot (Tel Aviv newspaper), 27, 28
Yeshiva University, 47

Zola, Emile, 182